DATE DUE

~~NO 4~~		
~~AG 1~~		
NO 15'04		

DEMCO 38-296

AMERICA'S INTERNATIONAL TRADE

A Reference Handbook

AMERICA'S
INTERNATIONAL
T R A D E

A Reference Handbook

E. Willard Miller
Department of Geography

Ruby M. Miller
Pattee Library

The Pennsylvania State University

CONTEMPORARY
WORLD ISSUES

ABC-CLIO

Santa Barbara, California
Denver, Colorado
Oxford, England

Library of Congress Cataloging-in-Publication Data

Miller, E. Willard (Eugene Willard), 1915–
    America's international trade : a reference handbook / E. Willard Miller, Ruby M. Miller.
        p. cm.—(Contemporary world issues)
    ISBN 0-87436-770-0 (cloth : alk. paper)
    1. United States—Commerce—Handbooks, manuals, etc. 2. United States—Commercial policy—Handbooks, manuals, etc. 3. Foreign trade regulation—United States—Handbooks, manuals, etc. 4. United States—Commerce—Bibliography. I. Miller, Ruby M. II. Title. III. Series.
    HF3035.M55 1995   95-14135
    382'.0973—dc20   CIP

02 01 00 99 98 97 96 95 10 9 8 7 6 5 4 3 2 1

ABC-CLIO, Inc.
130 Cremona Drive, P.O. Box 1911
Santa Barbara, California 93116-1911

This book is printed on acid-free paper ∞ .

Manufactured in the United States of America

Contents

Tables

Preface

Throughout much of the history of the United States, the domestic market provided the major outlet for the national economy. Accordingly, most legislation during this period protected the domestic economy. After World War II, the traditional policies changed as the United States rebuilt the world's economy. To reach the world market, policies of free trade have gradually developed. The United States is now part of the globalization of the world's economy. Fundamental changes are evolving as the United States competes in the world market.

This book begins with a short description of the evolution of the trade policies of the United States. A discussion of tariffs and trade barriers is followed by an analysis of trade promotion techniques such as trade fairs, advertising, catalogs, and trade missions. Since World War II, the development of global policies on trade relationships have become increasingly essential to the economy of individual nations. Beginning in 1947, the world's nations have attempted to develop a global policy, such as the General Agreement on Tariffs and Trade. More recently, free trade policies have evolved under regional systems. The United States has been a leader in the evolution of free trade in North America. The trade legislation of the

United States has evolved from a policy of trade protection to policies to reduce all trade barriers worldwide. The legislation has become more comprehensive and now includes policies to protect such activities as services, insurance, and banking.

Other chapters provide information on a variety of topics. A chronology lists important data in the evolution of national and international laws and regulations. Many public and private organizations at both the national and international levels provide information on trade relationships.

In recent years, there has been a massive increase in the amount of literature on trade. Chapter 5 presents an annotated bibliography of books on a variety of topics, as well as nearly 1,000 articles from journals and government publications. The references are arranged topically, and include a list of selected journals that publish articles on trade. The book concludes with an annotated list of films and a glossary.

International Trade of the United States

1

Evolution of U.S. Trade Policies

The evolution of the international trade policies of the United States reflects not only the dominance of the domestic economy but also the relationships that the United States has developed in the world economy. In the nineteenth century, Congress adopted a protectionist stance to protect the infant industries, and thus the comprehensive trade legislation of 1860 established tariffs on essentially all imports.

For nearly three-quarters of a century, the industrialists of the North were protected from foreign imports. In 1913, Congress attempted to lower the U.S. customs duties, but these changes were reversed in 1921. Although the United States had become the world's leading industrial nation, as well as the world's principal creditor nation, the protectionist policy persisted. This policy reached a climax in the Smoot-Hawley Tariff Act of 1930.

The response to this act was a dramatic reduction of world trade. The loss of U.S. exports at the time of a deep economic recession in the nation deepened the economic problems. Consequently, Congress enacted the 1934 Reciprocal Trade Agreement, which authorized the president to reduce existing

1

tariff duties up to 50 percent. A noteworthy aspect of the act was the inclusion of the most-favored-nation clause, which limited discrimination in trade by extending to third parties the same terms provided by contracting parties. The most-favored-nation clause is now a fundamental principle of U.S. trade policy.

The Reciprocal Trade Agreement encouraged the development of bilateral trade treaties to increase U.S. exports. These measures were initial steps toward the free trade policies of a later date. The act was extended every few years, and by 1945, trade agreements had been negotiated with 29 countries. The average rate of tariffs on taxable imports into the United States was reduced from 47 percent in 1934 to 28 percent in 1945. In 1945, Congress authorized the president to cut the tariff rate an additional 50 percent. While the cut reduced tariff rates, it had no effect on such trade barriers as quotas or internal taxes.

After World War II, it became evident that an international organization was needed to develop world trade policies. A world conference was convened out of which emerged in 1948 the first General Agreement on Tariffs and Trade (GATT). The act of 1934 provided the legal document for U.S. participation in the formation of GATT. From the 1950s to the 1980s, essentially all progress to reduce trade barriers was a response to the activities of GATT. The export of commodities from the United States flourished in the 1950s as this nation aided in the world recovery from the devastation of World War II.

By the late 1950s, the postwar recovery was completed, and the industrial nations, particularly Japan and the Western European countries, began exporting. These countries provided formidable competition to the United States. In order to expand U.S. trade, the Congress enacted the Trade Expansion Act of 1962, which authorized the president to (1) reduce tariffs up to 50 percent of the rates existing as of July 1, 1962, (2) eliminate tariffs on products in which the United States and the European Common Market countries together accounted for at least 50 percent of world trade, and (3) eliminate rates that did not exceed 5 percent. The 1962 act empowered the president to negotiate across-the-board (rather than item-by-item) tariff reduction and to modify the safeguard provisions of the old trade agreements program. This act not only increased U.S. trade but influenced the expansion of world trade.

In the 1970s, the trend of the past 35 years was somewhat reversed by a series of acts to restrict trade. The Trade Act of 1974 banned export-import credit via the Export-Import Bank, which was established to finance major exports such as aircraft. The Foreign Corrupt Practices Act of 1979 imposed jail terms and fines for overseas payoffs by U.S. companies. The Carter administration's human rights legislation denied export-import credits to rights violators. Loans were withheld from

South Africa, Uruguay, and Chile. U.S. trade embargoes banned exports to Cuba, Vietnam, Rhodesia, and other countries.

In the 1970s, the export of services increased. Significantly, the importance of such exports grew as deficits in commodity trade increased. The trade deficit was reduced to some extent by a growing balance attributed to services. In response to this trend, the U.S. government in 1981 adopted a policy to promote trade in services, and Congress passed a series of acts toward that end. This response has become a worldwide trend. For example, in the Uruguay Round of GATT in 1982, services were identified as significant areas for tariff reductions.

In 1988, Congress enacted legislation, the Omnibus Trade and Competitiveness Act, that provided a comprehensive policy for the development of American trade. This act provided the foundation for the initial Canada–United States Free Trade Agreement and the more comprehensive North America Free Trade Agreement.

Trade Controls

There are two types of trade barriers, tariff and nontariff, that limit trade between nations. Tariff barriers refer to taxes such as customs duties levied on goods entering a nation. Trade barriers consist of rules and regulations that control the flow of goods and services to a nation.

Tariffs

Tariffs have been the traditional means of reducing, or even eliminating, international trade. In newly developing countries, tariffs have frequently been imposed to protect the growth of new industries. In addition, tariffs have played a role in providing revenues for a nation. There are many types of tariffs. The simplest and most widely used is the simple tariff, called unilateral, that is imposed on all goods from all nations. Another type of tariff is known as the general-conventional tariff, which applies to all nations except those that have tariff treaties or conventions that specify particular conditions. There is also a specific duty tax, known as an ad valorem duty, that is determined on the basis of a tax permit, or as a percentage of the value of goods imported.

Since World War II, there has been a worldwide attempt to lower tariffs through GATT. When the General Agreement on Tariffs and Trade was established in 1947, tariffs worldwide added an average of almost 40 percent to the price of imported products. In 1987, at the beginning of the Uruguay Round of GATT, this figure was about 5 percent. When the tariff reduction of the Uruguay Round tax cuts have been implemented, tariffs and other trade barriers will be reduced further. The Organization for Economic Cooperation and Development estimates that worldwide trade will lead to a projected gain in economic output of $270 billion by 2002.

Trade Barriers

Nontax barriers include quotas, preferential treatment to domestic producers, antidumping measures, and subsidies. Quotas impose a limit on the quantity of specified goods that can be imported. Thus the United States has established quotas for textile imports from specific countries. A quota may be either directed against a single nation or applied universally. Antidumping measures are designed to prevent the practice, common among nations that have excess amounts of certain products, of selling those products at or even below cost in order to develop trade relations with the importing country. Many nations provide direct subsidies to designated industries to enable them to compete effectively against imports. In 1980, for example, the U.S. government subsidized certain types of steel in order to strengthen the nation's position against imports, particularly from Japan.

Monetary barriers can control exchange rates. There are three commonly used monetary restrictions. In the first type, blocked currency, imports are eliminated by restricting the availability of foreign exchange. This measure is usually imposed for specific commodities and may persist for a specified time. In 1975, for instance, Iran used a currency blockage to eliminate trade with the United States. The second currency control consists of differential exchange rates. This barrier sets different rates for converting currencies into foreign monies in order to control the amount of import goods from a given country. A government may set different rates on different goods to control the flow of a particular commodity. Finally, a government can set higher conversion rates on goods it does want imported. This method is rarely used, for it normally receives such bad publicity that the relations between governments deteriorate.

Trade barriers may be defined in such broad terms that they are difficult to interpret. In a number of countries, trade barriers are imposed at the direction of the government, as in Cuba, which has allowed no trade relations with the United States since the Castro regime assumed power over 30 years ago.

Unfair Trade Laws and Regulations

All countries condemn the use of unfair trade laws, but the practice persists. If, however, the United States believes an unfair trade situation exists, an investigation may be initiated. A special unit of the

Department of Commerce will determine whether and to what extent an unfair practice exists. If the decision is affirmative, the International Trade Commission (ITC)—a six-member independent agency—determines whether the practice is causing "material injury" to an American industry. Under the general rules of GATT, the unfair trade effects may be remedied by imposing import offsetting duties if both decisions are affirmative. The duty is recalculated each year when requested by the offending country in an "administrative review." The duty is discontinued when the unfair policy stops.

In the past, when a dispute developed over unfair trade practices, the discussion between the countries was carried out in a highly charged political atmosphere. To lessen the tensions, GATT developed procedures for the investigation of unfair trade practices. Well-established statutory standards now provide a sound basis for determining whether imports are or are not "fairly traded."

For many years, the United States rarely protested the use of unfair trade practices. As the United States expanded its trade in the 1980s, its policy changed. Between 1980 and 1989, the United States undertook 451 antidumping investigations against 54 countries, of which 327 were completed. More than half of these cases (54 percent) resulted in affirming dumping regulations or were settled. Of the countries investigated, Japan with 58 offenses had the most, followed by West Germany, 29; Taiwan, 28; Korea, 27; Italy, 26; Canada, 25; and France, 22 (Tables 1 and 2).

A lower but still substantial number of countervailing duty cases were also filed during the 1980s against 36 countries. Brazil had the most with 36, followed by France, 28; Italy, 24; Spain, 21; and the United Kingdom and West Germany with 18 apiece.

A wide variety of industries were targets of the U.S. Antidumping and Countervailing Duty (CVD) cases. Of the 451 antidumping investigations, 201 were directed against iron and steel and 58 against chemicals. Of the countervailing duty cases, 149 targeted iron and steel, 45 targeted food, and 37 targeted chemicals.

The unfair trading cases triggered the establishment of some of the most important trading policies since 1980. The "dumping" of iron and steel into the U.S. market formed the basis of a major "voluntary restraint agreement" in 1982, which limited steel imports from 18 nations. Another example is the countervailing duty filed by the U.S. lumber industry in 1985 that resulted in reduced imports from Canada. In 1986, the well-known semiconductor accord reached with Japan set floor prices for Japanese conductors. The list of commodities targeted for trade investigations has grown significantly. In 1989, dumping orders were imposed against computer diskettes and cellular

Table 1. Number of Antidumping and Countervailing Duty Investigations
by the United States, 1980–1989

	Antidumping	Countervailing Duty
1980	37	69
1981	15	17
1982	65	116
1983	46	8
1984	74	26
1985	63	31
1986	71	20
1987	15	3
1988	42	8
1989	23	3

Source: U.S. International Trade Commission, Annual Reports, Washington, DC.

Table 2. Target Industries of U.S. Antidumping and Countervailing Duty
Investigations, 1980–1989

Industry	Antidumping	Countervailing Duty
Chemicals	58	37
Food	16	45
Iron and Steel	201	149
Leather	—	6
Machinery	8	6
Nonferrous metals	16	5
Petroleum tubular goods	72	8
Textiles and apparel	15	6
Lumber	—	4
Other	125	34
Total	451	300

Source: U.S. International Trade Commission, Annual Reports, Washington, DC.

mobile telephones. In 1991, the United States imposed dumping duties against word processors and display screens. Dumping procedures were also initiated against the largest producer of Japanese minivans, and luxury cars were named as a possible target.

The unfair trade investigations have thus become a major element in U.S. trade policy. The United States was most influential in making unfair trade policies a part of GATT procedure, and indeed the United States has been the world's leading prosecutor of unfair trade practices. Other nations are now beginning to use these procedures to protect them from unfair trade practices. Notable among these are the European Union, Australia, and Canada.

Export Promotion

In order for companies to sell on a world market, a promotion program is desirable and possibly even necessary. Promotion promotes awareness in the foreign market as well as interest in purchasing the given commodity. Promotion includes advertising, personal selling, sales promotion, and publicity. For a U.S. company, the most inexpensive way to promote a product is through the U.S. Department of Commerce. The promotion of a product may also originate from state and local governmental agencies.

Company Promotional Efforts

Many of the largest firms have developed international organizations to sell their products, a trend encouraged in recent years by the globalization of industry. International companies must develop a distribution system that entails a complete sales organization, and considerable capital is required to develop a company's world marketing system. The motor vehicle industry and modern high technology are excellent examples of successful world marketing organizations.

Advertising is fundamental to the success of a company's international competition. Advertising represents a tangible resource, transferable from one export market to another, and for many industries, advertising may in fact constitute their sole contact with overseas markets. For an advertising campaign to succeed, it must provide fundamental information to the buyer and establish the importance of the product in the potential market.

Advertising is the most cost-effective method for communicating with potential buyers, but in order for it to work a complete campaign must be devised. The company must not only present its product in correct detail, but must also be aware of the local economy and culture. An experienced ad agency in the host country is normally desirable for an effective selling campaign.

The selection of the most appropriate media is a particularly important task. Although ads can be placed in the usual radio, television, newspaper, and magazine spots, other more specialized media, such as general trade and market directories, may be more effective venues, for they reach markets directly. Many business magazines also issue international editions.

Trade Center Shows

The U.S. Department of Commerce has 17 complete trade centers worldwide, located in such major centers as Paris, Vienna, Frankfurt,

Warsaw, London, Milan, Sydney, Singapore, Tokyo, Taipei, Seoul, and Mexico City. Each city has about ten trade shows annually to highlight a particular industry with export potential in the country. The trade shows provide an excellent opportunity to display products, demonstrate quality of goods, and provide information. In many fairs, contracts are negotiated at the exhibition. The trade shows are an excellent way to contact potential customers. For a modest fee, the trade center provides conference and press previews to attract customers.

International Trade Fairs

International trade fairs offer customers the opportunity to examine industrial products firsthand. A trade fair may be privately or governmentally sponsored. Many fairs specialize in a particular product, such as the Paris Air Show and the Frankfurt Book Fair. Many fairs are internationally known, such as the Hanover Fair in Germany, and attract a worldwide audience.

Many U.S. firms exhibit their products at international fairs. The first type is the private trade fair, sponsored by the U.S. Department of Commerce. An organization may plan an overseas trade fair and then acquire a certificate from the U.S. Department of Commerce if it meets the necessary standards.

The second type is the foreign buyer show. The U.S. and foreign commercial services select leading U.S. trade shows in industries that exhibit a high export potential. Foreign companies are then invited to attend these fairs.

The third type consists of U.S. pavilions at international trade fairs where products are displayed. A company or industry may rent a booth in a pavilion to display products. The U.S. Department of Commerce may arrange these trade fairs in order to provide attractive and functional exhibits.

The international trade fair requires careful planning and trained personnel to explain the value of the products shown.

Trade Missions

Trade missions are planned to provide information to major potential importers of U.S. goods. The trade missions may be developed by individual firms or governmental sponsors. The U.S. Department of Commerce plans missions to countries throughout the world to introduce U.S. industry and to provide information to foreign consumers. A trade mission may consist of 5 to 15 members.

Three types of trade missions may be distinguished. The first consists of personnel from the Department of Commerce who select a particular product and plan visits to countries where sales potential is greatest. The program is tailored to the specific needs of each participant. A major function of the mission is for U.S. citizens to meet with foreign governmental and industrial leaders.

A second type of mission is the state- and industry-organized mission that is government approved. These missions are created by state development agencies, trade associations, chambers of commerce, and other export-oriented groups. These groups must follow the guidelines provided by the U.S. Chamber of Commerce.

Finally, seminar missions promote the sale of a particular product. These seminars have an educational sales strategy that provides information on sophisticated products and technology.

Catalog Exhibitions

To provide information to foreign buyers, most companies produce catalogs, brochures, and other graphic materials. This material is usually distributed through U.S. embassies and consulates. Most catalogs are devoted to a specific product group so that the U.S. industry expert can provide technical information to the potential buyer. The cost of a catalog exhibition is modest. In recent years, video cassettes have added a new dimension to this promotional endeavor.

State and Local Governmental Promotion

Many states offer an array of promotional services to companies seeking an international market. In addition, many states maintain international offices in market areas around the world. These offices are most numerous in Japan and Western Europe. The state office supplies information about domestic producers, provides assistance to trade missions, and helps locate potential buyers. In recent years, states have encouraged foreign buyers to visit them, and the subsequent person-to-person relationships have aided successful commercial transactions. These promotional endeavors tend to stimulate new attitudes toward a company's product. Sales promotion techniques have become a standard procedure for the selling of U.S. goods. Sales promotion not only increases the sales potential but builds the morale of the distributors.

To succeed, this promotional program requires a clear definition of the objectives of the program, precise information about the product, a realistic budget, and a definite plan for implementing a sales contract once it is made. Moreover, the project manager must not only have precise information about the way business is conducted in a particular country but also a good understanding of the broad culture of the nation.

International Trade Agreements

After World War II, policymakers devoted much thought to the types of international economic organizations that should evolve. The international economic structure of the past was clearly completely inadequate. The isolation of nations created many of the political conditions that fostered fascism and military aggression. The negotiation to reconstruct the world's economy began at the Bretton Woods conference in the United States in 1944. As a response to these meetings, the International Monetary Fund (IMF) and the World Bank were established. The conference also recognized that barriers to trade had to be reduced.

General Agreement on Tariffs and Trade (GATT)

In 1947, the United States and 23 other countries met in Geneva to find ways to reduce tariffs and remove trade barriers. The fundamental principles were established at this meeting. The General Agreement on Tariffs and Trade stipulated that these 23 countries must treat foreign firms the same as domestic firms in all trade relationships. Consequently, GATT members agreed to extend to all their trading partners the concessions awarded to a single nation.

Evolution of GATT

The second meeting of GATT was held at Annecy, France, in 1949. Thirty-three countries participated in the second meeting. The Geneva and Annecy meetings established procedures to reduce tariffs and structure the organization.

The Torquay and Geneva Rounds, in 1951 and 1956, respectively, are regarded as less significant. The U.S. economy was believed to be so powerful that its predominance could never be threatened. As a consequence, the United States dominated the world's economy and controlled trade relationships, bringing great economic benefits to the world and fueling the belief its dominance would ensure ultimate world peace.

As the dominance of the United States declined in the 1960s, the need for freer trade was once again recognized. The Dillon Round in 1962 resulted in further reductions of average world tariff rates. Its goals, however, of an across-the-board 20 percent reduction of tariffs and the settlement of problems unresolved in the 1950s, especially those involving trade agreements with less-developed countries, were not met.

Seventy countries participated in the Kennedy Round, sixth in the series of negotiations, and major progress was accomplished in the size of the tariff reduction and the value of the world trade involved. The negotiation concluded in 1969 with tariffs reduced on some 60,000 commodities, valued at $40 billion in world trade. Again, however, its stated goals, such as a 50 percent across-the-board reduction in tariffs on industrial products, were not achieved. Overriding national interests of many countries forced exceptions to such a reduction for such commodities as chemicals, steel, aluminum, pulp, and paper.

By the early 1970s, a gradual erosion of the free trade principle necessitated the organization of the Tokyo Round in 1973. The basic goals remained the same as in previous rounds, that is, to expand and liberalize world trade. The Tokyo Round attempted to limit the scope of trade exceptions but recognized the special needs of developing countries in their trade negotiations. The Tokyo Round, concluding in 1978, was the most complex and comprehensive trade negotiating effort attempted to date, for it tried to develop a substantively free world trade system with different economies and political systems and needs. Again, expectations were high. For example, the Carter administration predicted that the free trade development would create more than $25 billion of new trade for the United States, creating more than 100,000 new jobs. These benefits did not accrue. In reality, trade disputes with Japan and other countries multiplied. Most countries did not sign the trade regulations introduced in the Tokyo Round.

In November 1985, 90 countries unanimously agreed to a U.S. proposal to launch a new round of global trade talks beginning in September 1986 at Punta del Este, Uruguay. The talks concentrated on the following sectors:

Agriculture. The development of worldwide agricultural policy has been one of the most difficult problems. The Uruguay Round attempted to reduce import barriers and pare government subsidies, including both European-style export subsidies and more traditional farm programs such as those in the United States.

Services. Initial negotiations began the process of developing broad rules and enforcement procedures to govern trade in services, such as banking, insurance, and data processing.

Intellectual Property. The round wrote rules to protect patents, trademarks, and copyrights from pirating and counterfeiting and set up new procedures for enforcement.

Investment. Regulations were proposed to regulate the use of restrictions in foreign investment that also limit trade, such as requirements that foreign companies use a certain proportion of local workers and materials or that they export a minimum percentage of their output.

Moratorium on Protectionism. GATT members agreed to eschew any further protectionist measures that violate existing GATT rules and to negotiate a phaseout of current violations. These provisions required the United States to submit unfair trade practices concerning trade in merchandise through GATT dispute-settlement policies rather than deciding such cases on its own.

Strengthening GATT Enforcement. It was recognized that in the past, enforcement procedures had been weak. Rules were now established for dispute-settlement and other enforcement procedures. A schedule was prepared for clearing up outstanding issues from previous negotiations, such as rules governing the use of subsidies and temporary restrictions to deal with sudden surges of imports.

Textiles. U.S. officials agreed to consider changing or replacing the Multifibre Agreement, an international compact that set worldwide textile import quotas, when it expired in 1991.

GATT and the U.S. Economy

How will the new Uruguay Agreement affect the American economy? There is general agreement that the freer trade area will provide a number of benefits. The Institute of International Economics predicts that the American annual trade deficit will be reduced by about $22 billion and boost the U.S. economy by nearly a full percentage point. Further, the institution projected that global tariff cuts should boost U.S. exports by $41.9 billion by 2000. The lower U.S. tariffs would result in an increase of $27.7 billion in imports. The report stated, in addition, that the Uruguay Round would provide more than 19 times the benefits of the free trade agreement with Mexico. The higher exports plus lower costs to consumers and U.S. businesses for imports should translate into a total gain for the U.S. economy of $65 billion by 2004.

Although the new agreement will not completely liberalize world trade, it moves the nations closer to free trade than any past agreement. To illustrate, the United States, Canada, Japan, and most countries of Europe will eliminate tariffs on pharmaceuticals, construction materials, agricultural equipment, furniture, paper products, and medical equipment. Unlike previous GATT agreements, it opens trade in commercial services and agriculture. For the first time, intellectual property trade is covered by GATT, which will greatly benefit the U.S. computer, software, telecommunications, and pharmaceutical industries.

To understand the importance of GATT, suppose there was no free trade between the states. The Commerce Clause of the U.S. Constitution ensures that the exchange of goods and services between the states be free and open. It is the free trade between the different regions—industrial Northeast, agrarian Midwest, and the resource-rich West and Southwest—that has allowed the U.S. economy as a whole to grow and achieve high living standards.

The global economy is in a similar situation today. The United States, Canada, Japan, and Western Europe have well-developed economies and produce most of the industrial material of the world. Many Third World economies are poised for growth. Economic barriers to growth will gradually disappear. In this way, GATT will benefit both developed and developing countries.

The agreement holds promise for different sectors of the U.S. economy. For example, the agreement will most likely provide greater opportunities for workers who specialize in services and in those commodities in which their nation is a leader. For the consumer, it will provide access to less expensive goods from around the world. In short, GATT can provide a decisive step toward a higher standard of living throughout the world.

The Uruguay Round concluded its negotiations in 1994. The United States Congress ratified the new agreement in December 1994.

International Commodity Agreements

The development of commodity agreements was initiated at the original Havana meeting of GATT. All member states of GATT were asked to participate. Member states could request study groups for each commodity. Consumers and producers were to have equal voting power on the commodity council set up under any agreement. The terms of an agreement had to be published in full and the agreement was limited to five years. The objective was to meet world demand at reasonable prices and ensure that increases in output should come from the most efficient producers. All agreements were to be subject to United Nations review.

In the early 1950s, due to fluctuations of commodity prices, study groups were created for lead, zinc, cocoa, coffee, tin, rubber, and wool, and the existing International Council for cotton, sugar, and wheat was reorganized. International agreements followed for wheat, sugar, coffee, and tin.

Each of these four agreements evolved differently. The Wheat Agreement was a system for allocating supplies through multilateral controls. Prices and stocks were effectively managed by the authorities in the United States and Canada, the two largest producers. In this manner, the Third World countries benefited from a smooth flow of wheat and from concessionary sales to countries with special needs, as determined under U.S. Public Law No. 480. At the same time, however, these provisions discouraged poor countries from exporting domestic wheat production. The Wheat Agreement was renewed from 1949 until 1970, when the Wheat Council became no more than a trade clearinghouse.

The International Sugar Agreement was established in 1954 to regulate sugar production through a quota system designed to maintain supplies at equitable and stable prices. The largest exporter was Cuba, the main importers were the United Kingdom, United States, and the Soviet Union. When the United States boycotted Cuban sugar by unilateral action, the scheme collapsed.

The two other major international commodity agreements, for tin and coffee, lasted longer and came closer to fulfilling the Havana principles. An international tin agreement came into existence in 1956 after nearly ten years of negotiation, but without the participation of the United States and the Soviet Union. It was based on regulation of exports and in the creation of a buffer stock (25,000 tons). Agreements were renewed every five years, and in 1971 a production quota system was added to ensure a more equitable sharing of the markets. This system led to divisional competition between the exporting countries with no increase in earnings. Since the price on the buffer stock could not be controlled by the producing countries, the agreement failed.

The International Coffee Agreement began when the Latin American producers established export quotas in 1958 following the collapse of prices or a response to overproduction, not only in Brazil but in Central America and East Africa. In 1962, an agreement was signed between all producers and the major consumers, including the United States. The purpose was to maintain the 1962 price level. Nevertheless, the price of coffee continued to fluctuate depending on availability. In 1968, when the agreement was renewed, an interesting innovation established a diversified fund to help with structural change designed to control the new planting of coffee. In 1973, a crisis occurred when a cartel similar to the Organization of Petroleum Exporting Countries (OPEC) was proposed, upsetting the importing countries. The agreement finally collapsed in 1989 when Brazil tried to control production. The United States, as the chief consumer, would not pay higher prices to Brazil when coffee could be bought cheaper elsewhere.

The most recent agreement among a group of countries occurred when OPEC members succeeded in raising the price of oil from $1.30

in the 1960s to $7.00 in 1974 and to an all-time high of $40.00 in 1978. This price hike stimulated production outside OPEC and world oil prices have dropped to about $18.00 a barrel in 1994. The OPEC nations, though still attempting to maintain oil quotas, have lost much of their economic power as a result of producers outside the OPEC cartel and the reduced consumption of oil products. Nevertheless, OPEC nations have had worldwide economic repercussions. High prices brought immense wealth to the OPEC nations. The rise in oil prices and the need to import oil into the United States has been a major factor in the great deficit in the U.S. balance of trade. It has also been devastating to Third World countries where commodity prices were declining when oil prices rose dramatically.

International commodity agreements have normally been temporary. None, including the present OPEC, has been able to control the flow of a particular commodity in international trade.

United States–Canada Free Trade Agreement (FTA)

Signed by the president of the United States and the prime minister of Canada on January 2, 1988, and later ratified by the governments, the Free Trade Agreement produced a historic link between these two nations. It provided a path-breaking resolution to some of the most difficult economic problems of international trade dividing the two neighbors.

Objectives of the Free Trade Agreement

Although economic relations between Canada and the United States were sometimes strained by national policies, the integration of the economies has made remarkable progress. By the mid-1980s, both nations were eager to avoid disputes that could disrupt bilateral commerce. Despite the progress achieved by GATT to reduce tariffs on trade between Canada and the United States, significant tariff and nontariff barriers remained. It was agreed that the removal of these barriers would benefit both nations.

In the initial stages of the free trade negotiations, each country had certain specific objectives that were essential to assure political acceptance of the overall pact. The objectives of the United States included the establishment of new rules to govern services and investment in order to retain traditional trade relationships with Canada and to resolve trade and investment problems in energy and motor vehicles. Canadian objectives were more precise, due to the dominance of trade with the United States. Canada centered on the need to attain greater security of access to the U.S. market, particularly through changes in U.S. trade laws.

These goals were defined in the negotiation process as the basic objectives:

1. To eliminate trade barriers to goods and services.
2. To promote fair trade.
3. To improve the investment climate.
4. To establish joint procedures to administer the Free Trade Agreement.
5. To resolve disputes.
6. To promote further cooperation on trade and investment issues both bilaterally and multilaterally.

Importance of the Free Trade Agreement

Since the acceptance of the Free Trade Agreement by both countries in 1988, notable gains in trade relationships have been achieved. Both countries were committed to liberalizing barriers to trade and investments and to expanding bilateral economic relations. Most significant, FTA has encouraged efficiency and increased productivity in both nations thus enlarging their position in the world market. Given the importance of increased exports from the United States to the world, arising from the present annual deficit of more than $100 billion, the systematic benefits that result from FTA may ultimately prove more significant than the bilateral economic benefits for the United States.

The Free Trade Agreement between Canada and the United States provided a small model for the Uruguay Round GATT. By elaborating national procedures such as the right of establishment and performance, FTA provides a foundation for multilateral negotiations. The regulations resulting from the Uruguay Round reflect some of these endeavors.

The Free Trade Agreement has not solved all trade problems between Canada and the United States. Five areas, including subsidies, investment in the energy sector, government procurements, transportation, and intellectual property rights, still require additional consideration.

North American Free Trade Agreement (NAFTA)

The initial concept of free trade between the United States, Canada, and Mexico dates from the early 1980s when the three governments met at Cancun to consider ways of cooperation and development. At that meeting, President Reagan elaborated on the principles guiding the United States in its efforts to ensure prosperity and stability for the world's developing nations. These efforts included (1) stimulating international trade by opening up markets, both within and among countries, (2) improving the elements for private investment, and (3) creating a political atmosphere that encourages practical solutions to problems of development and discourages policies that interfere with trade development. The United States adhered to the philosophy that full and unhindered trade between nations was the basis of economic prosperity. This belief continues to inform its views on future development.

Finally, in 1990, U.S. president George Bush, former Canadian prime minister Brian Mulroney, and Mexican president Carlos Salinas began the process of developing a free trade association between the three nations. By August 1992, they reached an accord, and they signed the agreement in December 1992. The three governments later ratified the trade agreement.

Objectives of NAFTA

The basic objectives of NAFTA are

1. To promote trade liberalization.
2. To improve the climate for bilateral investment.
3. To resolve problems arising from disputes over the use of subsidies and countervailing duties.
4. To create new rules to govern trade in services and liberalize the financial markets.
5. To promote multilateral concepts on trade and investment issues in GATT.

Implementation of NAFTA

The first effect of NAFTA is to liberalize trade. Over a period of 15 years, NAFTA plans to reduce and ultimately eliminate all tariffs and most nontariff barriers between the United States, Canada, and Mexico. In addition, none of the three nations can increase their tariffs on imports from other countries.

Currently, about 68 percent of goods imported from Mexico into the United States come without tariffs, and about 50 percent of U.S. exports to Mexico are tax free. Other less obvious merchandise trade barriers were removed. In the traditional in-bound or maquiladora industries, performance (export) requirements and restrictions on domestic sales were removed.

The North American Free Trade Agreement focuses on more than commodity trading alone. The agreement recognizes the need to liberalize trade in services and foreign investment, to increase sales abroad, and to strengthen the protection of intellectual property. In these achievements, NAFTA represents goals that have been part of the new GATT policies.

Restrictions under NAFTA

Although a significant percentage of tariff protection is removed, NAFTA retains protectionist elements, protecting such sensitive sectors as agriculture, minerals, textiles, apparel, and banking by extending the phase-in time. This protection is, however, temporary. The agreement contains other types of protection that are not only permanent but that also raise trade barriers above pre-NAFTA levels.

In several sectors—notably automobiles, textiles, and apparel—NAFTA imposes North American content rules, some of which appear to increase protectionism. Under the United States–Canada Free Trade Agreement, for example, automobiles could be imported duty-free if they contained at least 50 percent Canada–U.S. inputs. For auto imports to receive NAFTA benefits, the North American rule is 62.5 percent. For textiles and apparel to qualify for free trade under NAFTA, all components, starting with the yarn or fiber, must be made in North America. Thus, the NAFTA covenant extends and strengthens the protectionism inherent in the broader, multinational Multifibre Agreement.

Dispute Settlement

Before the passage of NAFTA, the settlement of trade disputes among the countries was difficult. If a disagreement arose, for example, between the United States and Canada or Mexico, the following steps were instituted to address the problem. The U.S. government began action through the Department of Commerce, which referred the results to the International Trade Commission. If the International Trade Commission rejected the appeal, there was a final appeal to the U.S. court system, a lengthy, expensive, and uncertain course.

Under NAFTA, there is, for the first time, a binational panel, consisting of two representatives of the United States, two Canadians or two Mexicans, and a fifth person chosen at random from a list agreed to by both parties to settle disputes. This has proved most important, for it removes the politics from international trade. In the implementation of NAFTA procedures, the Mexicans agreed to reform their own judicial system in order to comply with the established NAFTA adjudication system. The binational system has been successful and has become a permanent element of the overall agreement.

Opposition to NAFTA

The principal objection to NAFTA is based on the wide economic differences that separate the U.S. and Mexican economies. Specifically, opponents argue that low Mexican wages, about one-eighth, on average, of those in the United States, will attract manufacturing to Mexico, causing a direct loss of U.S. jobs. Furthermore, the argument persists that even if there is an eventual net gain in U.S. jobs, there will be no effective compensation, no meaningful retraining, and no financial assistance for those who have already lost their jobs.

Opponents also contend that Mexico does not enforce its labor or environmental laws, giving Mexico a further cost advantage in competing with U.S. industry. In addition, the Mexican worker lacks many of the amenities enjoyed by American workers, such as paid vacations and health insurance, that raise the cost of goods further.

In 1991, Mexico's Gross Domestic Product (GDP) was $203 billion, Canada's GDP was $500 billion, and the GDP of the United States was $5,673 billion. The U.S. economy had 87.8 percent of the total for the three nations. Some opponents argue that these disparities are simply too great. Never before has a developing nation like Mexico entered an agreement with an advanced industrial nation with the avowed purpose of changing its economy.

Support for NAFTA

Proponents of the agreement assert that the Mexican economy, like the Canadian economy, is already highly integrated with the U.S. economy. This integration is revealed in the importance of the two North American countries as markets for U.S. products. The value of goods exported to the two countries in 1991 approximated $85 billion to Canada and $33 billion to Mexico. These two countries occupy first and third places in U.S. trade; Japan occupies second place. Shipments of U.S. goods to Canada and Mexico together constituted 28 percent of all U.S. merchandise exported in 1991. The United States also invests heavily in both of these countries. Over half of the trade in manufactured goods is intracompany.

Supporters of NAFTA also dismiss the concern that the U.S. market will be swamped with cheap imports from Mexico. In recent years, U.S. exports to Mexico have increased much more rapidly than U.S. imports. Before the agreement was developed, tariff barriers had been greatly lowered. The tariffs averaged about 3 percent between the two countries. There is every indication that NAFTA will augment the economic integration that is already in progress among the three nations.

Studies indicate that Mexican potential to import from the United States outweighs the U.S. potential to import from Mexico. This finding suggests that the U.S. trade surplus from Mexico will continue to grow in tandem with the Mexican economy. The United States thus has a major stake in Mexico's economic growth.

Initial Trade Developments under NAFTA

As the first anniversary of NAFTA approaches, strong evidence exists that the treaty has erased national borders for business and created a new North American market. Companies are not limiting their developments in Canada, the United States, or Mexico but are now beginning to think in terms of North America.

In the first ten months of NAFTA, the U.S. Department of Commerce reported that U.S. trade with Mexico increased by 18 percent. U.S. exports to Mexico increased from an annual rate of $42 billion to $52 billion and Mexican exports to the United States have increased from $26 billion to $48 billion. The leading exports to Mexico were food, beverages, and consumer goods manufactures. Allied with the rise of trade on the continent, direct foreign investment is also increasing, knitting the economies more closely. Canadian and U.S. companies invested $24 billion in Mexico in the past eight months of 1994, accounting for 55 percent of Mexico's foreign direct investments. Other countries are also investing in North America to take advantage of lower tariffs. For example, in November 1994 the Toyota Motor Company announced a $450 million expansion in Ontario to make Corollas for the North American market. John M. Weiker, Canada's chief NAFTA negotiator states, "NAFTA is laying the foundation for something that will be a lot bigger."

The U.S. exports to Mexico are growing three times faster than U.S. exports to the rest of the world, and Mexico just passed Japan as the second largest consumer of U.S. products. Trade of the United States with Canada has grown by more than 10 percent—double the gain with Europe and Asia. About two-thirds of Canada's imports were from the United States, and U.S. purchases account for 25 percent of Canada's gross domestic products.

NAFTA has fostered dramatic change within the U.S. auto industry. Before the free trade pact was approved, the Big Three—Ford, General Motors, and Chrysler—had to purchase locally most of the cars they sold in Mexico. Now Ford can freely export cars to Mexico. In the meantime, Ford has spent $60 million to modernize its Cuantitlan plant near Mexico City to produce small cars and light trucks for global sales. The export of Ford cars to Mexico has increased from 1,200 in 1993 to 30,000 in 1994. Furthermore, the export of Mexican Ford cars to the United States is increasing. The trade in motor vehicles has increased, but there has been in fact no significant movement of jobs from the

United States to Mexico. Although the average Mexican labor cost is $6.00 per hour, including benefits, productivity is lower because of less automation. Almost 80 percent of the components in Ford's Mexican-assembled cars for export come from the United States; in other words, U.S. industry has benefited from the growth in Mexico.

In the initial developments of the trade patterns, it is somewhat disappointing that U.S. imports from Mexico and Canada have been rising faster than exports to both countries. Makers of high-value-added U.S. products were predicted to increase exports. Instead, electronics, computer products, and telecommunications equipment have been entering the United States from Mexico twice as fast as they have gone in the other direction. As a result, the United States imported about $48 billion of Mexican goods and $120 billion of Canadian goods in 1994.

NAFTA has not yet proven to be the significant creator of U.S. jobs predicted by some economists. The U.S. Labor Department estimated that in 1994 there would be fewer than 100,000 of the 1.7 million new jobs in the United States related to NAFTA. At the same time, there has been little migration of labor to Mexico. In the first ten months of 1994, only 12,015 U.S. workers have been certified for aid under NAFTA Adjustment Assistance Programs.

NAFTA and Environmental Protection

There has been concern in the United States that the lower environmental standard of Mexico will present a problem. In order to protect the United States, the Office of U.S. Trade Representatives has provided a set of guidelines to ensure that the agreement will promote environmental protection. The guidelines stipulate that

1. Federal and state environmental standards and the U.S. right to ban nonconforming imports will be maintained.
2. The parties to the agreement, including states and cities, will be allowed to enact standards that are more strict than international and national standards.
3. Each party is allowed to choose the level of protection of human, animal, or plant life it considers appropriate.
4. The parties are encouraged to improve harmonization of standards.
5. The parties may adopt regulations and sanitary and phytosanitary standards based on available information when there is insufficient evidence to conduct a risk assessment.
6. Each country and its nationals may review and comment on proposed regulatory action.

7. A committee on standard-related measures will be established to facilitate compatibility of standards.
8. A committee on sanitary and phytosanitary measures will be established to enhance food safety.

When a dispute arises that raises factual questions about a country's standard, a measure taken under international agreement, the complaining party may submit the issue for regulation under the NAFTA dispute settlement procedures, according to which the complaining party has the burden of proof.

Potential Western Hemisphere Free Trade Agreement

As a response to rapid development in the economies of Latin America, it is now possible to begin thinking seriously about the possibility of a free trade agreement covering the total Western Hemisphere (WHFTA). The world now possesses a global economy tied together by developments in information processing, communication technology, and transportation. Globalization makes possible the rapid and pervasive diffusion of production, consumption, and investment of goods, services, and capital.

Recently, three great regional economies have evolved: the European Union dominates Europe and the Middle East, Japan reigns economically over the Far East and Pacific, and the United States holds economic sway in North and South America. As a result, intraregional trade is now growing more rapidly than interregional trade. The competitive pressures following globalization and regionalization are leading to governmental policies to establish a hospitable economic environment.

In response to the relative decline in interregional trade, governments are taking steps to formulate concurrent subregional and global initiatives. There is now universal recognition that nations cannot exist in isolation. Within this context, it is evident that the North American Free Trade Agreement marks an important step toward the development of a regional trading policy for the Americas within a global region.

The North American Free Trade Agreement represents for the first time a coherent trade policy associated with a Latin American country. It establishes a legal framework that will allow a developing Latin country to constitutionalize external obligations, thus allowing the international trade regime to become an integral part of domestic economic policy.

Traditionally, the Latin American countries have looked inward with minimal outward contacts. A new perspective is now evident as country after country has developed outward-looking policies. Virtually every Latin American country has adopted international market-based economic policies. Many countries have adopted democratic pluralism and begun to forge a national consensus favoring quota integration into the global economy. The first steps toward a Western Hemisphere Free Trade Agreement appear within the realm of reality within the next decade.

Modern Trade Objectives of the United States

The modern objectives for establishing trade relations with other countries was enacted by Congress in Public Law 100-418, known as the Omnibus Trade and Competitiveness Act of 1988. In the development of the act, Congress found that "in the past ten years, there has arisen a new global economy in which trade, technological development, investment, and services form an integrated system. These activities affect each other and the health of the United States economy."

The overall trade objectives are (1) more open, equilateral reciprocal market access, (2) the reduction or elimination of barriers and other trade-distorting policies and practices, and (3) a more effective system of international trading disciplines and procedures.

Dispute Settlement

This policy is intended to provide more effective and expeditious procedures and to ensure that such mechanisms within the structure of GATT result in better enforcement of U.S. rights.

Improvement of GATT and Multinational Trade Negotiation Agreements

Such improvement would entail enhancing the status of GATT, improve the operation and extend the coverage of GATT, and respond to country participation with particular agreements and arrangements.

Transparency

A basic goal is to obtain broader application of the principle of transparency, that is, that all negotiations are on public record.

Developing Countries

The United States recognizes the need to treat developing nations with special consideration. The United States aims to ensure that developing countries have trade policies for achieving and maintaining an open international trading system and that they develop a system to reduce nonreciprocal trade benefits.

Current Account Balance

The United States aims to develop rules that address the current imbalances of countries, including imbalances that threaten the stability of international trading systems.

Coordination of Trade and Money

There is a need for monetary coordination to develop mechanisms to assure greater consistency and cooperation between trading and monetary systems.

Agriculture

Because the United States is an excess food producer, one of its principal objectives is to achieve to the maximum extent possible more open and fair conditions of trade in agricultural commodities. The United States hopes (1) to develop, strengthen, and clarify rules for agricultural trade, including restrictions on trade-distorting import and export practices, (2) to increase U.S. exports by eliminating barriers to trade, including the reduction or elimination of subsidization of agricultural products consistent with the national policy of agricultural stabilization in cyclical and unpredictable markets, (3) to create a free and more open world agricultural trading system vis-à-vis questions of exports and other trade-distorting subsidies, market pricing and market access, and other restraints to free trade, and (4) to seek the agreement of the major agricultural countries to pursue policies to reduce excessive production of agricultural commodities during periods of oversupply.

Reduction of Unfair Trade Practices

The United States has two principal negotiation objectives with respect to unfair trade practices. First, the United States seeks to improve the provision of the GATT and nontariff measure agreements in order to define, deter, discourage the persistent use of, and otherwise discipline unfair trade practices having adverse trade effects. Such unfair practices include resource import subsidies, diversionary dumping, dumped or subsidized imports, and export targeting. Second, the United States wishes to obtain enforcement of the GATT rules against state trading enterprises and against the acts, practices, or policies of any foreign government that, as a practical matter, unreasonably require substantial direct investment in the foreign country, the licensing of intellectual property to the foreign country or to a firm of the foreign country, or other collateral concessions as a condition for the importation of any product or service of the United States.

Trade in Services

The principal negotiating objectives of the Unites States regarding trade in services are twofold. First, the United States wishes to reduce or eliminate barriers, including barriers that deny national treatment and restrict an establishment and operation of such markets. Second, the United States seeks international agreement on rules, including dispute settlements that are consistent with the commercial policies of the United States, and the reduction and elimination of such barriers or distortions to ensure fair, equitable opportunities for foreign markets. The policies will take into account the legitimate U.S. domestic objectives, including health or safety, essential security, environmental, consumer or employment opportunities, and the related laws and regulations.

Intellectual Property

The United States has four principal objectives in regard to intellectual property. The first goal is to seek the enactment and effective enforcement of foreign countries of laws that recognize and adequately protect intellectual property, including copyrights, patents, trademarks, semi-conductor chips, layout designs, and trade secrets and provide protection against unfair competition. Second, the United States hopes to establish within GATT substantive standards based on existing international agreements that provide adequate protection, or, if international standards are inadequate or do not exist, to establish the standards in material laws. Third, the United States seeks the inclusion in GATT of adequate and effective substantive norms and standards for the protection and enforcement of intellectual property rights and dispute settlement provisions. These regulations are to be administered without prejudice to other complementary initiatives undertaken in other international organizations. Finally, the United States wants to supplement and strengthen standards for protection and enforcement in existing international intellectual property conventions, including the expanded coverage of new and emerging technologies and the elimination of discrimination and unreasonable exceptions as preconditions to protection.

Foreign Direct Investment

The first objective of the United States regarding foreign direct investment is to reduce or eliminate artificial or trade-distorting barriers to foreign direct investment, to expand the principle of national treatment, to reduce unreasonable barriers to establishment, and to develop internationally agreed rules, including dispute settlement procedures. The second U.S. goal is to protect security, environmental, consumer, health, safety, and employment opportunity interests and to ensure adherence to U.S. laws and regulations.

Safeguards

The principal objectives are to improve and expand rules and procedures covering safeguard measures, to ensure that safeguard measures are transparent, temporary, digressive, and subject to review and termination, and to require notification of and to monitor the use of import relief actions for domestic industries by GATT contracting parties.

Specific Barriers

The United States has a basic policy to reduce or eliminate specific tariff and nontariff barriers in order to maintain competitive trade positions in both exports and imports.

Workers' Rights

The negotiating objectives of the United States in regard to workers rights include the promotion of respect for workers' rights; the relating of workers' rights to GATT articles, objectives, and related instruments to guarantee that the benefits of the trading systems are available to all workers; and the adaptation, as a principle of GATT, of the position that the denial of workers' rights will not allow a country or its industries to gain a competitive advantage in international trade.

Access to High Technology

The principal negotiating objective of the United States regarding access to high technology is to reduce or eliminate foreign barriers to policies and practices by foreign governments that limit equitable access by U.S. personnel to foreign development technology. These practices include barriers, acts, policies, or practices that have the effect of restricting participation of U.S. citizens in government-supported research and development projects, denying equitable access by U.S. citizens to government-held patents, requiring the approval or agreement of governments as a condition for granting license to U.S. citizens, or otherwise denying equitable access to citizens of the United States.

Border Taxes

In order to redress the disadvantages to countries that rely primarily on direct (rather than indirect) taxes for revenue, the United States seeks a revision in GATT with respect to border adjustments for internal taxes.

Growth of U.S. International Trade

There has been a phenomenal rise in U.S. trade since 1970. In that year, the United States exported $42.1 billion out of a world total of $1,336 billion, or only 0.03 percent of the total. Since then the value of export trade has risen steadily and in 1990 totaled $393.6 billion out of a world total of $3,340 billion, or 11.76 percent of the total. Imports have also increased dramatically, rising from $39.9 billion in 1970 to $434.2 billion in 1992.

Importance of International Trade

Exports and imports presently constitute a considerable percentage of total domestic output. Most important for a growing number of industries, changes in trade patterns can result in significant gains and losses in domestic employment opportunities. For example, since about 1980, one out of every six jobs in the manufacturing sector has depended upon exports, and each of these jobs, in turn, supports a corresponding job in a supporting industry. Over 5 million domestic jobs, or about 5 percent of the total work force, depend on U.S. exports. Nearly two-thirds of U.S. imports are critical minerals such as petroleum, chromium, manganese, tin, cobalt, and other products that cannot be produced domestically. One out of every three dollars of U.S. corporate profits was derived from international activities. For each $1 billion of goods exported about 25,000 new jobs are created. An $8 billion increase in exports generates about 200,000 U.S. jobs both directly or indirectly, and a similar increase in imports eliminates about 180,000 jobs. Thus the exports generation effect is about 7.8 percent greater than the import job-loss effect (Table 3).

Balance of Trade

Until the 1970s, the United States had a small positive balance of payment. Thereafter, a negative balance of payment has increased, on the average, to more than $100 billion annually. Of the three major categories of goods traded in the 1990s, agricultural commodities provided a positive balance of trade of $186.20 billion. In contrast, a negative balance of $85 billion consisting of manufactured goods and mineral fuels had a negative balance of $43 billion (Table 4).

The trade deficit is one of the most serious economic problems facing the United States. Much effort has been devoted to tracing the causes of the deficit and offering possible solutions, and there have been efforts to increase trade. The economic recovery in the mid-1980s provided a favorable environment for increased American exports. The drop in the value of the dollar during the 1980s also furnished some impetus to U.S. exports.

It is now evident that government measures and favorable environmental trends alone cannot prompt higher exports; businesses must develop export relations. Currently, about 1 percent of U.S. companies, mostly multinational corporations, control about 85 percent of the export trade. To reduce the trade deficit, the following steps are required: (1) U.S. businesses must be made aware of export opportunities, (2) the federal government needs to develop a comprehensive plan to support U.S. companies, and (3) the firms that do export must obtain sufficient information about foreign markets. As a consequence of corporate ignorance of foreign markets, companies have developed a reputation for delays in delivery, poor maintenance of the products in the foreign country, poor economic relations with foreign purchasers, and other problems.

Importance of Exports to State Economies

Of the $448,156,000,000 of exports in 1992, states contributed directly $379,263,000,000 (Table 5). In addition, $64,900,000 of exports were unreported, including special categories, estimated shipments, foreign trade zones, re-exports, and timing adjustments. Of the specified export shipments, the 12 leading states had 69.2 percent of the total. California led in value of exports with $56,300 million, 14.8 percent of the total, followed by Texas with $43,553 million, 11.4 percent of the total. Hawaii had the lowest exports of the states, totaling less than $20 million.

Table 3. U.S. Share of World Trade, 1960–1990 (Millions of Dollars)

	World	United States	U.S. Percentage of Total
1960	620	19.6	0.03
1965	869	26.7	0.03
1970	1,336	42.7	0.03
1975	1,769	107.7	0.06
1980	2,353	220.6	8.69
1985	2,585	213.1	8.23
1990	3,340	393.6	11.76

Source: *Statistical Abstract of the United States,* U.S. Department of Commerce, Washington, DC.

Table 4. U.S. Balance of Trade, 1950–1992 (Millions of Dollars)

	Exports	Imports	Balance of Trade
1950	9,997	8,954	+1,043
1955	14,298	11,566	+2,732
1960	19,659	15,073	+4,586
1965	26,742	21,520	+5,222
1970	42,681	42,833	–152
1975	107,652	105,935	–1,716
1980	220,626	256,984	–36,358
1985	213,133	361,624	–148,493
1990	394,030	516,987	–122,657
1991	421,730	508,363	–86,633
1992	446,164	554,023	–105,659

Source: *Statistical Abstract of the United States,* U.S. Department of Commerce, Washington, DC.

Table 5. U.S. Exports by State of Origin, 1992 (Millions of Dollars)

	Exports	Percentage
1. California	56,307	14.84
2. Texas	43,553	11.47
3. Washington	28,041	7.39
4. New York	22,628	5.96
5. Michigan	20,414	5.38
6. Ohio	16,306	4.29
7. Louisiana	16,151	4.25
8. Illinois	15,329	4.04
9. Florida	14,431	3.80
10. Massachusetts	10,400	2.74
11. Pennsylvania	10,329	2.72
12. Virginia	9,784	2.57

Source: *Statistical Abstract of the United States,* U.S. Department of Commerce, Washington, DC.

Commodity Trade

Exports and imports fall into three major categories: agricultural commodities, manufactured goods, and minerals (Table 6).

Agricultural Commodities

Exports of agricultural commodities consisted of about $45,590 million, or 9.2 percent, of the total exports of $445,156 million in 1992. Imports of agricultural commodities made up $23,400 million, or 4.4 percent, of the $532,498 million total imports. Agricultural exports garnering more than $1,000 million were vegetables and fruit, $5,716 million; corn, $4,944 million; soybeans, $4,416 million; animal feed, $3,521 million; dairy products and eggs, $2,010; unmanufactured tobacco, $1,651 million; and hides and skins, $1,260 million. Agricultural commodity imports of $1,000 million or more in 1992 consisted of vegetables and fruits, $5,698 million; meats, $2,723; coffee, $1,562 million; and live animals $1,434 million (Table 7).

The United States produces an excess of food products and has become the largest exporter of foods in the world. Accordingly, agricultural commodities exports produced a positive balance of payments in international trade. It is essential for the U.S. economy that the United States remain the food basket for the world.

Manufactured Goods

There were great contrasts in the value of manufactured goods imported and exported in 1992, although in many categories exports and imports were at a par. For example, automatic data processing (ADP) equipment and office machines exported goods valued at $29,968 million and imported products valued at $36,383 million. Likewise, general industrial machinery showed $18,436 million in exports and $15,572 million in imports, and electrical machinery $32,039 million in exports and $39,729 million in imports. In general, the manufactured goods that enjoyed large exports were expensive products. The foreign products most in demand by U.S. companies also tended to be highly valued articles (Table 8). The U.S. motor vehicle industry was built on a domestic market, and for decades very few foreign cars were imported. In the 1950s, however, the unique styling of West Germany's Volkswagen earned the acceptance of U.S. buyers. The peak impact of the Volkswagen occurred in 1970 when 674,945 cars were imported. With competition from Japan in the 1970s, German imports declined, and in 1991 only 172,000 German cars were imported.

Table 6. Commodity Trade and Balance of Payments, 1992
(Millions of Dollars)

	Exports	Imports	Balance of Payments
Total	448,156	532,498	−84,342
Agricultural commodities	42,078	23,437	+18,645
Manufactured goods	347,512	434,236	−86,724
Mineral fuel	11,122	55,028	−43,906

Source: Statistical Abstract of the United States, U.S. Department of Commerce, Washington, DC.

Table 7. Trade in Agricultural Commodities,[1] 1992 (Millions of Dollars)

	Export	Import	Balance of Payments
Total	42,237.7	23,374.9	+18,863
Vegetables and fruit	5,736.3	5,687.6	+39
Corn	4,968.8	68.5	+4,900
Wheat	4,503.2	191.1	+4,312
Soybeans	4,462.8	15.8	+4,440
Meat and preparations	4,207.9	2,711.5	+1,496
Other agriculture	4,111.6	5,897.9	−1,786

[1]Products with a value of $4 million or more.
Source: Statistical Abstract of the United States, U.S. Department of Commerce, Washington, DC.

With the rising price of gasoline in the 1970s, the small, efficient, well-equipped Japanese cars gained a major market in the United States. Peak imports occurred about 1985 when 2,527,000 cars were imported. By the late 1980s the U.S. motor vehicle industry recognized that its survival depended on matching the Japanese competitors. With the improvement of U.S. cars and the development of Japanese factories in the United States, imports of Japanese cars declined to 1,769,000 in 1991 (Table 9).

In recent years, South Korea has been the only country where exports of automobiles to the United States have risen significantly. In 1991, the total reached 200,000. Other countries exporting a small number of cars to the United States include Italy, France, and the United Kingdom.

Minerals

Imports exceed exports in the mineral trade of the United States. In 1992, there was a total import-export total of $52,033 million, of which $44,823 million, or 86 percent, was imports. Of the imported minerals,

Table 8. Trade in Manufactured Goods, 1992[1] (Millions of Dollars)

	Export	Imports	Balance of Payments
TOTAL	347,493.7	434,348.8	-86,855
Electrical machinery	32,172.4	39,710.4	-7,538
ADP equipment	26,999.9	36,377.1	-9,378
Airplanes	26,285.7	3,859.8	+22,426
General industrial	18,479.6	15,519.7	-2,960
Power generating	17,994.7	15,888.1	+2,106
Vehicles/parts	16,753.1	15,838.3	+915
Specialized industrial	16,688.6	11,814.4	+4,874
Scientific instruments	14,374.5	7,602.0	+6,773
Telecommunication equipment	11,247.8	25,802.8	-14,555
Chemicals, organic	10,992.6	9,408.1	+1,584
Chemicals, inorganic	10,257.9	4,252.0	+6,005

[1]Goods with a value of more than $10,000 million.
Source: *Statistical Abstract of the United States*, U.S. Department of Commerce, Washington, DC.

petroleum and its products dominate trade with $42,796 million, or 95 percent of the total. In 1992, petroleum and its products made up $42,055 million, or 42 percent, of the total trade deficit of $99,714 million (Table 10).

The United States was essentially self-sufficient in petroleum and its products to the mid-1960s. Demand continued to rise after this date, however, and output remained nearly stable. In the continental United States, the last major discovery of oil was the East Texas Field in the early 1930s, and the last major discovery of oil in the United States was in 1967 in the North Slopes of Alaska.

Until the early 1970s, the United States controlled the world price of oil. In 1972, however, during the oil crisis, the OPEC nations gained control of the oil reserves in the Middle East, North Africa, Nigeria, and Venezuela. They immediately raised the price of oil to about $3.00 per barrel, beginning a trend that reached a maximum in 1979 with a barrel price of $40.00. As oil production increased worldwide after 1980, the price of petroleum declined to between $18 and $19 per barrel by the mid-1990s.

The reduction of petroleum imports is fundamental to the development of a sound U.S. economy, but although Congress has enacted legislation to increase, for example, the miles per gallon in motor vehicles, the overdependence on imported oil persists. It has been suggested that a heavy tax be placed on gasoline. A gas tax might indeed

Table 9. Passenger Car Imports, 1965–1990

	1965	1970	1975	1980	1985	1990
Japan	25,538	381,338	695,573	1,991,502	2,527,467	1,867,754
West Germany	376,950	674,945	370,012	338,711	473,110	245,266
Italy	9,509	42,523	102,344	46,899	8,689	11,045
United Kingdom	66,565	76,257	67,106	32,517	24,474	27,271
Sweden	26,010	57,844	51,903	61,496	142,640	93,084
France	24,941	37,114	15,647	47,386	42,882	1,976
South Korea	NA	NA	NA	NA	NA	201,475
Mexico	NA	NA	0	1	13,647	215,986
Canada	33,728	692,783	733,766	594,770	1,144,805	1,220,221
Total	563,673	2,013,420	3,255,444	3,116,448	4,397,679	3,944,602

Source: Statistical Abstracts of the United States, U.S. Department of Commerce, Washington, DC.

Table 10. Trade in Minerals, 1992 (Millions of Dollars)

	Export	Import
Total	11,254.1	55,255.6
Coal	4,427.0	418.1
Crude oil	32.4	38,553.1
Petroleum preparation	4,011.3	11,277.1
Liquid propane/butane	257.2	707.1
Natural gas	352.5	3,000.8
Electricity	62.9	589.2
Other minerals	2,110.9	678.5
Metal ore/scrap	3,470.4	3,399.8

Source: Statistical Abstract of the United States, U.S. Department of Commerce, Washington, DC.

decrease gasoline consumption, but it would also certainly raise food prices, for the mechanized agriculture of the United States is a major consumer of gasoline. Moreover, the tax would penalize the lower-income workers who must use a car to reach their workplace. All transportation costs would escalate. An alternative approach is to develop renewable resources. Indeed, Congress passed a number of laws in the 1970s to increase the use of renewable energy, but implementation of these laws was essentially abandoned after 1980, and no new efforts have been made. Although observers and policymakers recognize that the huge importation of petroleum is a major problem, no solution appears in the foreseeable future.

Aside from petroleum, most mineral imports are metallic—iron ore, copper, lead, and zinc. Canada is the leading supplier, but many other countries also export these metals to the United States.

Geographical Distribution of U.S. Trade

Although the United States carries on trade with virtually every nation, Canada, Japan, and Mexico take about 40 percent of the U.S. exports and provide 50 percent of the imports. The eight countries that received more than $10 billion of U.S. imports in 1990 were Canada, Japan, Mexico, United Kingdom, Germany, South Korea, France, and Taiwan (Tables 11 and 12).

United States–Canada Trade Relations

Prior to the Free Trade Agreement, efforts to achieve free trade between the United States and Canada were beset with difficulties. There was a reluctance to develop trade relationships, either because of the protectionist attitude of the United States or the nationalistic sentiment of Canada. Efforts—and failures—to regularize trade between the two countries date from the implementation of a reciprocity treaty in 1854. This treaty was abrogated in the early 1860s by the United States as a result of disputes with Great Britain over the support of the South during the Civil War. An attempt to negotiate another reciprocity treaty in 1874 was also rejected by the United States. In response, Canada turned inward with its National Policy of 1879, which placed high tariffs on United States imports.

The high tariffs imposed by both countries continued until the 1930s. With the beginning of the world depression in 1930, Canada's economy suffered severely, and between 1929 and 1932, Canada's exports plunged by 50 percent. The two governments recognized the need to reduce these tariffs. In 1935, the first comprehensive bilateral trade agreement between the United States and Canada was negotiated by U.S. Secretary of State Cordell Hull and Canadian Prime Minister Mackenzie King. Each party granted the most-favored-nation status and tariffs were reduced below the intermediate rates for certain commodities.

In 1941, with war raging in Europe, the United States and Canada signed the Hyde Park Agreement on Defense Production Sharing. By 1945, the U.S. share of Canadian trade had risen to 83 percent, and the United Kingdom accounted for only 13 percent. These bilateral trade agreements provided the basis for the organization of the multilateral agreements begun by GATT in 1948.

In the late 1940s, Canada and the United States explored the possibility of establishing free trade policies. The agreement envisioned almost unrestricted free entry of goods across both borders after a five-year phase-in period. Both nations would retain the right to maintain

Table 11. U.S. Imports by Country of Origin, 1985 and 1990[1] (Millions of Dollars)

Country	1985		1990	
	Total	Percentage	Total	Percentage
Canada	91,380	18.9	89,086	25.7
Japan	89,664	18.1	68,783	19.9
Mexico	30,157	6.0	19,132	5.5
Germany	28,162	5.6	20,239	5.8
Taiwan	22,666	4.5	16,396	4.7
United Kingdom	20,188	4.0	14,907	4.3
South Korea	18,485	3.7	10,013	2.9
France	13,153	2.6	9,482	2.7
Italy	12,751	2.5	NA	
Total	345,276		495,310	

[1]Countries with more than $10,000 million of exports to the United States.
Source: Statistical Abstract of the United States, U.S. Department of Commerce, Washington, DC.

Table 12. U.S. Exports to Countries, 1985–1990[1] (Millions of Dollars)

Country	1985		1990	
	Total	Percentge	Total	Percentage
Canada	83,674	21.2	45,461	21.9
Japan	41,580	12.3	22,042	10.6
Mexico	28,279	7.2	18,578	8.9
United Kingdom	23,490	5.9	10,802	5.2
Germany	18,760	4.7	8,684	4.1
South Korea	14,404	3.6	11,591	5.6
France	13,664	3.4	7,651	3.6
Taiwan	14,404	3.4	11,591	5.6
Total	206,920		393,592	

[1]Countries importing more than $10,000 million of U.S. exports, 1985–1990.
Source: Statistical Abstract of the United States, U.S. Department of Commerce, Washington, DC.

their own third-party tariffs, thus removing one of the traditional objections of Canada. In addition, the agreement would establish the principle of consultation in the sensitive tariff relationships of agricultural marketing. King decided, however, that the agreement was politically unacceptable and the proposal was abandoned.

During the 1950s and 1960s, both countries sought to develop their trade policies within the framework of GATT. Trade between the two countries grew, and by 1960, Canada's exports to the United States were 60 percent of its total exports. Tariff rates continued to decrease, and by 1967 duties had been reduced by an average of 37 percent. Canada and the United States were moving ever closer toward trade liberation.

The increased trade was symbolized in 1965 by the signing of the Canada-U.S. Automobile Trade Agreement. Transportation equipment was by far Canada's largest manufacturing industry and was dominated by subsidiaries of the major U.S. automobile companies. This agreement provided for duty-free trade over an array of products, subject to certain performance standards. The U.S. Congress accepted the auto pact after major persuasion from President Johnson.

After 1960, Canada became concerned about the possible dominance of foreign investments, primarily from the United States, in the nation's economy. Popular concerns led the Liberal government of Lester Pearson to appoint a royal commission to determine the extent of foreign investment in Canada. Their report led to the passage of the Corporation and Labour Union's Act, which required all corporations to report detailed data on their sales, assets, and degree of foreign ownership.

Despite the integration of the two economies, Canadian economic nationalism grew throughout the 1960s and 1970s. Although still following GATT guidelines, the Canadian government attempted to reduce foreign influences on its economy. In 1966, a nonbinding report on "Guidelines to Good Corporate Citizenship" was prepared to discourage the sale of mines, petroleum concessions, and other natural resources to foreign buyers. This report was reinforced in 1968 by the Watkins Report on "Foreign Ownership and Structure of Canadian Industry." This report stated that the U.S. multinational corporations limited the establishment of an independent economic development policy in Canada. Although it was recognized that foreign direct investment raised the Canadian standard of living, such investments hindered domestic Canadian economic growth. The Watkins Report called for the establishment of a governmental agency to monitor foreign operations and investments and to consider the use of performance requirements of such firms.

In 1970, the Watkins Report established the Standing Committee on External Affairs and National Defense, which extended the nationalist philosophy on foreign investments and recommended the goal of Canadian ownership of at least 51 percent of all corporations over time. It also called for all corporate boards to seat a majority of Canadians. Finally, the proposed new agency was to have both screening and decision-making powers. This nationalist policy was continued in the Gray Report of 1972 on Foreign Direct Investment in Canada, which proposed a method for screening direct investments based on cost-benefit analysis.

In 1973, under Prime Minister Pierre Trudeau, the process culminated in the enactment of the Foreign Investment Review Act. The threshold for review was set at sales of over $3 million. In 1980, the Liberal government added performance reviews to the test of significance, and in 1982 the United States challenged the process before a GATT panel. The panel ruled that the procurement requirements were unfair but allowed the export requirement to remain; Canada complied with the ruling and amended the guidelines.

The implementation of these plans depended upon the policies of the prime minister in power. Under Herb Gray, for example, Canada accepted 73 percent and 70 percent of foreign firms applying to invest in 1980 and 1982, respectively. In the energy sector, the acceptance rate fell to only 18 percent in 1982. In addition, the National Energy Policy led to a capital outflow of slightly more than CDN $15 billion between 1980 and 1985.

In 1984, the newly elected Conservative government of Brian Mulroney abolished the old policies and established a new Investment Canada policy. Investment Canada was charged to increase foreign investments by promoting an "open for business" stance. New establishments were no longer subject to review. Furthermore, investments were assessed for a "net benefit," not a "significant benefit." It had become evident that Canada required foreign investments to develop economically. In 1983, accordingly, the Canadian Manufacturers Association abandoned its century-old support for tariffs and protection and called for a bilateral Canada–United States fair trade agreement. This policy furnished Prime Minister Mulroney the initiative to begin the negotiations for the Canada–U.S. Free Trade policy that was approved in 1988.

The United States is the dominant trading partner with Canada, taking from 66 to 70 percent of both imports and exports (Tables 13 and 14). Canada's economy is thus heavily dependent on the U.S. market. In the development of trade between Canada and the United States, regional differences are apparent. Traditionally, resistance to U.S. trade has been led by Ontarian industrialists trying to retain their tariff protection. Western provinces have advanced free trade as a means of obtaining low-cost manufactured goods. In recent years, these regional differences have gradually disappeared, forcing Canada to become more specialized and to realign its manufacturing base. Canada is thus now able to compete more successfully with U.S. plants. The pattern of free trade with the United States that has developed in recent years reflects Canada's response to the grim prospect of lacking free access to a market of 250 million people with high purchasing power. As the only industrialized nation without such access, Canada could not have

Table 13. Canadian Export-Import Dollars from the United States
(Millions of Dollars)

	Total Exports	Exports to U.S.	%	Total Imports	Imports from U.S.	%
1980	67,730	41,028	61	61,000	41,201	68
1990	131,278	95,388	73	118,000	75,252	63

Source: *Statistical Abstract of the United States*, U.S. Department of Commerce, Washington, DC.

Table 14. Canadian Commodity Exports to the United States, 1990–1992
(Percentage of Total)

Transport equipment	32–36
Crude materials	19–20
Wood and paper	12–13
Machinery	9–10
Chemicals	5–6
Agriculture	5
Others	13–15

Source: *Statistical Abstract of the United States*, U.S. Department of Commerce, Washington, DC.

achieved the economies of scale enjoyed by its international competitors, a competitive disadvantage that could have devastating results for the Canadian economy.

United States–Japan Trade Relations

The growth of Japanese international trade after the early 1960s has been spectacular. This export growth stimulated much of the protectionist action taken by the industrialized countries in the 1960s and 1970s. A number of these actions effectively removed significant areas of trade from the GATT multilateral trading system. In developing its international trade, Japan has focused on exporting while stringently controlling imports.

Japan developed a trade based on low prices and high-quality products. Consequently, they gained an advantage over most of the world's nations. To protect domestic industries, trade restrictions against Japan gradually evolved. The low cost of Japanese textile exports caused the first formal restrictions to be imposed in 1955 as a condition of Japanese inclusion in GATT. As Japanese exports of steel, electronic consumer goods, and motor vehicles rose, they too became subject to barriers and restraints in many countries, including the United States. Indeed, a nearly continuous pattern of U.S. and European trade barriers and restrictions levied against Japanese imports has prevailed since the 1960s. Most of these arrangements have not been recognized in GATT, for although they are not technically illegal, they certainly do not reflect the spirit of free trade. In the mid-1980s, Japan began to protect its foreign trade vigorously, and Japanese industry quietly persisted by developing new products, seeking local partners, and constantly improving old products. As a consequence, Japanese exports on the international market flourished, with an exceptional increase to the United States. Meanwhile, imports remained a small share of the Japanese market. The exporting nations asserted that low imports were a result of governmental policy. Japanese officials rejoined that exporters from Europe and the United States did not make the same efforts as Japanese exporters to understand consumer tastes and to produce a high-quality product.

The great surge in Japanese exports came with the export of the small gas-economy car after the energy crisis of the 1970s. As the trade developed, the Japanese exports included electrical goods, office machines, stereo equipment, computers, and other high-cost products. In contrast, the United States exports to Japan consisted primarily of low-cost goods such as lumber, waste paper, scrap metal, grass seed, resins, and hay. As a consequence, the annual trade deficit with Japan has risen in recent years to about $60 billion

In the 1990s, the United States began to protest vigorously Japan's closed markets. In October 1994, after 20 months of negotiations, a major agreement was reached to open the Japanese market to American telecommunications and medical equipment, glass, and insurance. Regrettably, the negotiations failed to produce a deal to increase the Japanese importation of cars and auto parts from the United States. President Clinton expressed satisfaction with the program but simultaneously threatened to initiate limited trade sanctions against Japan for failure to open its markets completely. The sanctions process, however, requires a 12- to 18-month period of investigation and further consultation before tariffs are imposed on Japanese exports to the United States.

Admission to the important $320 billion Japanese insurance market is the most sweeping agreement between the two nations. Penetration of the Japanese market by foreign companies has been about 3 percent, compared with 10 percent in the United States. The accord provides for both governments to track the foreign share of the Japanese market with several quantitative indicators and to try to make the U.S. share increase.

The agreement calls for extensive changes in the secretive and biased rules by which the Japanese government allotted contracts in telecommunications, an area that was 95 percent controlled by Japanese companies. Although the changes will apply to the purchase of telecommunications equipment by the Japanese government and the largely state-owned Nippon Telegraph and Telephone Corporation, the final negotiation does not guarantee the United States any specific market share. Likewise, there is no guarantee to assure Japanese government purchases of medical equipment. The United States share of the market stood at 23 percent, compared, for example, to its 40 percent share of the European market. The glass agreement consists of a set of "principles which will be defined in the future." Companies from the United States have enjoyed less than 1 percent of the $4.5 billion Japanese flat glass markets.

Traditionally, the Japanese have avoided market-share targets for U.S. imports. The present agreement perpetuates this policy but allows regulatory change that makes it easier for U.S. companies to gain a market share. The Japanese have agreed in each new market area to track whether or not the Japanese markets are becoming more open: a positive step in the trade relationship between the two nations. It is, however, only the first step, and many years of negotiation remain before a free trade policy evolves that will achieve the equity desired in the trade relationships among Canada, the United States, and Mexico.

United States–Mexico Trade Relations

Developing Trade Policies

Traditionally, Mexico's trade policy restricted imports in various ways in order to encourage domestic industrialization. Besides high tariffs, Mexico has sought to reduce imports through official import reference prices, domestic content requirements, subsidies, and import licenses. Foreign investors frequently had to agree to export an established percentage of their output.

Mexico did not become a member of GATT until 1986, for it feared that acceptance of GATT principles would compromise its import-substituting industrialization strategy. Finally, however, Mexico joined GATT and agreed to bring its entire tariff schedule to a maximum ad valorem rate of 50 percent, reducing tariffs to a maximum rate of 20 percent and a weighted average rate of 11 percent. Import licensing arrangements were also liberalized, and Mexico agreed to sign five of the nontariff barrier codes of the Tokyo Round. In 1987, the Mexican government announced the Economic Solidarity Pact, which further liberalized trade and which involved a wider set of reforms aimed to reduce inflation.

Before 1987 the United States and Mexico had few formal trade relations. In the signing of the Framework of Principles and Procedures for Consultation Regarding Trade and Investment, governing principles for both trade and investments were established. Both the United States and Mexico hoped that this structure would help alleviate the tensions and mistrust that had often characterized the bilateral relationship. The Framework of Principles established a consultative mechanism in which the two countries agreed to discuss within 30 days any trade or investment problems that either country raised. Trade officials have been consulted, for instance, on such matters as intellectual property protection, investment restructing, agricultural trade, motor transport, and unfair trade cases.

Another step in the evolution of the trade relationship between Mexico and the United States occurred in 1989, when the presidents of the two nations met to discuss the liberalization of trade and investments. Trade officals from the two nations identified mutual problems, and in February 1990 Mexico and the United States resolved their basic differences and began the negotiations that led to the comprehensive free trade agreement. In the course of discussions, it became evident that Canada should be a part of the developing trade relations. By 1992, a comprehensive trade policy had been developed between the three countries, and the governments of the three nations ratified the North American Free Trade Agreement (NAFTA) in 1994.

Trade between Mexico and the United States

Mexico is the third largest U.S. trading partner, exceeded only by Canada and Japan. Although the present Mexican market is only one-tenth the size of the U.S. market in GDP terms, it is expanding rapidly. In recent years, manufactured goods consisted of three-fourths of the U.S. exports and two-thirds of the imports. About 60 percent of Mexican manufactured exports to the United States are exchanges between multinational corporations located in both countries (Tables 15 and 16).

After the reduction of Mexican tariffs in 1987, U.S. exports rose from $14 billion to $40.6 billion in 1992. In 1991, Mexico accounted for 9.2 percent of total U.S. exports and 6 percent of its imports, compared with Mexican dependence on the United States for about 20 percent of both its imports and exports. According to the U.S. Department of Commerce, for every $1 billion in U.S. exports to Mexico, approximately 20,000 U.S. jobs are created.

In 1983, 44 percent of Mexican exports entered the U.S. duty free. With the implementation of GATT, the United States has agreed to reduce tariffs further but has shown reluctance to reduce the tariffs on certain products, such as textiles and steel. NAFTA has strict rules that neither Canada nor Mexico can be used as a "packaging station" by countries seeking a back door to U.S. markets. Before NAFTA, the Mexican government believed that U.S. quotas and high tariffs made its markets relatively more closed than Mexican markets. The Mexicans argued that U.S. protectionist policies resulted in effectively blocking a comparative advantage with the United States. For example, Mexican agricultural products (cotton, dairy products, sugar, peanuts) exported to the United States have traditionally been limited by significant quotas.

Because Mexico depends so heavily on exports to the United States, a recession in the United States is extremely detrimental to the Mexican economy. In the past, Mexico has tried to avert increased dependence on the United States by nationalizing industries, subsidizing import substitution, raising trade barriers, and limiting foreign investments. In recent years, however, as trade has grown, traditional restraints have loosened, finally culminating in the North American Free Trade Agreement. Although it is too soon to evaluate the long-term effects of a trade relationship between the United States and Mexico, trade has grown rapidly in the few months since the passage of NAFTA. As each nation benefits from free trade, other benefits will follow automatically. Thus Carla Hill, the U.S. trade representative, noted that U.S. exports to Mexico following Mexico's reduction of its tariffs doubled to $28 billion. She concluded that the bilateral FTA is really a "job-creating" mechanism for both nations.

Mexican Trade Potential

The economy of Mexico has experienced a number of remarkable changes in recent years. Under the leadership of President Salinas, Mexico initiated an ambitious program of economic reform measures and has reduced its fiscal deficit from 16 percent of gross national product (GNP) a few years ago to 0.5 percent of GNP in 1990. Inflation was reduced from 200 percent in 1987 to less than 30 percent in 1990. Moreover, Mexico has sold over 85 percent of the more than 1,200 state-owned companies to private enterprises. These newly private businesses include mining companies, airlines, a telephone company, and industrial plants. Mexico has also eliminated most of its import license requirements, formerly Mexico's most potent nontariff barrier, and tariffs on imports have been reduced to an average of 10 percent, just slightly above the average tariff imposed by the United States and Canada.

In response to this liberalization of the economy, the Mexicans are approaching free trade more favorably. In the 1980s, the United States adopted the stance that one of the best ways to aid Mexico was to provide greater access to the American markets. The U.S. government's

Table 15. U.S. Trade with Mexico (Billions of Dollars)

	U.S. Exports	U.S. Imports	Balance of Payments
1985	13.6	19.1	–5.5
1986	12.4	17.3	–4.9
1987	14.6	20.3	–5.7
1988	20.6	23.2	–2.6
1989	25.0	27.2	–2.2
1990	20.0	32.6	–2.7
1991	33.3	31.2	+2.1

Source: *Statistical Abstract of the United States*, U.S. Department of Commerce, Washington, DC.

Table 16. Mexican Commodity Export-Import Trade with the United States (Millions of Dollars)

	Total Exports	Exports to U.S.	%	Total Imports	Imports from U.S.	%
1980	15,537	10,072	65	19,456	11,979	62
1990	29,982	21,922	73	32,687	23,144	71

Source: *Statistical Abstract of the United States*, U.S. Department of Commerce, Washington, DC.

Table 17. Commodities in U.S.–Mexican Trade (Billions of Dollars)

	1989	1990	1991	1992
Principal U.S. Exports to Mexico				
Electrical machinery apparatus	3.6	3.8	4.4	5.3
Auto/motor vehicle parts	2.0	2.9	3.2	3.9
Chemicals	2.2	2.3	2.7	3.2
Telecommunications equipment	1.0	1.2	1.3	1.5
Office machinery and computers	0.8	0.8	1.1	1.3
Principal U.S. Imports from Mexico				
Electrical machinery apparatus	4.2	4.6	4.8	5.5
Crude oil	4.0	4.8	4.3	4.4
Autos/motor vehicles	1.2	2.2	2.6	2.6
TVs and radios	1.6	1.5	1.6	1.9
Auto/motor vehicle parts	1.1	1.2	1.4	2.0

Source: *Statistical Abstract of the United States*, U.S. Department of Commerce, Washington, DC.

position, expressed by President Bush, was that "the size and sophistication of United States–Mexican trade today only hints at our potential as we can create and show unprecedented prosperity and jobs."

When the economy of Mexico experiences a downturn, the United States now recognizes that it must be stabilized. In early 1995 the value of the peso declined precipitously and the Mexican economy faltered. In order to prevent a Mexican depression the United Staes guaranteed $20 billion to stabilize the situation, acknowledging that the welfare of one nation is important in this interrelated economic world.

Future of U.S. International Trade

Because the dollar plays such a dominant a role in international currencies, the United States has become a major force in structuring the world's economy. Through the United Nations, the World Bank, and other financial institutions, the United States has assumed a global role and has encouraged free trade worldwide. The increasing globalization of the economy will only increase the world trade relationships of the United States.

Chronology 2

U.S. Trade Legislation

Basic Trade Legislation

1861   Tariff Act

1922   Tariff Act

1930   Tariff Act

1962   Trade Expansion Act

1974   Trade Act

1978   Trade Act

1979   Trade Agreement Act

1982   Export Trading Company Act

1983   Trade and Development
        Enhancement Act

1984   Trade and Tariff Act

1988   Omnibus Trade and
        Comprehensive Act

1990   Customs and Trade Act

Tariff Acts

1882   Tariff Commission

1909   Tariff Board Act

1962   Tariff Classification Act

1965   Tariff Schedule Technical
        Amendments Act

Export Trade Act
1918   Export Trade Act

Export Enhancement Acts
1971   Export Expansion Finance Act

1988   Export Enhancement Act

1989   Export Enhancement Act

1992   Export Enhancement Act

Customs Acts
1890   Custom Administration Act

1912   Custom Reorganization Act

1927   Customs Bureau Act

1928   Customs Employees Salary Act

1953   Customs Simplification Act

1954   Customs Simplification Act

1956   Customs Simplification Act

1970   Customs Administration Act

1970   Customs Courts Act

1978   Customs Procedural Reform and Simplification Act

1980   Customs Courts Act

1986   Customs Enforcement Act

1990   Customs and Trade Act

Export-Import Bank Acts
1939   Export-Import Extension Act

1945   Export-Import Bank Act

1949   Export-Import Bank and Reconstruction Finance
        Corporations Appropriations Act

Export-Import Bank Amendments
1974   Export-Import Amendments

1976   Export-Import Bank Act Amendments

1983   Export-Import Bank Act Amendments

1986   Export-Import Bank Act Amendments

1988   Export Bank and Trial Aid Act Amendments

Export-Import Bank of Washington

1951   Export-Import Bank of Washington

1952   Export-Import Bank of Washington Appropriations Act

1954   Export-Import Bank of Washington and Reconstruction
Finance Corporation Appropriations

Export Trading Companies

1982   Export Trading Company Act

1988   Export Trading Company Act Amendment

Merchant Marine Acts

1920   Merchant Marine Act

1928   Merchant Marine Act

1936   Merchant Marine Act

1941   Merchant Marine Priorities Act

1942   Merchant Marine Emergency Act

1946   Merchant Ships Labor Act

1970   Merchant Marine Act

1970   Merchant Marine Decorations and Medals Act

1990   Merchant Marine Memorial Act

Related Trade Acts

Market and Finance Acts

1962   Market Access to Trade Expansion Act

1968   Buy American Act

1974   International Air Transportation Fair Competition Practices Act

1978   Bank Export Services Act

1983   Caribbean Basin Economic Recovery Act

1984   Generalized System of Preferences Renewal Act

1984   Wine Equity and Export Expansion Act

1988   Exchange Rates and International Economic Policy

Coordination Act

1988   International Debt Management Act

1988   Foreign Corrupt Practices Act Amendment

1988   Multilateral Development Bank Procurement Act

1988   Education and Training for a Competitive America

1988   Financial Reports Act

1988   Foreign Shipping Act

1988   Small Business Trade and Competition Act

1988   Pricing Dealers Act

Agriculture

1937   Agricultural Marketing Agreement Act

1949   Agricultural Act

1954   Agricultural Development and Assistance Act

1986   Food and Peace Act

1988   Agricultural Competitiveness and Trade Act

1988   Food Security Act

1988   Pesticide Monitoring Improvement Act

Forest

1978   Cooperative Forestry Conservation Act

1990   Forest Resources Conservation and Shortage Relief Act

International Trade Agreements

1947–   General Agreement on Tariffs and Trade

1994   1947   Geneva Round

          1949   Annecy Round

          1951   Torquay Round

          1956   Geneva Round

          1962   Dillon Round

1965   Kennedy Round

1973   Tokyo Round

1986   Uruguay (Punta del Este) Round

1947   International Commodity Agreements

1949   Wheat

1954   Sugar

1956   Tin

1958   Coffee

1988   United States–Canada Free Trade Agreement

1994   North American Free Trade Agreement

Laws and Regulations 3

The Tariff Act of 1861 established the modern tariff legislation of the United States. Its primary purpose was to provide revenue and protect the infant industry of the United States. The 1930 legislation provided barriers to the expansion of international trade. The legislation since 1930 has gradually developed policies to increase U.S. trade. This shift reflects the expansion of world trade, acknowledged generally by the signatories to the international General Agreement on Tariffs and Trade (GATT). To encourage free trade between nations, the United States and Canada agreed to a free trade policy in 1990; in 1994 the agreement was extended to Mexico under the North American Free Trade Agreement (NAFTA). The possibility of extending the free trade agreement to all of Latin America is already under discussion.

Basic Trade Legislation

Tariff Act of 1861

(March 2, 1861, Chapter 68, 12 Statute 178)

Revised seven times, in 1883, 1890, 1894, 1897, 1909, 1913, and 1922.

Until 1930, the 1861 act and the seven subsequent amendments provided the basic tariff legislation for this 69-year period

The 1861 law stated:

> In lieu of the duties heretofore imposed by law on the articles hereinafter mentioned, and on such as may now be exempt from duty, there shall be levied, collected, and paid, on the goods, wares, and merchandise, herein enumerated and provided for, imported from foreign countries, the following duties and rates of duty.

This law was comprehensive and specifically listed the goods subject to import duty and the amount to be paid. For example, there was a duty of four cents per pound on refined sugar and on sheet iron twenty dollars per ton.

Among the items subject to duty tax were sugar, brandy, cigars, bar iron, old scrap iron, band and hoop iron, rice, sheepskins, woolen cloth, shawls, cotton goods, hemp, flax, china and porcelain wares, periodicals, sheet iron, steel, coal, lead, copper, pork, spices, carpets, yarns, delaines, shirts, cordage, silk, earthen- and stoneware, white bread, linseed oil, candles, salt, beef, corn, wood, mats and rugs, blankets, oil and floor cloths, linens, cotton bagging, gloss, and books.

Tariff Act of 1922

(September 21, 1922, Chapter 356, 42 Statute 858 [Titles 19 and 46])

The Tariff Act of 1922 updated the original Tariff Act of 1861. It enumerated hundreds of items imported into the United States and specified the specific duty on each item reflecting the change of price since 1901. The act was to provide revenue, to regulate commerce with foreign countries, to encourage the industries of the United States, and to develop domestic industry.

Tariff Act of 1930

(June 17, 1930, Chapter 497, 46 Statute 590)

The Tariff Act of 1930, known as the Hawley-Smoot Act, is the basic modern tariff act. It was revised 228 times in the years between 1930 and 1992.

The act was intended to provide revenue, to regulate commerce with foreign countries, to encourage the industries of the United States, and to protect U.S. labor, among other purposes.

Title I of the act provided a "Dutiable List" of goods. Section 1 states:

Except, as otherwise specially provided for in this Act, there shall be levied, collected and paid upon all articles when imported from any foreign country into the United States or into any of its possessions (except the Philippine Islands, the Virgin Islands, American Samoa, and the island of Guam) the rates of duty which are prescribed by the schedules and paragraphs of dutiable list of this title.

The act contains 15 schedules listing the dutiable products:

Schedule 1, Chemicals, Oils, Acids and Paints. Each product is specifically mentioned and the exact tariff listed. For example, under acids are acid anhydrides, the duty on phosphoric acid is 2 cents per pound; gallic acid, 6 cents per pound; vinyl alcohol, 6 cents per pound; caffeine, $1.25 per pound.
Schedule 2, Earth, Earthenware, and Glass Ware
Schedule 3, Metals and Manufacturers of
Schedule 4, Wood and Manufacturers of
Schedule 5, Sugar, Molasses, and Manufacturers of
Schedule 6, Tobacco and Manufacturers of
Schedule 7, Agricultural Products and Provisions
Schedule 8, Spirits, Wines and Other Beverages
Schedule 9, Cotton Manufacturers
Schedule 10, Flax, Hemp, Jute, and Manufacturers of
Schedule 11, Wood and Manufacturers of
Schedule 12, Silk Manufacturers
Schedule 13, Manufacturers of Rayon and Other Synthetic Textiles
Schedule 14, Papers and Books
Schedule 15, Sundries

Title II provided a list of goods and stated that "the articles mentioned in the following paragraphs, when imported into the United States or into any of its possessions, shall be exempt from duty." The list basically covered goods that were not available in the United States, including animals for breeding purposes, vaccines, argols, asbestos, Brazilian beans, dried blood, and tea.

Title III included the following special provisions:

Sections 301 and 302 provided special tax provisions for the Philippines and Puerto Rico.
Section 303, Countervailing Duties, provided levies on imports receiving bounty if manufactured abroad.

Section 304, Marking of Imported Articles, indicated that all imported articles must be conspicuously marked in English and the country from which it originates.

Section 305, Immoral Articles, prohibited importation of same

Section 306, Cattle, Sheep, Swine, and Meat, prohibited importation in certain cases.

Section 307, Convict-made Articles, prohibited importation of same.

Section 308, Temporary, Free Importation under Bond for Exportation, designated such items duty free.

Section 309, Supplies for Certain Vessels, designated the supplies as untaxed.

Section 310, Free Importation of Merchandise recovered from Sunken and/or Abandoned Vessels.

Section 311, Bonded Manufacturing Warehouses

Section 312, Bonded Smelting Warehouses

Section 313, Drawback and Refunds

Section 314, Reimportation of Tax-Free Exports

Section 315, Effective Date of Rates of Duty

Section 316, Cuban Reciprocity Treaty not Affected

Section 317, Tobacco Products—Exportation Free of Duty Based on Interval Revenue Tax

Section 318, Emergencies

Section 319, Duty on Coffee imported into Puerto Rico

Section 320, Reciprocal Agreements Relating to Advertising Matters

The Hawley-Smoot Act also established a Tariff Commission to investigate the administration and fiscal and industrial effects of the customs laws of their country now in force or which may be hereafter enacted, the relation between the rates of duty on new materials and finished or partly finished products, the effects of ad valorem and specific duties and of compared specific ad valorem and specific duties, all questions relative to the arrangement of schedules and classification of articles in the several schedules of the customs law, and in general, to investigate the operation of custom laws, including their relation to the Federal revenues, their effect upon the industries and labor of the country, and to submit reports of its investigations.

In addition, the commission was invested with power to investigate commercial treaties, preferential provisions, and economic alliances, as well as to discern the effect of export bounties and preferential transportation rates, the volume of importations compared with domestic production and consumption, the tariff relations between the United States and foreign countries, and the conditions, causes, and effects relating to competition of foreign industries to those of the United States, including dumping and cost of production.

Trade Expansion Act of 1962
(Public Law 87-794, October 11, 1962, 76 Statute 872)

Revised six times, in 1963, 1975, 1977, 1980, 1985, and 1987.

The purpose of this act was to promote the general welfare, foreign policy, and security of the United States. The act was designed to

1. Stimulate economic growth of the United States and maintained or enlarge foreign markets for the products of United States agriculture, industry, mining, and commerce.
2. Strengthen economic relations with foreign countries through the development of open and nondiscriminatory trade.
3. Prevent commercial penetration.

The basic authority of this act gives the president the right to determine that any existing duties or other import restrictions of any foreign country or of the United States are unduly burdensome and restrictions of foreign trade of the United States. If he discovers restrictions, the president may enter into trade agreements with foreign countries between 1962 and 1967, and he may proclaim the modification or continuance of any existing duty or import restriction he determines necessary or appropriate to carry out trade agreements.

In order to implement the act, the U.S. Trade Commission must provide advice to the president. The commission must therefore

1. Investigate conditions, causes, and effects relating to competition between the foreign industries producing the articles in question and the domestic industries producing like or directly competing articles.
2. Analyze the production, trade, and consumption of each like or directly competitive article, taking into consideration employment, profits, use of production facilities, prices, wages, sales, inventories, patterns of demand, capital investment, obsolescence of equipment, and diversification of production.
3. Describe the probable nature and extent of any significant change in employment, profit levels, use of production

facilities, and any other conditions relevant to the domestic industries.
4. When warranted, undertake special studies of particular proposed modifications affecting U.S. industry, agriculture, and labor, utilizing the facilities of the U.S. attachés abroad and other appropriate personnel of the United States.

In order to carry out the provisions of this act, the president shall establish an Interagency Trade Organization that will

1. Make recommendations to the president on basic policy issues arising in the administration of the trade agreement program.
2. Make recommendations to the president as to what action, if any, he should take with respect to tariff adjustment submitted to him by the Tariff Commission.
3. Advise the president of the results of hearings concerning foreign impact on the U.S. economy.
4. Perform other functions as designated by the president.

This act provided for foreign import restrictions in the event that unjustifiable foreign imports imposed unfair conditions on the value of tariff commitments made to the United States, oppressed the commerce of the United States, or prevented the expansion of trade on a mutually advantageous basis. When unjustifiable restrictions exist, the president is enjoined to

1. Take all appropriate and feasible steps within his power to eliminate such restrictions.
2. Refrain from negotiating the reduction or elimination of any United States import restrictions in order to obtain the reduction or elimination of the restrictions imposed by another country.
3. Impose duties or other import restrictions on any foreign country establishing or maintaining foreign import restrictions against U.S. agricultural products, when he deems such duties for other import restrictions necessary to prevent the establishment or to obtain the removal of such foreign import restriction and to provide access for United States agricultural produce to the markets of such country on an equitable basis.

Title III of the act also provides for trade tariff adjustment and outlines the procedure for seeking assistance in determining other adjustments. A petition for tariff adjustment may be filed with the trade commission by a trade association, a firm, a certified or recognized union, or any other representative of the industry. After the Tariff Commission makes a decision, the president may

1. Provide tariff adjustment to such industry.
2. Provide eligibility to firms for adjustment assistance.
3. Provide that the workers in the industry may apply to the secretary of labor for certification of eligibility to apply for adjustment assistance.
4. Provide any combination of the above.

The assistance to firms may be technical, financial, or protective. Workers may also receive assistance in cases of unemployment. To assure that the readjustment of adversely affected workers is kept to a minimum, the act stipulates a retraining program. Workers may apply for supplemental aid to defray the expenses of transportation and subsistence during the training program. If workers must relocate, an allowance may be provided to defray moving expenses.

Trade Act of 1974

(Public Law 93-618, January 3, 1975, 88 Statute 1978)

Revised 25 times, in 1979, 1980, 1981, 1982, 1983, 1984, 1985, 1986, 1987, 1988, 1989, 1990, and 1992.

By pursuing trade agreements that afford mutual benefits, this act seeks

1. To foster economic growth and full employment in the United States and to strengthen economic relations between the United States and foreign countries through open and nondiscriminatory world trade.
2. To harmonize, reduce, and eliminate barriers to trade in a manner that ensures substantially equivalent competitive opportunities for the commerce of the United States.
3. To establish fairness and equity in international trading relations, including reform of the General Agreement on Tariffs and Trade.
4. To provide adequate procedures to safeguard American industry and labor against unfair or injurious import competition, and to assist industries, firms, workers, and communities to adjust to changes in the flow of international trade.
5. To open up market opportunities for United States commerce in nonmarket economies.

6. To provide fair and reasonable access to products of less developed countries in the U.S. market.

Six titles compose the act. Title I, Negotiating and Other Authority, provides the basic authority for trade agreements. Whenever the president determines that any existing duties or other important restrictions of any foreign country or the United States are unduly burdensome and restricting foreign trade of the United States, he

1. May enter into trade agreements with foreign countries during the five-year period that begins with the enactment of this act.
2. May proclaim modifications or continuance of any existing duty, free or excess treatment, or any additional duties as he determines to be required to carry out a trade agreement.

If nontariff barriers distort trade, the president is urged to take all appropriate and feasible steps within his power, including the negotiation of new trade agreements, to harmonize, reduce, or eliminate them. Likewise, if the president determines that bilateral trade agreements will effectively promote the economic growth or full employment in the United States, he shall negotiate as necessary to fulfill these objectives.

Title I also includes a provision to ensure that the United States has access to supplies. This agreement may be concluded so as to assure the United States the continued availability of important articles at reasonable prices, provide reciprocal concessions on comparable trade obligations, or both.

The trade laws of the United States must not conflict with the provisions of the regulations of the General Agreement on Tariffs and Trade (GATT), including

1. The extension of GATT articles to conditions of trade not presently covered in order to move toward fair trade practices.
2. The adopting of international fair labor standards and the use of public petition in order to conform to procedures in GATT.
3. The revision of decision-making procedures in GATT to more nearly reflect the balance of economic interests.
4. The improvement and strengthening of the provisions of GATT and other international agreements governing access to supplies of food, raw materials, and manufactured products.

This portion of the act also considers the balance-of-payments authority wherever international payment problems require special import measures to restrict imports, such as

1. Dealing with large United States balance of payment deficits.
2. Preventing an imminent and significant depreciation of the dollar in foreign exchange markets.
3. Cooperating with other countries in correcting an international balance-of-payment disequilibrium.

Other aspects of this chapter include compensation authority, two-year residual authority to negotiate duties, reciprocal nondiscriminatory treatment, and reservation of articles for national security or other resources. Chapter 3 considers hearings and advice concerning negotiations; chapter 4 establishes the Office of the Special Representative for Trade Negotiations in the executive office of the president; chapter 5 addresses congressional procedures with respect to presidential actions; and, finally, chapter 6 establishes an international trade commission.

Title II, Relief from Injury Caused by Import Competition, specifies that in order to be eligible for import relief, the complainant must file a petition with the International Trade Commission. The petition must include a statement describing the specific purposes for which import relief is being sought. To remedy the problem the president may

1. Proclaim an increase in any duty on the article causing or threatening to cause injury to the petitioning industry.
2. Proclaim a tariff-rate quota on such articles.
3. Proclaim a modification or imposition of any quantitative restriction on the import into the United States of such articles.
4. Negotiate orderly marketing agreements limiting export from foreign countries, and
5. Pursue any combination of the above.

Other conditions of Title II include adjustment assistance for workers, firms, and communities.

Title III treats the issue of relief from unfair trade practices. Unfair trade practices include subsidies, unjustifiable or unreasonable tariffs, discriminatory or other acts or policies that are unjustifiable or unreasonable, and other restrictions. In the event of unfair practices, the president may choose

1. To suspend, withdraw, or prevent the application of benefits of trade agreements or concessions to carry out a trade agreement with such country.
2. To impose duties or other import restrictions on the product of the offending foreign country.

Other aspects of Title III include antidumping duties, countervailing duties, and unfair import practices.

Title IV details trade relations with countries not currently receiving nondiscriminatory treatment. This title asserts the continued dedication of the United States to fundamental human rights. Notwithstanding any other provision of law, the product from any non-market-economy country will not be eligible for nondiscriminatory treatment (most-favored-nation treatment), the country will not participate in any program of the government of the United States that extends credit or credit guarantees as investment guarantees, and the president of the United States will not conclude any commercial agreement with any such country. These limitations would apply to any country that

1. Denies its citizens the right or opportunity to emigrate.
2. Imposes more than a nominal tax on emigration.
3. Imposes more than a nominal tax, levy, fine, fee, or other charge on any citizen as a consequence of the desires of such citizens to emigrate to the country of his choice.

Title V considers a generalized system of preferences, and Title VI provides general provisions.

Trade Agreement Extension Acts

Trade Agreement Extension Act of 1948
(June 26, 1948, Chapter 678, 62 Statute 1053)

Trade Agreement Extension Act of 1949
(September 26, 1949, Chapter 585, 63 Statute 697)

Trade Agreement Extension Act of 1951
(June 16, 1951, Chapter 141, 65 Statute 72)
Revised three times, in 1953, 1955, and 1958.
Trade Agreement Extension Act of 1953
(August 7, 1953, Chapter 348, 67 Statute 472)

Trade Agreement Extension Act of 1955
(June 21, 1955, Chapter 169, 69 Statute 162)

Trade Agreement Extension Act of 1958
(Public Law 85-686, August 20, 1958, 72 Statute 673)

Trade Agreement Act of 1979

(Public Law 96-39, July 25, 1979, 93 Statute 144)

Revised seven times, in 1980, 1983, 1984, and 1988.

This act updates the Tariff Act of 1930 by providing basic guidelines for carrying out the trade relations of the nation. Congress determined the need for the act

1. To approve and implement new trade agreements.
2. To foster the growth and maintenance of an open world-trading system.
3. To expand opportunities for the commerce of the United States in international trade.
4. To improve the rules of international trade and to provide for the enforcement of such rules.

The act consists of 11 titles:

1. Countervailing and Antidumping Duties
2. Customs Valuation
3. Government Procurement
4. Technical Barriers to Trade (Standards): Obligations of the United States, Functions of Federal Agencies, Administrative and Judicial Proceedings, Representations Allegings, United States Violations of Obligations, Proceedings Regarding Custom Standards and Related Activities, Definitions and Miscellaneous Provisions
5. Implementation of Certain Tariff Negotiations
6. Civil Aircraft Agreement
7. Certain Agricultural Measures
8. Treatment of Distilled Spirits: Tax Treatment, Tariff Treatment
9. Enforcement of United States Rights
10. Judicial Provisions
11. Miscellaneous Provisions

Titles II through V illustrate the trade guidelines provided by the act. Title II provides regulation for customs valuation. Except as otherwise specified in this act, imported merchandise shall be appraised on the basis of the transaction value and the transaction value of identical merchandise. If the transaction value cannot be determined, or if the importer does not request alternative valuation, imported merchandise shall be appraised on the basis of the deductive value.

The transaction value of imported merchandise is the price actually paid or payable for the merchandise when sold for exportation to the United States, plus amounts equal to

1. The packing costs incurred by the buyer.
2. The selling commission, if any.
3. The value, apportioned as appropriate, of any other office.
4. Any royalty or license fee related to the imported goods.
5. The proceeds of any subsequent resale, disposal, or use of the imported merchandise.

Title III considers the special regulations for government procurement. With respect to eligible production of any foreign country or instrumentality, the president may waive, in whole or in part, the application of any law, regulation, procedure, or practice regarding government procurement that would result in treatment less favorable than that accorded to U.S. products and suppliers of such products and to eligible products of a foreign country that is party to the agreement and supplier of such products.

The act also designates eligible countries. The president determines that parties to the agreement will provide appropriate reciprocal competitive government procurement opportunities, are not major industrial countries, and are among the least-developed countries.

Title IV identifies technical barriers to trade standards. The title states that no federal agency may create standards that are unnecessary obstacles to the foreign commerce of the United States.

Title V provides rules for the implementation of tariff negotiations. Tariffs may be reduced when the appropriate concessions have been received from foreign countries developed under prior trade agreements.

The other titles are devoted to specific trade situations.

Export Trading Company Act of 1982
(Public Law 97-290, Title I, 101–104, October 8, 1982, 96 Statute 1233–1235)

The purpose of this act was to increase U.S. exports of products and services by encouraging more efficient provisions of export trade services to U.S. producers and suppliers. The act establishes an office within the Department of Commerce to promote the formation of export trade associations and export trading companies. This office reduces trade financing provided by financial institutions and modifies the application of antitrust laws in order to permit bank-holding companies, bankers' banks, Edge Act corporations, and agreement corporations that are subsidiaries of bank-holding companies to invest in export-trading companies.

Congress had numerous reasons to pass this act:

1. Exports create and maintain one out of every nine manufacturing jobs in the United States and generate one out of seven dollars of total U.S. goods produced.
2. The rapidly growing service-oriented industries are vital to the well-being of the U.S. economy, for they create jobs for seven out of every ten Americans, provide 65 percent of the nation's gross national products and offer the greatest potential for significantly increased industrial trade in finished products.
3. Trade deficits contribute to the decline of the dollar on international currency markets and have an inflationary impact on the United States economy.
4. Tens of thousands of small and medium-sized United States businesses produce exportable goods or services but do not engage in exporting.
5. Although the United States is the world's leading agricultural exporting nation, many farm products are not marketed as widely and effectively abroad as they could be through export trading companies.
6. Export trade services are fragmented into a multitude of separate functions in the United States, and companies attempting to offer export trade services lack the financial leverage to reach a significant number of potential United States exporters.
7. The United States needs well-developed export trade intermediaries that can achieve economies of scale and acquire expertise that will enable them to export goods and services profitably, at a low per-unit cost to producers.
8. The development of export-trading companies in the United States has been hampered by business attitudes and by government regulations.
9. States and local governmental authorities that initiate, facilitate, or expand exports of goods and services can provide an important source for expansion of total U.S. exports, as well as for experimentation in the development of innovative export programs keyed to local state and regional economic needs.
10. If U.S. trading companies are to be successful in promoting exports and in competing with foreign trading companies,

they should be able to draw on the resources, expertise, and knowledge of the U.S. banking system, both in the United States and abroad.
11. The Department of Commerce is responsible for the development and promotion of U.S. exports and especially for facilitating the export of finished products by U.S. manufacturers.

Title II of this act, known as the Bank Export Services Act, establishes regulatory policies that

1. Provide for the establishment of export trading companies with sufficient power to compete with similar foreign-owned institutions in the United States and abroad.
2. Afford to U.S. commerce, industry, and agriculture, especially to small and medium-sized firms, a means of exporting at all times.
3. Foster the participation by regional and smaller banks in the development of export-trading companies.
4. Facilitate the formation of joint-venture export-trading companies between bank-holding companies and nonbank firms. Such joint ventures would provide complementary trade and financing services that could handle all of an exporting company's needs.

Title III establishes policies for issuing export trade certificates of review. The certificates (intended to promote trade) are issued to any applicant that engages in any trade export activities that

1. Result in neither a substantial lessening or restraint of trade within the United States, nor a substantial restraint of the export trade of any competitor of the applicant.
2. Not unreasonably enhance, stabilize, or depreciate prices within the United States of the goods, wares, merchandise, or services of the class exported by the applicant.
3. Do not constitute unfair methods of competition against competitors engaged in the export of goods, wares, merchandise, or services of the class exported by the applicant.
4. Do not undertake any act that may reasonably be expected to result in the sale for consumption or resale within the United States of the goods, wares, merchandise, or services exported by the applicant.

Title IV is cited as the Foreign Trade Antitrust Improvement Act of 1982.

Trade and Development Enhancement Act of 1983

(Public Law 98-181, November 30, 1983, 97 Statute 1263)

The purpose of this act is

1. To expand employment and economic growth in the United States by expanding U.S. exports to the markets of the developing world.
2. To stimulate the economic development of countries in the developing world by improving their access to credit for the importation of U.S. products and services for developmental purposes.
3. To restore export competition to a market basis by neutralizing the predatory financing practiced by many nations whose exports compete with U.S. exports.
4. To encourage foreign governments to enter into effective and comprehensive agreements with the United States that allow the use of credit for exports and to limit and govern the use of export credit subsidies generally.

The president is directed to negotiate rules and limitations for the use of tied aid for exports. The objectives here are

1. To define the various forms of tied-aid credit, particularly mixed credits under the arrangement or guidelines for officially supported export credits established through the Organization for Economic Cooperation and Development.
2. To phase out the use of government mixed credits.
3. To set rules governing the use of public-private cofinancing, or other forms of mixed financing, which may have the same result as government-mixed credits of drawing on concessional development assistance to produce subsidized export financing.
4. To raise the threshold of notification of the use of tied-aid credit to a 50 per centum level of concessionality.
5. To improve notification procedures so that advance notification must be given on all uses of tied-aid credit.
6. To prohibit the use of tied-aid credit for production facilities for goods that are oversupplied on the world market.

The term "tied-aid credit" is defined as credit

1. That is provided for development aid purposes.
2. That is tied to the purchase of exports from the country granting the credit.
3. That is financed either exclusively from public funds or, as a mixed credit, partly from public and partly from private funds.
4. That has a grant element, as defined by the Development Assistance Committee of the Organization for Economic Cooperation and Development, greater than 0 percent.

The term "government-mixed credits" means the combined use of credits, insurance, and guarantees offered by the Export-Import Bank of the United States with concessional financing or grants offered by the Agency for International Development to finance exports.

The term "public-private cofinancing" means the combined use of official development assistance or official export credit with private commercial credit to finance exports.

The term "blending of financing" refers to the use of various combinations of official development assistance, official export credit, and private commercial credit, integrated into a single package with a single set of financial terms, to finance exports.

The term "parallel financing" refers to the related use of various combinations of separate lines of official development assistance, official export credits, and private commercial credit, not combined into a single package with a single set of financial terms, to finance exports.

To implement the legislation, the chairman of the Export-Import Bank of the United States established a program of tied-in credits administered by the Agency for International Development. The tied-in credit program was to offer or arrange for financing for the export of U.S. goods and services.

Trade and Tariff Act of 1984

(Public Law 98-573, October 30, 1984, 98 Statute 2989

Revised five times.

This act amended the trade laws, authorized the negotiation of trade agreements, extended trade preferences, and changed the tariff treatment.

Title I considers amendments to tariff schedules, permanent changes in tariff treatment, temporary change in tariff treatment and technical amendments, and effective dates.

Title II provides customs and miscellaneous amendments, including amendments to the Tariff Act of 1930, small business trade assistance, and miscellaneous provisions.

In amending the Trade Act of 1974, Title III purposes

1. To foster economic growth and full employment in the United States by expanding competitive U.S. exports via commercial opportunities in foreign markets substantially equivalent to those accorded by the United States.
2. To improve the ability of the president to identify and to analyze barriers to (or restrictions on) U.S. trade and investment, and to achieve the elimination of such barriers and restrictions as exist.
3. To encourage the expansion both of international trade in services through the negotiation of agreements (both bilateral and multilateral) that reduce or eliminate barriers to international trade in services and of U.S. service industries in foreign commerce.
4. To enhance the free flow of foreign investment by negotiating agreements (both bilateral and multilateral) that reduce or eliminate the trade-distorting effects of certain investment-related measures.

Title III, Chapter 8, is cited as Barriers to Market Access of Trade Expansion Act of 1962 and is amended to

1. Identify and analyze acts, policies, or practices that constitute significant barriers to or distortions of U.S. export of goods and services (including agricultural commodities, and property protected by trademarks, patents, and copyrights reported or licensed by United States persons, and foreign direct investment by citizens of the United States, especially if such investments have implications for trade in goods and services.
2. Estimate the trade-distorting impact on U.S. commerce of any act, policy, or practice identified above.

The following factors are to be taken into account in making analyses and estimates:

1. The relative impact of the act, policy, or practice on domestic commerce.
2. The availability of information to document prices, market shares, and other matters necessary to demonstrate the effects of the act, policy, or practice.

3. The extent to which the act, policy, or practice is subject to international agreements to which the United States is a party.
4. Any advice given through appropriate committees.

Title IV specifically addresses trade with Israel, amending the Trade Act of 1974 by providing for the reduction or elimination of any duty imposed by the United States if

1. An article is the product of or produced in Israel or if it is a new or different article of commerce that has been grown, produced, or manufactured in Israel.
2. An article is imported directly from Israel into the custom territory of the United States.
3. And if the sum of the value of the material produced in Israel plus the direct costs of processing operation performed in Israel is not less than 35 percent of the appraised value of the article at the time it entered the United States.

Title V is cited as the "Generalized System of Preferences Renewal Act of 1984." Its purpose is to

1. Promote developing countries, which often need temporary preferential advantages to compete effectively with industrialized countries.
2. Promote the notion that trade, rather than aid, is a more effective and cost-efficient way of promoting broad-based, sustained economic growth.
3. Take advantage of the fact that developed countries provide the fastest-growing markets for U.S. exports and that foreign exchange earnings from trade with such countries through the Generalized System of Preferences can further stimulate U.S. exports.
4. Allow for the fact that significant differences exist among developing countries with respect to their general development and international competitiveness.
5. Encourage provision of increased trade-liberalization measures, thereby setting an example to be emulated by other industrialized countries.
6. Recognize that a large number of developing countries must generate sufficient foreign-exchange earnings to meet international debt obligations.
7. Promote the creation of additional opportunities for trade among the developing countries.

8. Integrate developing countries into the international trading system in a manner commensurate with their development.
9. Encourage developing countries to eliminate or reduce significant barriers to trade in goods, services and investments; to provide effective measures under which foreign nationals may secure, exercise, and enforce exclusive intellectual property rights; and to afford workers internationally recognized worker rights.
10. Address these concerns in a manner that does not adversely affect U.S. producers and workers and that conforms to the international obligations of the United States under its General Agreement on Tariffs and Trade.

Title VI amends the Tariff Act of 1930 and the later amendments.

Title VII provides Authorization of Appropriations for Customs and Trade Agreements.

Title VIII, the Steel Import Stabilization Act, considers enforcement authority for steel industry policy. The Congress finds therein that

1. The U.S. steel industry must modernize its plants and equipment in order to enhance its international competitiveness; furthermore, it requires increased capital investments to effect that modernization.
2. The ability of the domestic steel industry to be internationally competitive has been impeded by the enormous federal budget deficit, the overvalued dollar, and increasing trade deficits; its competitiveness has been seriously injured by subsidies, dumping, and other unfair and restrictive foreign trade practices.
3. The extent of the unfair trade practices practiced on the international market imposes unusually harsh burdens on the U.S. steel industry, which must combat these practices through the trade remedy laws.
4. Expenditures and effective action under the president's national policy for the steel industry, including more vigorous efforts by the executive branch to self-initiated remedies against these practices, are needed to eliminate the adverse effects of unfair trade practices.
5. Import relief will be ineffective and will not serve the national economic interest unless the industry engages in simultaneous concerted efforts to substantially modernize and to improve its international competitiveness.

6. Full and effective implementation of the national policy for the steel industry will substantially improve the economy and employment in the sectors that produce steel and iron ore.

The purposes of this title are, then,

1. To supplement the president's authority to achieve policy goals for the steel industry by granting the president enforcement powers over bilateral arrangements that are entered into or undertaken in order to implement the national policy.
2. To subject the continuation of those powers to the condition that the steel industry undertakes a comprehensive modernization of its plant and equipment.

Title IX is cited as the Wine Equity and Export Expansion Act of 1984.

Congress finds that

1. The substantial imbalance in international wine trade results in part from the relative accessibility of foreign wines to the United States market; the U.S. wine industry, by contrast, faces restrictive tariff and nontariff barriers in virtually every existing or potential foreign market.
2. The restricted access to foreign markets and the continued low prices for U.S. wine and grape products adversely affect the economic position of the nation's winemakers and grape growers as well as all other domestic sectors that depend upon wine production.
3. The competitive position of U.S. wine in international trade has been weakened by foreign trade practices, high domestic interest rates, and unfavorable foreign exchange rates.
4. Wine consumption per capita is very low in many major non–wine-producing markets, and the demand potential for U.S. wine is significant.
5. The U.S. wine-making industry has the capacity and the ability to export substantial volumes of wine, and any increases in the U.S. wine exports will create new jobs, improve the nation's balance of trade, and otherwise strengthen the national economy.

The purposes of this title are

1. To provide wine consumers with the greatest possible choice of wines from wine-producing countries.

2. To encourage an export promotion program to develop, maintain, and expand foreign markets for U.S. wine.
3. To achieve greater access to foreign markets for U.S. wine and grape products through the reduction or elimination of tariff barriers and nontariff barriers to (or other distortions of) trade in wine.

Omnibus Trade and Competitiveness Act of 1988

(Public Law 100-418, 102 Statute 1107, August 23, 1988)

Revised six times, in 1988, 1990, and 1992.

Congress discovered the need for this law in the new global economy that has emerged in the last ten years. Trade, technological development, investments, and service form an integrated system, and these activities affect one another other and the health of the U.S. economy.

Moreover, the United States is confronted with a fundamental disequilibrium in the trade and current account balance and a rapid increase in the net external debt. This disequilibrium stems from numerous factors, including disparities between the macroeconomic policies of the major trading nations, the large U.S. budget deficit, instabilities and structural defects in the world monetary system, growth of debt throughout the developing world, structural defects in the world trading system and inadequate enforcement of trade agreement obligations, governmental distortions and barriers, serious shortcomings in U.S. trade policy, and inadequate growth in the productivity and competitiveness of United States firms and industries relative to their overseas competition.

Congress deems it essential that the U.S. government pursue a broad array of domestic and international policies to prevent future decline in the U.S. economy and standard of living, to ensure future stability in external trade of the United States, and to guarantee the continental vitality of the technological, industrial, and agricultural base of the United States.

The president should be authorized and encouraged to negotiate trade agreements and related investments, financial, intellectual property, and service agreements. For although the United States cannot dictate economic policy to the rest of the world, it is in the national interest for the United States to lead the world, which it can do.

The purposes of this act are to

1. Authorize the negotiation of reciprocal trade agreements.
2. Strengthen U.S. trade laws.

3. Improve the development and management of U.S. trade strategy.
4. Improve standards of living in the world.

Title I treats trade, customs, and tariff laws. The first part of this section is devoted to negotiation and implementation of trade agreements. The overall trade negotiations are

1. To be more open, equitable, and have reciprocal market access.
2. To reduce or eliminate barriers and other trade-distorting policies and practices.
3. To develop a more effective system of international trading disciplines and procedures.

Other sections of Title I include discussions on trade agreements and negotiation provisions, implementation of the harmonized tariff schedule, enforcement of U.S. rights under trade agreements and response to foreign trade practices, improvement in the enforcement of the antidumping and countervailing duty laws, protection of intellectual property rights, telecommunication trade, adjustment to import competition, market disruptions, trade adjustment assistance, national security, functions and organization of trade agencies, U.S. International Trade Commission, interagency trade organization, trade policy negotiations and agreements, and tariff provision agreements.

Title II, the Export Enhancement Act of 1988, stipulates rules to deal with Mexico, Japan, China, Taiwan, Poland, and other countries. The act affirms its support for the Overseas Private Investment Corporation as a U.S. government agency serving investment goals. It also addresses barter and countertrade, protection of intellectual property, workers rights, loan guarantees, export promotion, and export controls.

Title III considers international financial policy. It consists of a number of separate acts, the first of which is the Exchange Rates and International Economic Policy Coordination Act of 1988. In passing this act, Congress found that

1. Macroeconomic policies, including the exchange-rate policies of the leading industrialized nations, require improved coordination and are not consistent with long-term economic growth and financial stability.
2. Currency values have a major role in determining the patterns of production and trade in the world economy.
3. The rise in the value of the dollar in the early 1980s contributed substantially to the current U.S. trade deficit.

4. Exchange rates among major trading sections have become increasingly volatile.
5. Capital flows between nations have become very large compared to trade flows.
6. The policy of some major trading nations that manipulates value of their currencies in relation to the dollar to gain competitive advantages continues to create serious competitive problems for U.S. industries.
7. A more stable exchange rate for the dollar at a level consistent with a more appropriate and substantial balance in the U.S. current account should be a major force of national economic policy.
8. Procedures for improving the coordination of macroeconomic policy need to be strengthened considerably.
9. Intervention by the United States in foreign-exchange markets as part of a coordinated international strategic intervention effort could produce a more orderly adjustment of the foreign exchange markets.

This title also includes the International Debt Management Act of 1988. Congress found that

1. The international debt problem threatens the safety and soundness of the international financial system.
2. Orderly reduction of international trade imbalances require very substantial growth in all parts of the world economy, particularly in the developing nations.
3. Growth in developing countries with substantial external debts has been significantly constrained over the last several years by a combination of high debt service obligations and insufficient financial help to these countries.
4. Substantial interest payment outflows from debtor countries, combined with inadequate payment outflows from debtor countries and inadequate net new capital inflows, have produced a significant net transfer of financial resources from debtor to creditor countries.
5. Negative resource transfers at present levels severely depress both investments and growth in the debtor countries.
6. The United States has borne a disproportionate share of the burden of absorbing increased exports from debtor countries, whereas other industrialized countries have increased their imports from developing countries only slightly.

7. Current approaches to the debt problem should not rely solely on new lending.
8. New international mechanisms to improve the management of the debt problem and to expand the range of financing options available to developing countries should be explored.
9. Industrialized countries with strong currency account surpluses have a disproportionate share of the world's capital resources and bear an additional responsibility for contributing to a viable long-term solution to the debt problem.

Title III also includes the Multilateral Development Bank Procurement Act of 1988, the Export-Import Bank and Tied-Aid Credit Amendments of 1988, the Export Trading Company Act Amendment of 1988, the Pricing Dealers Act of 1988, and the Financial Reports Act of 1988.

Title IV, the Agricultural Competitiveness and Trade Act of 1988, is based on congressional findings that

1. U.S. agricultural exports have declined by more than 36 percent since 1981.
2. The U.S. share of the world market for agricultural commodities and products has dropped by 20 percent during the last six years.
3. For the first time in 15 years, the United States incurred monthly agricultural trade deficits in 1986.
4. The loss of $1 billion of U.S. agricultural exports causes the loss of 35,000 agricultural jobs and the loss of 60,000 nonagricultural jobs.
5. The loss threatens family farms and the economic well-being of rural communities.
6. Factors contributing to the loss include addition of new exporting nations, innovation in agricultural technology, increased use of export subsidies, existence of barriers to agricultural trade, slow-down of growth to world food demand, and rapid build-up of surplus stocks.
7. Increasing the volume and value of exports is important to the financial well-being of farmers in the United States.
8. Food aid and export assistance programs in developing countries should stimulate activity.

Other acts cited under agricultural trade include the Food Security Act of 1985, the Agricultural Development and Assistance Act of 1954, the Agricultural Act of 1949, the Food for Peace Act of 1986, the Cooperative Forestry Assistance Act of 1978, the Agricultural Marketing Agreement Act of 1937, and the Pesticide Monitoring Improvement Act of 1988.

Title V is the Foreign Corrupt Practices Act Amendments of 1988.

Title VI is the Education and Training for a Competitive America Act of 1988.

Title VII is the Buy American Act of 1988, an amendment of the 1933 act.

Title VIII, the Small Business International Trade and Competitiveness Act, seeks to increase the ability of small businesses to compete in international markets by enhancing their ability to export, facilitating technology transfer, enhancing their ability to compete effectively and efficiently against imports, increasing access of small business to long-term capital, disseminating information concerning state, federal, and private programs, and ensuring that the interests of small businesses are adequately represented in bilateral and multilateral trade negotiations.

Title IX is cited as the Process Patent Amendment Act of 1988.

Title X, the Foreign Shipping Producer Act of 1988, devotes its Section B to international air transportation under the International Air Transportation Fair Competitive Practice Act of 1974.

Customs and Trade Act of 1990

(Public Law 101-382, 104 Statute 629, August 20, 1990)

This act revises the Tariff Act of 1930. It considers trade agency authorizations, customs user fees, and other provisions.

Title II, the Caribbean Basin Economic Recovery Expansion Act of 1990, is based on congressional findings that

1. A stable political and economic climate in the Caribbean region is necessary for the development of the countries in that region and for the security and economic interests of the United States.
2. The Caribbean Basin Economic Recovery Act was enacted in 1983 to assist in the achievement of such a climate by stimulating the development of the export potential of the region.
3. The commitment of the United States to the successful development of the region, as evidenced by the environment of the Caribbean Basin Economic Recovery Act, should be affirmed and further strengthened by amending that act to improve its operation.

Title III lists tariff provisions in three parts. Part I details new duty suspensions and temporary reduction, Part II gives existing temporary duty suspensions and other tariff and miscellaneous provisions, and Part III considers tariff classification and other technical amendments.

Title IV, the Forest Resources Conservation and Shortage Relief Act of 1990, aims to

1. Promote the conservation of forest resources.
2. To take action essential for the acquisition and distribution of forest resources or products in short supply in the western United States.
3. To ensure sufficient supplies of certain forest resources as products that are essential to the United States.
4. To continue and refine the existing federal policy of restricting the export of unprocessed timber harvested from federal lands in the western United States.
5. To effect measures that will meet these objectives in conformity with the obligation of the United States under the General Agreement on Tariffs and Trade (GATT).

Specialty Trade Acts

Trading with the Enemy Act of 1917
(October 6, 1917, Chapter 106, 40 Statute 411)

Revised 45 times, in 1918, 1919, 1920, 1921, 1922, 1923, 1926, 1928, 1929, 1930, 1933, 1934, 1937, 1940, 1941, 1946, 1947, 1948, 1950, 1953, 1954, 1956, 1962, 1964, 1966, 1972, 1976, 1977, 1982, 1985, and 1988.

This act was passed by Congress during World War I to prevent the United States from trading with the enemy. An enemy is deemed to be any individual, partnership, or other body of individuals of any nationality resident within the territory (including that occupied by the military and rival forces) of any nation with which the United States is at war, or resident outside the United States and doing business within such territory, or any corporation incorporated within the territory of any nation with which the United States is at war or incorporated within any country other than the United States and doing business with a country with which the United States is at war.

This act makes it unlawful

1. For any person in the United States, except with the license of the president, to trade, or attempt to trade, either directly

or indirectly, with, to, or from or for, or on account of, or on behalf of, or for the benefit of, any person who may reasonably be suspected of being an enemy or ally of the enemy or who is conducting or practicing such trade, directly or indirectly, for the benefit of an enemy or ally of an enemy.

2. For any person, except with the license of the president, to transport or attempt to transport into or out of the United States, any subject or citizen of an enemy or ally of an enemy nation, with knowledge or reasonable cause to believe that the person transported or attempted to be transported is such a subject or citizen.

3. For any person to send or take out of the United States any letter or other writing or tangible form of communication such as a book, map, plan, picture, cablegram, or wireless message.

4. When the president deems it necessary, he may cause to be censored, under rules that he may establish from time to time, communication by mail, cable, radio, or other means of transmission passing between the United States and any foreign county. Any person who willfully evades these regulations by use of a code or other device for the purpose of concealing from censors the intended meaning of such communication shall be punished by a fine of $10,000 or ten years in prison, or both.

Export-Import Bank Act of 1945

(July 31, 1945, Chapter 341, 59 Statute 526)

Revised 35 times, in 1945, 1947, 1951, 1953, 1954, 1957, 1958, 1961, 1963, 1968, 1971, 1974, 1977, 1978, 1980, 1981, 1983, 1986, 1987, 1988, 1989, 1990, and 1992.

The Export-Import Bank of Washington is organized as an agency of the United States to make loans and to discount, rediscount, or guarantee notes, drafts, bills of exchange, and other evidence of debt for the purpose of financing and facilitating exports and imports and the exchange of commodities between the United States and any foreign country. The bank is authorized to use all of its assets in pursuit of these activities.

It is the policy of the bank not to compete with private capital. The management of the bank is vested in a board of governors consisting of five members of which not more than three are members of the same political party.

The initial capital of the bank was $1 billion. The bank provides annual reports to the U.S. Congress of its activities.

Export Control Act of 1949

(February 26, 1949, Chapter 11, 63 Statute 7)

Revised 11 times, in 1951, 1953, 1956, 1958, 1960, 1962, 1965, 1968, and 1970.

This act was based on the findings of Congress that

certain materials continue in short supply at home and abroad so that the quantity of United States exports and their distribution among importing countries affect the welfare of the domestic economy and have an important bearing upon the fulfillment of the foreign policy of the United States.

The policy of the United States is thus to use export controls as necessary to

1. Protect the domestic economy from the excessive drain of scarce materials and to reduce the inflationary impact of abnormal foreign demand.
2. Further the foreign policy of the United States and aid in fulfilling its international responsibilities.
3. Exercise the necessary viligance over exports from the standpoint of their significance to the national security.

This act authorized the president to prohibit or curtail the exportation from the United States of any articles, materials, or supplies. The president may also delegate this power to an appropriate department or agency. The authority of this act can be used with respect to any agricultural commodity, including fats and oils, when these products are determined by the secretary of agriculture to be in excess of domestic economy.

Trade Fair Act of 1959

(Public Law 86-14, April 22, 1959, 73 Statute 18)

This act is intended to foster trade by holding fairs in the United States. When the secretary of commerce is satisfied that the public interest in promoting trade would be served by according the privileges stipulated in this act to any fair to be held in the United States, he shall advise the secretary of the treasury, designating the name, place, date, and name of the operator of the fair.

Any article imported or brought into the United States that is continuously under customs custody, is covered by an exhibition at the fair, or is a foreign trade zone, and on which no duty or internal revenue tax has been paid may, without payment of any duty or internal revenue tax, be entered under bond for the purpose of exhibition at a fair, or for use in constructing, installing, or maintaining foreign exhibits at a fair.

Export Administration Act of 1969
(Public Law 91-184, December 30, 1969, 83 Statute 841)

Revised 13 times, in 1971, 1972, 1974, 1975, 1977, 1978, and 1979.

This act is based on congressional findings that

1. The availability of certain materials at home and abroad varies so that the quantity and composition of U.S. exports and their distribution among importing countries may affect the welfare of the domestic economy and may significantly influence the fulfillment of the foreign policy of the United States.
2. The unrestricted export of materials, information, and technology without regard to whether they make a significant contribution to the military potential of any other nation or nations may adversely affect the national security of the United States.
3. The unwarranted restrictions of exports from the United States has a serious adverse effect on our balance of payments.
4. The uncertainty of policy toward certain categories of export has curtailed the efforts of U.S. businessmen in those categories and has undercut the overall attempt to improve the trade balance of the United States.

Accordingly, Congress establishes the following policy:

1. To encourage trade with all countries with which the United States has diplomatic or trading relations and to restrict the export of goods and technology that would make a significant contribution to the military potential of any other nation which would prove detrimental to the national security of the United States.
2. To use export controls as necessary to protect the domestic economy from the excessive drain of scarce materials and to reduce the serious inflationary impact of abnormal foreign demand.

3. To further the foreign policy of the United States and to fulfill the international responsibilities.
4. To exercise the necessary vigilance over exports to maintain a sound national security.
5. To formulate and apply necessary controls to the maximum extent possible in cooperation with all nations with which the United States has defense treaty commitments.
6. To formulate a unified trade control policy to be observed by all nations.
7. To use enormous resources and trade potential of the United States to further the sound growth and stability of its national security.
8. To oppose restrictive trade production or boycotts fostered or imposed by foreign countries against other countries friendly to the United States.
9. To encourage domestic enterprises engaged in the export of articles, materials, supplies, or information.

The secretary of commerce has the authority to implement this act. If an individual violates a provision of the act, he may be either fined or given a prison term.

In order to enable U.S. exporters to coordinate their license activities with the export control policy, the U.S. government has official responsibility to

1. Inform each exporter of the considerations that may cause his export license request to be denied or subject to long examination.
2. Inform each exporter of the circumstance behind any delays in licensing.
3. Give each exporter the opportunity to present evidence and information to expedite licensing.
4. Inform each exporter of the reasons for a denial of an export license.

Other Trade Acts

April 10, 1918, Chapter 50, 40 Statute 516.

September 30, 1976, Public Law 94-435. Title III, 90 Statute 1397.

Export Enhancement Act of 1988
(Public Law 100-418, August 23, 1988, Title II, 102 Statute 1325)

Export Enhancement Act of 1989
(Public Law 102-429, October 21, 1992, Title II, 106 Statute 2199)

Export Enhancement Act of 1992
(Public Law 102-429, October 21, 1992, 106 Statute 2186)

Export Expansion Finance Act of 1971
(Public Law 92-126, August 17, 1971, 85 Statute 345)

Export Grape and Plum Act of 1960
(Public Law 86-687, September 2, 1960, 74 Statute 734)

Tariff Acts

Tariff Board Act
(Chapter 6, August 1909, 36 Statute 83)

Tariff Classification Act of 1962
(Public Law 87-456, May 24, 1962, 76 Statute 72)
Revised 1962, 1988.
(Public Law 100-418, August 23, 1988, Title I, 102 Statute 1155)

Tariff Schedules Technical Amendments Act of 1965
(Public Law 89-241, October 7, 1965, 79 Statute 933)
Revised 1967.

Tariff Commission of 1882
(Chapter 146, May 15, 1882, 22 Statute 64)
Revised 1986.
(Public Law 99-514, October 1986, 100 Statute 2332)

Custom Acts

Custom Administration Act of 1890
(June 10, 1890, Chapter 407, 26 Statute 131)
Revised four times, in 1909, 1922, 1930, and 1938.
(June 25, 1938, Chapter 679, 52 Statute 1077)

Custom Reorganization Act of 1912
(April 24, 1912, Chapter 355)

Customs Bureau Act of 1927
(March 3, 1927, Chapter 348, 44 Statute 138)

Customs Employees Salaries Act of 1928
(May 29, 1928, Chapter 865, 45 Statute 955)

Customs Simplification Act of 1953
(August 8, 1953, Chapter 397, 67 Statute 507)

Customs Simplification Act of 1954
(September 1, 1954, Chapter 1213, 68 Statute 1136)

Customs Simplification Act of 1956
(August 2, 1956, Chapter 887, 70 Statute 943)

Customs Courts Act of 1970
(Public Law 91-271, June 2, 1970, Title I, 84 Statute 274)

Customs Administrative Act of 1970
(Public Law 91-271, June 2, 1970, 84 Statute 282)

Customs Procedural Reform and Simplification Act of 1978
(Public Law 95-410, October 3, 1978, 92 Statute 888)
Revised eight times, in 1983, 1984, 1986, 1987, 1988, 1989, and 1990.
(Public Law 101-382, August 20, 1990, Title I, 104 Statute 634)

Customs Courts Act of 1980
(Public Law 96-417, October 10, 1980, 94 Statute 1727)

Custom Enforcement Act of 1986
(Public Law 99-570, October 17, 1986, Title III, 100 Statute 3207-79)

Customs and Trade Act of 1990
(Public Law 101-382, August 20, 1990, 104 Statute 629)

Export-Import Bank

Export-Import Bank Extension Act
March 4, 1939, Chapter 5, 53 Statute 510.

March 2, 1940, Chapter 34, 54 Statute 38.

Export-Import Bank and Reconstruction Finance Corporation
Appropriation Act, 1950
(June 30, 1949, Chapter 286, Title III, 63 Statute 374)

Export-Import Bank Amendments of 1974
(Public Law 93-646, January 4, 1975, 88 Statute 2333)

Export-Import Bank Act Amendments of 1976
(Public Law 95-630, November 10, 1978, Title XIX, 92 Statute 3724)

Export-Import Bank Act Amendments of 1983
(Public Law 98-181, November 30, 1983, Title VI, 97 Statute 1254)

Export-Import Bank Act Amendment of 1986
(Public Law 99-472, October 15, 1986, 100 Statute 1200)

Export-Import Bank and Tied Aid Credit Amendment of 1988.
(Public Law 100-418, August 23, 1988, Title III, 102 Statute 1383)

Export-Import Bank of Washington

Export-Import Bank of Washington, and Reconstruction Finance
Corporation Appropriation Act, 1955
(May 28, 1954, Chapter 242, Title III, 68 Statute 149)

Export-Import Bank of Washington Appropriation Act, 1952
(August 11, 1951, Chapter 301, Title III, 63 Statute 182)

Export-Import Bank of Washington Appropriation Act, 1953
(June 30, 1952, Chapter 523, Title III, 66 Statute 293)

Export Trading Company Acts

Export Trading Company Act of 1982
(Public Law 100-418, August 23, 1988)

Export Trading Company Act Amendment of 1988
(Public Law 100-418, August 23, 1988, Title II, 102 Statute 1346; Title III,
102 Statute 1384)

Merchant Marine Acts

Merchant Marine Act of 1920
(June 5, 1920, Chapter 250, 41 Statute 988)
Revised 21 times, in 1956, 1958, 1959, 1960, 1965, 1968, 1971, 1975, 1978,
1979, 1981, 1982, 1984, 1986, 1988, 1989, 1990, and 1992.
(Public Law 102-587, November 4, 1992, 106 Statute 5085)

Merchant Marine Act of 1928
(May 22, 1928, Chapter 675, 45 Statute 689)
Revised three times, in 1980 and 1989.
(Public Law 101-225, December 12, 1989, 163 Statute 1925)

Merchant Marine Act of 1936
(June 29, 1936, Chapter 858, 49 Statute 1985)
Revised 138 times, in 1937, 1938, 1940, 1941, 1942, 1943, 1944, 1950,
1952, 1953, 1954, 1955, 1956, 1957, 1958, 1959, 1960, 1961, 1962, 1963,
1964, 1965, 1966, 1967, 1968, 1969, 1970, 1972, 1973, 1975, 1976, 1977,
1978, 1980, 1981, 1983, 1984, 1985, 1986, 1988, 1989, 1990, and 1992.
(Public Law 102-587, November 4, 1992, Title VI, 106 Statute 5093)

Merchant Marine Act of 1970
(Public Law 91-465, October 21, 1970, 84 Statute 1018)

Merchant Marine Decorations and Medals Act
(Public Law 100-324, October 21, 1970, 84 Statute 1018)

Merchant Marine Emergency Act
(June 16, 1942, Chapter 416, 56 Statute 370)

Merchant Marine Memorial Act of 1990
(Public Law 101-595, November 16, 1990, 104 Statute 2996)

Merchant Marine Priorities Act of 1941
(July 14, 1941, Chapter 297, 55 Statute 591)

Merchant Ship Sales Act of 1946
(March 8, 1946, Chapter 82, 60 Statute 41)
Revised 16 times, in 1947, 1948, 1949, 1950, 1954, 1956, 1960, 1981, 1986, 1989, 1991, and 1992.
(Public Law 102-587, November 4, 1992, 106 Statute 5894)

Special Trade Acts

Foreign Trade Zones Act
(Chapter 590, June 18, 1934, 48 Statute 908)
Revised in 1984, 1988, and 1990.
(Public Law 101-382, August 20, 1990, Title III, 104 Statute 706)

Import Milk Act
(Chapter 221, July 12, 1943, Table II, 57 Statute 498)

Impoundment Control Act of 1974
(Public Law 93-344, July 12, 1974, Title X, 88 Statute 332)
Revised in 1984 and 1987.
(Public Law 100-119, September 29, 1987, Title II, 101 Statute 785)

Foreign Trade Antitrust Improvements Act of 1982
(Public Law 97-290, October 8, 1982, Title IV, 96 Statute 1246)

Imported Vehicle Safety Compliance Act of 1988
(Public Law 100-562, October 31, 1988, 102 Statute 2818)

Foreign Operations, Export Financing and Related Programs Appropriations Act of 1988
(Public Law 100-202, December 22, 1987, 101, Statute 1329-131)
Revised in 1988, 1989, 1990, and 1991.

International Trade Laws

United States–Canada Free Trade Agreement Implementation Act of 1988

(Public Law 100-149, September 28, 1988, 102 Statute 1851)

The purposes of this act are

1. To approve and implement the free trade agreement between the United States and Canada negotiated under the authority of Section 102 of the Trade Act of 1974.
2. To strengthen and develop economic relations between the United States and Canada for their mutual benefit.
3. To establish a free trade area between the two nations through the reduction and elimination of barriers to trade in goods and services and to investment.
4. To lay the foundation for further cooperation to expand and enhance the benefits of such agreements.

The act consists of five titles. Title I, Approval of United States–Canada Free Trade Agreement and Relationship of Agreement to United States Law, states, "No provision of the Agreement nor the application of any such provision to any person or circumstance which is in conflict will apply to any law of the United States."

Title II, Tariff Modifications, User Fees, Drawbacks, Enforcement, and Other Customs Provisions, stipulates that the president may make certain tariff modifications, including

1. Continuance of any existing duty.
2. Continuance of existing duty-free or excise treatment.
3. Additional duties as the president determines to be necessary or appropriate.

According to the rules of origin, goods originate in the territory of a given party if they are wholly obtained or produced in the territory of either party or both parties, or if they have been produced in the territory of either party or both parties.

Title III, Application of Agreement to Sectors and Services, lists a number of specific provisions. The secretary of agriculture may recommend that the president impose a temporary duty on any Canadian fresh fruit or vegetable entered into the United States if the following conditions are met:

1. For each of five consecutive working days the import price of the Canadian fresh fruit or vegetable is below 90 percent of the corresponding five-year average monthly import price for such fruit or vegetable.
2. The planted acreage in the United States for the like fresh fruit or vegetable is no higher than the average planted acreage over the preceding five years, excluding the years with the highest and lowest acreage.

Nothing in this act shall preclude discussion or negotiation between the United States and Canada of voluntary restraint agreements or mutually agreed quantitative restrictions on the volume of steel products entering the United States from Canada.

Other provisions of Title III include plant and animal health regulations and the control of goods produced in Canada and imported into the United States in such quantities that they constitute a substantial cause of serious injury to the domestic industry producing an article similar to, or directly competitive with, the imported article. Other conditions of Title III include relief from imports from all countries and the lowered threshold for government procurement under the Trade Agreements Act of 1979 in the case of certain Canadian products.

Title IV, Binational Panel to Settle Disputes or Antidumping and Countervailing Duty Cases, is self-explanatory: the panel considers all disputes and, if necessary, directs them to the courts.

Title V provides for effective duties.

Directory of Organizations

4

Organizations that consider the development and importance of international trade of the United States fall into the four major categories outlined in this chapter. The first category includes the principal agencies of the U.S. government. These agencies play an important role in establishing the international trade policies of the nation. The second group lists many intergovernmental advisory committees that have specific, limited objectives and that provide information on trade relations to governmental agencies and private organizations. The third group, national organizations, provide advice on specific areas and nations. The fourth group features international organizations. Finally, the leading world trade centers are listed, and the chapter concludes with the organizational sources. These sources are revised annually.

Government Organizations of the United States

United States Department of Commerce
14th Street and Constitution Avenue, NW
Washington, DC 20230

Description: Founded as the Department of Commerce and Labor on February 14, 1903.

Renamed on March 4, 1913, as Department of Commerce. Labor transferred to Department of Labor. The Department of Commerce (DOC) is composed of the Office of the Secretary and its operating units.

Trade Units: Bureau of Export Administration. The Bureau of Export Administration was established on October 1, 1987. This unit oversees export licensing, technology and policy analysis, and foreign availability determinants. Its goal is to reduce processing times for granting export licenses, decontrolling technologies that offer no real threat to U.S. security and eliminating unilateral controls in areas where widespread foreign availability exists. The office also attempts to develop stronger, more uniform ways to control strategic exports. Investigates breaches of U.S. export control laws and analyzes export intelligence to assess diversion risks. The office also administers and enforces the antiboycott provision of the Export Administration Act.

Purpose: To encourage, serve, and promote the nation's international trade, economic growth, and technological advancement. Its basic goal is to promote the national interest by encouraging the competitive free-enterprise system. The department offers assistance and information to increase U.S. competitiveness in the global economy; administers programs to prevent unfair foreign trade competition; provides social and economic statistics and analyses for business and government planners; provides research and support for the increased use of scientific, engineering, and technological development; works to improve our understanding of the Earth's physical environment and oceanic resources; grants patents and registers trademarks; develops policies and conducts research on telecommunication; provides assistance to promote domestic economic development; promotes travel to the United States by residents of foreign countries; and assists in the growth of minority businesses.

The International Trade Administration was established on January 25, 1980. It promotes world trade and strengthens the international trade and investment position of the United States. It coordinates all issues concerning import administration and international economic policy, programs, and trade development. It is responsible for non-agricultural trade operations of the U.S. government, as well as for international trade-policy planning and interdepartmental coordination. It makes recommendations concerning the analysis, formulation, and implementation of international economic policies of a bilateral, multilateral, or regional nature. The administration defends U.S. industry against injurious and unfair trade practices by administering efficiently, fairly, and in a manner consistent with U.S. international trade obligations the antidumping and countervailing duty laws of the

United States. The office also provides advice on international trade and investment policies pertaining to U.S. industry, in the process of which programs are developed to strengthen domestic export competitiveness to promote U.S. industry in international markets.

Other units of the Department of Commerce are the Economic and Statistics Administration, the Bureau of the Census, the Bureau of Economic Analysis, the Economic Development Administration, the Minority Business Development Agency, the National Oceanic and Atmospheric Administration, the Natural Telecommunications and Information Administration, the Patent and Trademark Office, the National Institute of Standards and Technology, the National Technical Information Service, and the U.S. Travel and Tourism Administration.

Commodity Futures Trading Commission
2033 K Street, NW
Washington, DC 20581

Description: The federal regulating agency for futures trading was established by the Commodity Futures Trading Commission Act of 1974. Its authority to regulate future trading was renewed by Congress in 1978, 1982, 1986, and 1992. The commission consists of five members of which not more than three can be members of the same political party.

Purpose: To regulate trading on the 12 U.S. futures exchanges, which offer active futures and option contracts. It also regulates the activities of numerous commodity exchange members, public brokerage houses, commission-registered futures, industry salespeople and associated individuals, commodity trading advisers, and commodity pool operators. The commission's regulation and enforcement efforts are designed to ensure that futures trading is fair and that it protects both the rights of the customers and the financial integrity of the marketplace. It approves the rules under which the exchange operates, monitors exchange enforcement of those rules, and reviews the terms of futures contracts.

Offices: Large regional offices are maintained in Chicago and New York, and smaller offices exist in Kansas City, Los Angeles, and Minneapolis.

Export-Import Bank of the United States
811 Vermont Avenue, NW
Washington, DC 20571

Description: The Export-Import Bank of Washington was organized as a banking corporation organized under the laws of the District of Columbia by Executive Order 6581 on February 1, 1934. The bank was continued as an agency of the United States by acts of Congress in 1935, 1937, 1939, and 1940. It was made an independent agency of the U.S. government by the Export-Import Bank Act of 1947 and amended in that same year to incorporate the bank under federal charter. The name was changed to Export-Import Bank of the United States by the act of March 13, 1968.

Purpose: To help U.S. exporters meet government-supported competition from other countries and to correct market imperfections so that commercial export financing can take place.

Activities: The bank is authorized to have outstanding dollar loans, guarantees, and insurance in aggregate amounts not in excess of $75 billion. The bank is authorized to have a capital stock of $1 billion and to borrow up to $6 billion from the U.S. Treasury. Eximbank operates a loan program and a guarantee program for both medium- and long-term export transactions. The programs provide up to 85 percent financing, operate on preliminary and final commitments, and are open to any responsible party. The Eximbank loans also carry the minimum interest rate allowed by the Organization for Economic Cooperation and Development.

By providing a variety of insurance programs, the Eximbank reduces the risks of default for U.S. exporters. It also insures against risk of default and export transactions. Other programs include benefits for small business exporters, including the Working Capital Guarantees Program, a loan guarantee program, and access to capital.

Federal Maritime Commission
800 North Capitol Street, NW
Washington, DC 20573-0001

Description: The Federal Maritime Commission was established by Reorganization Plan No. 7 of 1961. It is an independent agency that regulates shipping according to the following statutes: Merchant Marine Acts of 1920, 1928, 1936, and 1966; the Shipping Act of 1984; and the Foreign Shipping Practices Act of 1988.

Purpose: To regulate the waterborne foreign and domestic offshore commerce of the United States, assures that U.S. international trade is open to all nations on fair and equitable terms, and protects against unauthorized concerted activity in the waterborne commerce of the United States. These tasks are accomplished through maintaining surveillance over steamships and common carriers by water. The commission guarantees equal treatment to shippers, carriers, and other persons subject to the shipping statutes.

Activities: The commission reviews all legal agreements. It accepts and rejects tariff filings, including filings dealing with service control, of common carriers engaged in the foreign and domestic offshore commerce of the United States, and conference of such carriers. The commission issues licenses to individuals, partnerships, corporations, or associations desiring to engage in ocean freight forwarding activities. It also administers passenger indemnity provisions and reviews illegal or suspected violations of the shipping statutes and rules and regulations. The commission promulgates rules and regulations to interpret, enforce, and ensure compliance with shipping and related statutes by common carriers and other persons. Finally, the commission prescribes and administers programs to ensure compliance with the provisions of the shipping statutes.

The commission has seven district offices.

Federal Trade Commission
Pennsylvania Avenue at Sixth Street, NW
Washington, DC 20580

Description: The Federal Trade Commission was created by the Federal Trade Commission Act of 1914 (September, 26, 1914, Chapter 311, 38 Statute 717; revised 23 times, in 1933, 1938, 1950, 1952, 1958, 1960, 1970, 1973, 1975, 1976, 1979, 1980, 1982, 1984, 1987, 1989, and 1992; Public Law 102-550, October 28, 1992, 106 Statute 4082), the Federal Trade Commission Improvements Act of 1980 (Public Law 96-252, May 28, 1980, 94 Statute 374; revised; Public Law 98-620, November 8, 1954, Title IV, 98 Statute 3358), and the Clayton Act (Anti-Trust Act) (October 15, 1914, Chapter 323, 38 Statute 730, revised ten times, in 1950, 1955, 1959, 1976, 1980, 1982, 1984, 1989, and 1990; Public Law 101-588, November 16, 1990, 104 Statute 2879). The Federal Trade Commission Act prohibits "unfair methods of competition" and "unfair or deceptive acts or practices" in areas affecting commerce. The Clayton Act outlines specific practices recognized as instruments of monopoly.

Purpose: To maintain competitive enterprise as the keystone of the economic system of the United States. The fundamental goal is to prevent the free-enterprise system from being filtered by monopoly or restraints on trade or corrupted by unfair or deceptive trade practices. Completion must be free and fair.

Activities: The principal functions of the commission are

1. To promote competition through the prevention of general trade restraints such as price fixing, boycotts, and illegal combinations of competition.

2. To avoid problems by preventing the dissemination of false or deceptive advertisements of consumer products generally.
3. To prevent pricing discrimination, exclusive dealing and tying arrangements, corporate mergers, and acquisition or joint ventures when such practices or arrangements may substantially lessen competition.
4. To stop fraudulent telemarketing schemes.
5. To regulate packaging and labeling of certain consumer commodities according to the Federal Packaging and Labeling Act.
6. To supervise the registration and operation of the Association of American Exporters engaged in export trade.
7. To achieve accumulative credit cost disclosure by consumer creditors as called for in the Trade in Lending Act.
8. To protect consumers against circulation of inaccurate or obsolete credit reports and to ensure that consumer-reporting agencies exercise their responsibilities.
9. To gather and make available to the Congress, the president, and the public factual data concerning economic and business conditions.

Trade and Development Agency
Room 309, State Annex 16
Washington, DC 20523-1602

Description: The Trade and Development Agency (formerly the Trade and Development Program) was established on July 1, 1980, as a component organization of the International Development Cooperation Agency in the Omnibus Trade and Competitiveness Act of 1988.

Purpose: To simultaneously promote economic development exportation of U.S. goods and services to developing and middle-income countries.

United States International Development Cooperation Agency
320 Twenty-First Street, NW
Washington, DC 20523-0001

Description: The Agency for International Development (AID) administers foreign economics and humanitarian assistance programs of the United States in the developing world, Central and Eastern Europe, and the newly independent states of the former Soviet Union. The agency is independent and has a worldwide network of programs.

Purpose: To plan and coordinate policy on international economic issues affecting developing countries. The agency makes decisions on trade, financing and monetary affairs, technology, and other activities and supplies strong direction to U.S. economic policies toward the developing world.

Activities: The agency carries on many functions in education, health, environment, agriculture, governance, energy, economic growth, housing, urban development, and others.

U.S. International Trade Commission
500 E Street, SW
Washington, DC 20436

Description: The U.S. International Trade Commission is an independent agency created by an act of September 8, 1916, and originally named the United States Tariff Commission. The commission functions under the Tariff Act of 1930, the Agricultural Adjustment Act, the Trade Expansion Act of 1962, and the Trade Act of 1974.

Purpose: To investigate customs laws of the United States and foreign countries. Checks on volume of importation in connection with domestic production and consumption. Looks at competition of foreign countries.

Activities: The commission enjoys broad investigative power relating to the customs laws of the United States and foreign countries; the volume of importation in comparison with domestic products and consumption; the conditions, causes, and effects relating to competition of foreign industries with those of the United States; and all other factors affecting competition between articles of the United States and imported articles.

The commission reports to the president, the Committee on Ways and Means of the House of Representatives and to the Committee on Finance of the Senate. The commission engages in extensive research, conducts specialized studies, and maintains a high degree of expertise in all matters relating to the commercial and international trade policies of the United States.

U.S. Intergovernmental Advisory Committees

**Advisory Committee for Trade Policy
and Negotiations (ACTPN) (International Trade)**
Office of the U.S. Trade Representative
600 17th Street, NW
Washington, DC 20506

Description: Established as the Advisory Committee for Trade Negotiations on June 3, 1975, by Public Law 93-618, the Trade Act of 1974, dated January 3, 1975, as amended by Public Law 96-39, the Trade Agreements Act of 1979. Name changed August 23, 1988. It is a public advisory committee of the Office of the U.S. trade representative. The committee meets at the request of the U.S. trade representative.

Purpose: To advise on operation of trade agreements.

Activities: In addition to advising and consulting duties, it makes recommendations to the president of the United States, Congress, and the U.S. trade representative regarding operation of trade agreements entered into by the United States and other matters concerning administration of the trade policy of the United States.

Membership: Its 45 members are appointed by the president. They represent labor, industry, agriculture, business, service industries, retailers, consumer interests, and the general public.

**Advisory Committee on the European Community
Common Approach to Standards Testing and
Certification in 1992 (International Trade)**
Office of European Community Affairs
Room 3036, Department of Commerce
14th Street and Constitution Avenue, NW
Washington, DC 20230

Description: Established February 23, 1990, as a public advisory committee of the International Trade Administration, Department of Commerce. It holds meetings three or four times a year.

Purpose: To serve as advisory committee to the secretary of commerce.

Activities: Advises secretary of commerce on the European Community's 1992 impact on U.S. exports. Makes recommendations regarding the European Community's 1992 program to create a single standards policy and assesses U.S. competitiveness as result of the European program. Suggests ways to improve coordination of U.S. federal, state, local, and private sector standards activities.

Membership: The committee includes 40 members, appointed for two-year terms by the secretary of commerce, representing chief executive officers, standards organizations, and test laboratories.

**Agricultural Policy Advisory Committee for Trade
(International Trade)**
Foreign Agricultural Service
Department of Agriculture
South Building, Room 5065
Washington, DC 20250

Description: Established January 9, 1981, under the authority of the Trade Act of 1974, as amended by the Trade Agreements Act of 1979 and the Omnibus Trade and Competitiveness Act of 1988. It is a joint public advisory committee of the Department of Agriculture and the Office of the U.S. trade representative and Agricultural Advisory Program. Meetings are closed to the general public because of trade sensitivity and confidential material.

Purpose: To advise secretary of agriculture and the U.S. trade representative on trade agreements.

Activities: Offers advice on negotiating objectives before the United States enters into trade agreements, on operation of the agreement once it has been signed, and on matters in connection with the administration of the trade policy of the United States.

Membership: The committee consists of 25 members representing United States agricultural interests. It is co-chaired by the secretary of agriculture and the U.S. trade representative.

**Committee of Chairs of Industry Advisory Committees
for Trade Policy Matters (International Trade)**
Trade Advisory Center, Room H2015B
International Trade Administration
Department of Commerce
Washington, DC 20230

Description: Established March 21, 1980, by the secretary of commerce and the U.S. trade representative as a public advisory committee. It is a joint committee of the Department of Commerce and the Office of the U.S. Trade Representative and part of the Industry Consultations Program established under the Trade Act of 1974 and amended by the Trade Agreements Act of 1979. The committee meets four times a year.

Purpose: To provide advice concerning trade agreements the United States enters into and other matters U.S. trade policy.

Activities: Provides the secretary of commerce and the U.S. trade representative with information about negotiating objectives and bargaining positions before entering any trade agreement affecting the

Industry Sector Advisory Committees for Trade Policy. Advises on other matters concerning the administration of the trade policy of the United States.

Membership: The committee has 20 members, 17 who use chairs of the Industry Sector Advisory Committees and 3 who use chairs of the Industry Functional Advisory Committees. The committee is co-chaired.

Foreign-Trade Zones Board (International Trade)
Herbert Hoover Building, Room 3716
14th Street and Pennsylvania Avenue, NW
Washington, DC 20230

Description: Established as an interagency board by Public Law 73- 397, dated June 18, 1934, and amended by Public Law 81-566. It operates within the International Trade Administration of the Department of Commerce.

Purpose: To serve in advisory capacity.

Activities: Grants authority to qualified corporations to establish foreign-trade zones in and near U.S. ports of entry and issues rules and regulations. Studies annual report of each grantee. Votes on zone matters. Follows international commerce and economic development.

Membership: There are three members: the secretary of commerce, the secretary of the treasury, and the secretary of the army. Chaired by the secretary of commerce.

Industry Functional Advisory Committee on Standards
for Trade Policy Matters (International Trade)
Trade Advisory Center, Room H2015B
International Trade Administration
Department of Commerce
Washington, DC 20230

Description: Established March 21, 1980, by the secretary of commerce and the U.S. trade representative as a public advisory committee. It is a joint committee of the Department of Commerce and the Office of the U.S. Trade Representative and part of the Industry Consultations Program, established under the Trade Act of 1974 as amended by the Trade Agreements Act of 1979.

Purpose: To advise concerning trade agreements and other matters relating to administration of U.S. trade policy.

Activities: Furnishes policy and technical advice to the secretary of commerce and the U.S. trade representative. Makes recommendations regarding the effect of standards on trade and the implementation of trade agreements negotiated under the Trade Act.

Membership: Committee consists of 40 members. Twenty are elected by membership of the Industry Sector Advisory Committees and 20 are appointed from the private sector by the secretary of commerce and the U.S. trade representative. Support services are provided by the Trade Advisory Center, International Trade Administration.

Industry Sector Advisory Committee on Capital Goods for Trade Policy Matters (International Trade)
Trade Advisory Center, Room H2015B
International Trade Administration
Department of Commerce
Washington, DC 20230

Description: Established March 21, 1980, by the secretary of commerce and the U.S. trade representative as a public advisory committee. It is a joint committee of the Department of Commerce and the Office of the U.S. Trade Representative and part of the Industry Consultations Program, established under the Trade Act of 1974, as amended by the Trade Agreements Act of 1979.

Purpose: To provide advice concerning trade agreements and other matters relating to the administration of U.S. trade policy.

Activities: Provides secretary of commerce and the U.S. trade representative with advice with respect to negotiating objectives and bargaining points before entering into a trade agreement concerning capital goods and other matters regarding administration of the trade policy of the United States.

Membership: Consists of not more than 30 members representing the capital goods industry. The Task Force on Market Access is a subsidiary unit.

Industry Sector Advisory Committee on Consumer Goods for Trade Policy Matters (International Trade)
Trade Advisory Center, Room H2015B
International Trade Administration
Department of Commerce
Washington, DC 20230

Description: Established March 21, 1980, by the secretary of commerce and the U.S. trade representative as a public advisory committee. It is a joint committee of the Department of Commerce and the Office of U.S. Trade Representative and part of the Industry Consultations

Program, established under the Trade Act of 1974, as amended by the Trade Agreements Act of 1979.

Purpose: To provide advice concerning trade agreements and other matters relating to administration of U.S. trade policy.

Activities: Provides the secretary of commerce and the U.S. trade representative with information and advice on negotiating objectives and bargaining positions before entering into a trade agreement concerning the consumer goods industry and other matters dealing with the administration of U.S. trade policy.

Membership: Consists of not more than 50 members representing the consumer goods industry.

Industry Sector Advisory Committee on Services
for Trade Policy Matters (International Trade)
Trade Advisory Center, Room H2015B
International Trade Administration
Department of Commerce
Washington, DC 20230

Description: Established March 21, 1980, by the secretary of commerce and the U.S. trade representative as a public advisory committee. It is a joint committee of the Department of Commerce and the Office of the U.S. Trade Representative and part of the Industry Consultations Program, established under the Trade Act of 1974, as amended by the Trade Agreements Act of 1979.

Purpose: To provide advice concerning trade agreements and other matters relating to the administration of U.S. trade policy.

Activities: Provides the secretary of commerce and the U.S. trade representative with information and advice specifically regarding negotiating objectives and bargaining positions before entering into a trade agreement concerning service industries, as well as advice on other matters relating to the administration of U.S. trade policy.

Membership: Consists of not more than 50 members representing the service industries.

Industry Sector Advisory Committee on Small and Minority
Business for Trade Policy Matters (International Trade)
Trade Advisory Center, Room H2015B
International Trade Administration
Department of Commerce
Washington, DC 20230

Description: Established as a public advisory committee on March 21, 1980, by the secretary of commerce and the U.S. trade representative. It is a joint committee of the Department of Commerce and the Office of the U.S. Trade Representative and part of the Industry Consultations Program, established under the Trade Act of 1974, as amended by the Trade Agreements Act of 1979.

Purpose: To provide advice concerning trade agreements and other matters relating to the administration of U.S. trade policy.

Activities: Provides the secretary of commerce and the U.S. trade representative with information and advice regarding negotiating objectives and bargaining positions before entering into a trade agreement concerning small and/or minority business, and advises on other matters connected with the administration of U.S. trade policy.

Membership: Consists of not more than 35 members representing small and minority business.

**Industry Sector Advisory Committee
on Transportation, Construction, and
Agricultural Equipment for Trade Policy Matters
(International Trade)**
Trade Advisory Center, Room H2015B
International Trade Association
Department of Commerce
Washington, DC 20230

Description: Established March 21, 1980, by the secretary of commerce and the U.S. trade representative as a public advisory committee. It is a joint committee of the Department of Commerce and the Office of the U.S. Trade Representative and part of the Industry Consultations Program, established under the Trade Act of 1974, as amended by the Trade Agreements Act of 1979.

Purpose: To provide advice concerning trade agreements and other matters relating to the administration of U.S. trade policy.

Activities: Provides the secretary of commerce and the U.S. trade representative with information and advice regarding negotiating objectives and bargaining positions before entering into an agreement concerning transportation, construction, and agricultural equipment industries, and advises on other matters relating to the administration of U.S. trade policy.

Membership: Consists of not more than 30 members representing transportation, construction, and agricultural industries.

Industry Sector Advisory Committee on Wholesaling and Retailing for Trade Policy Matters (International Trade)
Trade Advisory Center, Room H2015B
International Trade Administration
Department of Commerce
Washington, DC 20230

Description: Established March 21, 1980, by the secretary of commerce and the U.S. trade representative as a public advisory committee. It is a joint committee of the Department of Commerce, Office of the U.S. Trade Representative, and the Industry Consultations Program, established under the Trade Act of 1974, as amended by the Trade Agreements Act of 1979.

Purpose: To provide advice concerning trade agreements and other matters relating to the administration of U.S. trade policy.

Activities: Provides the secretary of commerce and the U.S. trade representative with information and advice about negotiating objectives and bargaining positions before entering trade agreements concerning wholesale and retailing industries, and advises on other matters relating to the administration of U.S. trade policy.

Membership: Consists of not more than 30 members representing the wholesaling and retailing industries.

Interagency Group on Countertrade (International Trade)
Office of the Secretary
Department of Commerce
14th Street and Constitution Avenue, NW
Washington, DC 20230

Description: Established by President Reagan under authority of Public Law 100-418, the Omnibus Trade and Competitiveness Act of 1988.

Purpose: As an interagency policy group, chaired by the Department of Commerce, to provide information on countertrade.

Activities: Reviews and evaluates current trends in international countertrade and recommends ways to offset the impact of those trends on the U.S. economy. Evaluates countertrade in U.S. exports and bilateral U.S. foreign economic assistance programs. Reviews need for and feasibility of negotiation with other countries through the Organization for Economic Cooperation and Development and other organizations. Reports to the president and Congress.

Membership: Representatives of 12 federal agencies and departments designated by the president of the United States.

Interagency Trade Data Advisory Committee (International Trade)
Office of Business Analysis, Room 4578
Department of Commerce
14th Street and Constitution Avenue, NW
Washington, DC 20230

Description: Established by the secretary of commerce under authority of the Omnibus Trade and Competitiveness Act of 1988 (15 USC 4901-13).

Purpose: To act as an interagency advisory committee.

Activities: Advises the secretary of commerce on the establishment, structure, contents, and operation of the National Trade Data Bank (NTDB). The Omnibus Trade and Competitiveness Act of 1988 directs the Department of Commerce to establish and manage the NTDB. The data bank provides access to data on international economics and trade. Assures timely and accurate collection of information and provides access to the data by the private sector and government officials.

Membership: Consists of U.S. trade representative, secretaries of agriculture, defense, labor, treasury, and state; director of Office of Management and Budget; director of Central Intelligence Agency; chairperson of Federal Reserve Board; chairperson of International Trade Commission; president of Export-Import Bank; president of Overseas Private Investment Corporation; and administrator of Small Business Administration or representative. Chaired by secretary of commerce.

**Intergovernmental Policy Advisory Committee
(International Trade)**
Office of Private Sector Liaison, Room 100
Office of the U.S. Trade Representative
600 17th Street, NW
Washington, DC 20506

Description: Established August 19, 1983, by the U.S. trade representative. Meets three or four times a year; meetings called by the U.S. trade representative.

Purpose: To serve as a public advisory committee of the Office of the U.S. Trade Representative.

Activities: Advises, consults with, and makes recommendations to the U.S. trade representative and relevant cabinet agencies on policy issues that may affect U.S. trade policy objectives, statutes, regulations, and other acts promulgated or enacted by the federal government that may affect the relationship between international trade and state and local governments.

Membership: Composed of 35 representatives of state and local governments who are familiar with international trade policy.

Joint American-Romanian Economic Commission (International Trade)
HCHB Room 3413, Office of East European and Soviet Affairs
Department of Commerce
Washington, DC 20230

Description: Established by President Nixon and the president of the Socialist Republic of Romania in their joint statement on economic, industrial, and technical cooperation on December 5, 1973. Commission meets alternately in Washington, DC, and Bucharest.

Purpose: To develop international trade between the United States and Romania.

Activities: Considers questions and problems concerning reciprocal establishment of business facilities to promote trade and economic cooperation. Facilitates establishment of joint consulting groups among representatives of firms, companies, and economic organizations of the two countries on matters of interest.

Membership: Administrative support furnished by the International Trade Administration.

Services Policy Advisory Committee (International Trade)
Office of Private Sector Liaison, Room 100
Office of the U.S. Trade Representative
600 17th Street, NW
Washington, DC 20506

Description: Established March 17, 1980, by Public Law 93-618, the Trade Act of 1974, as amended by Public Law 96-39, the Trade Agreements Act of 1979. Meets three or four times a year.

Purpose: To act as a public advisory committee of the Office of the U.S. Trade Representative.

Activities: Advises, consults with, and makes recommendations to the U.S. trade representative concerning U.S. government negotiations in the Uruguay Round of the General Agreement on Tariffs and Trade and in regional and bilateral negotiations to remove impediments to international trade in services. Provides policy advice for improving existing conditions in international trade in services. Offers advice on international investment problems.

Membership: Composed of 40 members representing U.S. industries. Members serve two terms.

Trade Policy Committee (International Trade)
600 17th Street, NW, Room 414
Washington, DC 20506

Description: Established November 25, 1957, by President Eisenhower in Executive Order 10741. It was terminated by Executive Order 11075, dated January 15, 1968, and reconstituted as the Trade Extension Act Advisory Committee under Public Law 87-749. The Trade Expansion Act Committee was terminated and reconstituted as the Trade Policy Committee by Executive Order 11846, dated March 27, 1975.

Purpose: To serve as an interagency committee of the executive branch.

Activities: Makes recommendations to the president on basic policy issues arising in the administration of the trade agreement programs. Recommends action the president should take on reports dealing with tariff adjustments submitted to him by the Tariff Commission. Advises the president of results of hearings concerning foreign import restrictions. Performs other functions as requested by the president. It has several subsidiary units.

Membership: Consists of the secretaries of agriculture, defense, commerce, energy, interior, labor, state, transportation, treasury; the U.S. attorney general; the director of the Office of Management and Budget; the chairperson of the Council of Economic Advisors; the assistant to the president for national security affairs; the director of the U.S. International Development Cooperation Agency, and the U.S. trade representative.

Trade Policy Review Group (International Trade)
Office of the U.S. Trade Representative
600 17th Street, NW
Washington, DC 20506

Description: Originally established as the Trade Executive Committee, December 11, 1971; abolished and reconstituted as the Trade Policy Review Group by Executive Order 11846, dated March 27, 1975, implementing the provisions of Public Law 93-618, the Trade Act of 1974.

Purpose: To serve as an interagency committee and work with the Trade Policy Committee.

Activities: Coordinates interagency activities concerning the trade agreements program and related matters at the level of the assistant secretary. Recommends policies and actions to the U.S. trade representative concerning trade agreements program. Reviews and approves recommendations of the Trade Policy Staff Committee on policies and actions concerning proposed trade agreements and related trade policy matters.

Membership: Composed of representatives chosen by the secretaries of agriculture, commerce, defense, energy, interior, labor, state, transportation, and treasury; the U.S. attorney general; the director of the Office of Management and Budget; the chairperson of the Council of Economic Advisors; the director of the International Development Cooperation Agency; and the assistant to the president for National Security Affairs.

Trade Policy Staff Committee (International Trade)
Office of the U.S. Trade Representative
600 17th Street, NW
Washington, DC 20506

Description: Established March 27, 1975, by President Ford under Executive Order 11846, as amended by Executive Order 12188, dated January 1, 1980. It absorbed the functions of the Trade Staff Committee and the Trade Information Committee, both established December 15, 1971.

Purpose: To serve as an interagency committee and as a subcommittee of the Trade Policy Committee.

Activities: Monitors trade agreements program. Obtains information and advice from other government departments and the private sector concerning any proposed trade agreements or concerning the Generalized System of Preferences. Provides opportunity for public hearings so that interested parties can present their views on matters relevant to proposed trade agreements or the Generalized System of Preferences.

Membership: Composed of representatives designated by the secretaries of agriculture, commerce, defense, energy, interior, labor, state, transportation, and treasury; U.S. attorney general; director of the Office of Management and Budget; chairperson of the Council of Economic Advisors; director of the International Development Cooperation Agency; and assistant to the president for National Security Affairs.

Trade Promotion Coordinating Committee (International Trade)
Department of Commerce, Room H3867
14th Street and Constitution Avenue, NW
Washington, DC 20230

Description: Established May 1990 by President Bush.

Purpose: To serve as an advisory committee under the International Trade Administration, Department of Commerce.

Activities: President Bush developed a Commercial Opportunities Initiative to help U.S. firms in exporting and to unify federal trade promotion activities. Offers U.S. business a one-stop shop for trade promotion services. Publishes a guide to U.S. government trade promotion resources. Provides a telephone service for quick information on promotion activities and events. Maintains a calendar of events that appears in the National Trade Data Bank. Coordinates future overseas trade missions led by secretary of commerce to new or neglected foreign markets. Has several subsidiary units.

Membership: Consists of representatives from the Department of State, the Treasury, Defense, Agriculture, Commerce, Labor, Transportation and Energy; Office of Management and Budget; Office of Technology Assessment; Council of Economic Advisors; Environmental Protection Agency; Small Business Administration; Agency for International Development; Export-Import Bank of the United States, Overseas Private Investment Corporation; Trade and Development Program; and United States Information Agency.

Transportation and Related Equipment
Technical Advisory Committee (International Trade)
EA/BXA, Department of Commerce
14th Street & Constitution Avenue, NW
Washington, DC 20230

Description: Established January 3, 1985, pursuant to Section 5(h)(l) of 50 USC 2401, the Export Administration Act of 1979, as amended. Meets quarterly.

Purpose: To serve as a public advisory committee of the Department of Commerce.

Activities: Advises secretary of commerce and other federal agencies referred to in the act with respect to technical specifications and policy issues of concern to the department, worldwide availability of products and systems, licensing procedures that affect the level of export controls applicable to goods or technology, exports subject to unilateral and multilateral controls that the United States establishes or in which it participates.

Membership: No more than 25 members, appointed by the secretary of commerce, representing the transportation industry and related equipment industries or government employees knowledgeable in the areas. Members serve for terms of not more than four years.

**United States Automotive Parts Advisory Committee
(International Trade)**
Office of Automotive Parts
Basic Industries Sector, Trade Development
Main Commerce, Room 4036
Washington, DC 20230

Description: Established by the secretary of commerce under authority of Public Law 100-418, the Omnibus Trade and Competitiveness Act of 1988. Also known as Auto Parts Advisory Committee.

Purpose: To serve as advisory committee of the International Trade Commission, Department of Commerce.

Activities: Advises government officials on matters relating to the implementation of the Fair Trade in Auto Parts Act of 1988. Reports annually to the secretary of commerce on barriers to sales. Assists secretary in reporting to Congress on progress of sales of U.S.–made auto parts in Japanese markets. Reviews data collected on sales of U.S.–made auto parts to Japanese markets. Advises secretary during consultation with Japan on these issues. Assists in establishing priorities for the department's initiatives to increase U.S.–made auto parts sales to Japanese markets. Helps carry out these initiatives.

Membership: None given, but two members of the Office of Automotive Affairs, Basic Industries Sector, and Trade Development serve as staff contacts.

National Organizations

**American Association of Exporters and Importers
(International Trade) (AAEI)**
11 West 42nd Street
New York, NY 10036

Description: Founded 1921. Has 1,200 members and 16 on staff. Budget is $1,000,000 and has regional groups. Meets on the last Monday and Tuesday in October in New York City. Members deal in exports and imports.

Purpose: To watch for problems to arise in laws and regulations that might affect members.

Activities: Gathers and disseminates data on world trade. Creates and supports legislation promoting balanced international trade. Maintains liaison with government committees and agencies. Testifies for exporters and importers before official groups. Offers advice and support to members facing problems in their businesses. Conducts forums and workshops on timely topics and developments. Holds seminars on exporting and importing. Has library of research information, records, and government data. Works occasionally through committees.

Publications: AAEI Membership Directory, annual; *Alertfax,* daily; *Bulletin,* periodic; *Export Controls Progress Report,* 5-6 per year, *GSP Red Flag Alerts,* 5-6 per year; *International Trade Alert,* weekly; *International Trade Alert Index,* quarterly; *Newsletter,* quarterly; *Textile Quota Report,* weekly; also publishes a broad range of import/export documents.

American Countertrade Association (International Trade) (ACA)
121 S. Meramec Avenue, No. 1102
St. Louis, MO 63105-1725

Description: Founded 1986. Has 156 members from among U.S. manufacturers engaged in countertrade. Semiannual meetings are held in spring and fall.

Purpose: To assist countries in the generation of hard currency to purchase U.S. products. Promotes trade and commerce between companies based in the United States and countertrade customers outside the United States.

Activities: Disseminates information on countertrade requirements and their impact on U.S. commerce. Provides a forum for countertrade professionals. Holds annual training sessions. Compiles matrix of countertrade activities.

Publications: ACA Newsletter, periodic.

American League for Exports and Security Assistance (International Trade) (ALESA)
122 C Street, NW, Suite 740
Washington, DC 20001

Description: Founded 1976. Has 38 members and 4 staff. Members include corporations, unions, and other interested organizations. Holds annual meeting.

Purpose: To support and encourage the sale of American defense products abroad.

Activities: Develops and implements a national export policy. Agrees to sale of U.S. defense products abroad in accord with the foreign policy, security, and economic goals of the nation. Ensures favorable treatment for exports in all legislation and national priorities to help create more jobs for U.S. workers.

Publications: None.

American Traders Group (International Trade) (ATG)
2318 Cleveland Street
Hollywood, FL 33020

Description: Founded 1983. Has two members from U.S. Exporters of U.S. Goods. Budget is $100,000. Membership is local, but the group plans to expand nationally. Meetings held periodically.

Purpose: To promote international trade.

Activities: Promotes good trade relations between the United States and other countries to develop international trade, specifically to increase exportation of U.S. products overseas. Specializes in supply and operation of supermarket operations.

Publications: Validated Export Price Lists, quarterly; *Validated Sheets,* quarterly; also publishes registers, directories, and brochures; plans to publish product catalog.

**American West Overseas Association
(International Trade) (AWOA)**
19451 195th Avenue
Hudson, CO 80642

Description: Founded 1976. Has 63 members and 5 staff. Members are manufacturers, wholesalers, and sales representatives engaged in the export of western wear. Holds annual meeting.

Purpose: To keep manufacturers, wholesalers, and sales representatives informed about changes and government programs that affect business.

Activities: Conducts foreign publicity and public relations programs aimed at foreign consumers and generates trade publications, such as product releases for the trade press featuring merchandise placed on display at export trade shows. Acts as liaison with officers in U.S. embassies and with officers of the U.S. Department of Commerce. Presently inactive.

Publications: AWOA Update: Export Newsletter for Association Members, monthly; *Association and Industry Newsletter,* includes trade requirements and regulations and sales opportunities; *Buyers Guide*, annual; *Directory Export*, annual.

Association of Foreign Trade Representatives (International Trade) (AFTR)
P.O. Box 300
New York, NY 10024

Description: Founded 1984. Members are representatives of foreign governments interested in promoting foreign trade. Has monthly luncheon.

Purpose: To promote and expand trade.

Activities: Serves as forum for trade representatives.

Publications: None.

Committee for Small Business Exports (International Trade) (COSBE)
P.O. Box 6
Aspen, CO 81612

Description: Founded 1979. Has 100 members including small manufacturers involved in exports.

Purpose: To protect the small manufacturer.

Activities: Lobbies to improve conditions and reduce financial and legal regulation of small companies that export their products.

Publications: Newsletter, periodic.

Council on Competitiveness (Trade) (CC)
900 17th Street, NW, No. 1050
Washington, DC 20006

Description: Founded 1986. Has 161 members and 11 staff. Members are chief executive officers of corporate, educational, and labor organizations. Holds annual meeting.

Purpose: To maintain and improve the competitiveness of the United States in trade.

Activities: Favors incremental changes in business, labor, academia, and government. Establishes an agenda of issues crucial to U.S. competitiveness, including policies that encourage investment. Seeks to develop an educated and skilled workforce. Maintains a solid scientific and technological infrastructure. Gives assistance to organizations engaged in building competitiveness. Consults with members of Congress and the executive branch. Testifies at congressional hearings. Appraises national budgets. Assesses effects of government policies on U.S. international competitiveness. Conducts media education campaign for domestic and foreign commentators and journalists. Maintains speakers' bureau. Plans to establish alliances with similar organizations nationwide. Conducts public opinion polls. Holds conferences.

Publications: Challenges, monthly; *Competitiveness Index,* annual; also publishes *America's Competitive Crisis: Confronting the New Reality; Restoring America's Trade Position; Governing America; A Competitive Policy for the New Administration; Reclaiming the American Dream: Fiscal Policies for a Competitive Nation; Picking up the Pace: The Commercial Challenge to American Innovation* (papers).

Czech and Slovak–U.S. Economic Council (International Trade) (CSUSEC)
c/o Chamber of Commerce of the United States
1615 H Street, NW
Washington, DC 20062

Description: Founded 1975. Has 60 members interested in trade. Holds annual meeting.

Purpose: To promote trade with Czech Republic and Slovakia.

Activities: Promotes trade via a trilateral council of U.S., Czech, and Slovak companies. Holds forums to discuss trilateral trade and investment issues. Forms policy issues to promote and expand economic relations between United States, Czech Republic, and Slovakia.

Publications: None.

Emergency Committee for American Trade (International Trade) (ECAT)
1211 Connecticut Avenue, NW, Suite 801
Washington, DC 20036

Description: Founded 1967. Has 65 members and staff of four. Members interested in international trade. Holds annual meeting.

Purpose: To disseminate information on international trade and policies.

Activities: Supports liberal international trade and investment policies. Opposes import quotas and capital controls and any legislation restricting trade and investment.

Publications: Membership List, periodic.

Federal Credit International Business/National Association of Credit Management (International Trade) (FCIB/NACM)
Metro Center 1
100 Wood Avenue S
Iselin, NJ 08830

Description: Founded 1919. Has 1,000 members and 12 staff. Has 22 regional groups and 22 local groups, including exporters and banks. Holds annual meeting in May.

Purpose: To protect exporters.

Activities: Manufacturing exporters and banks make market surveys, conduct research on countries, discuss current credit conditions, and collect overdue foreign accounts. Sponsors international credit workshops. The organization surveys worldwide credit conditions, operates a placement service, maintains a library, and compiles statistics.

Publications: FCIB Country Credit Report, periodic; *FCIB/NACM-International Bulletin,* monthly; *FCIB/NACM-Membership Roster,* biennial; *FCIB/NACM-Minutes of Round Table Conference,* monthly; *FCIB/NACM-Newsletter,* monthly; also publishes credit reports on individual foreign firms.

Federation of International Trade Associations (FITA)
1851 Alexander Bell Drive
Reston, VA 22091

Description: Founded 1985. Has 150 members interested in international trade. No meeting scheduled.

Purpose: To promote interest in international trade clubs.

Activities: Holds conferences and seminars. Sponsors export seminars by the U.S. Department of Commerce. Maintains research library.

Publications: Membership Directory, annual; *Newsletter,* periodic.

Foreign Commerce Club of New York (International Trade) (FCC)
c/o Frank Fills
One World Trade Center, Suite 3147
New York, NY 10048

Description: Founded 1914. Has 650 members and a staff of two. Members are executives interested in international trade. Holds annual meeting.

Purpose: To promote foreign trade.

Activities: Industrial and transportation executives engage in foreign trade using the port of New York. Bestows awards. Works through committees.

Publications: Journal, annual.

**Foreign Sales Corporation/Domestic
International Sales Corporation
(FSC/DISC) Tax Association (International Trade)**
2975 W. Chester Avenue
Purchase, NY 10577

Description: Founded 1982. Has 400 members and two staff. Budget is $105,000. Members include corporations, professional firms, and individual tax advisors. Holds annual conference.

Purpose: To help members understand U.S. tax incentives and other offshore benefits that can be used by exporters.

Activities: Conducts educational programs for companies that operate foreign sales corporation or domestic international sales corporation in order to obtain tax incentives for the export of U.S. goods. Holds seminars on international tax, export lease finance, and incentives for companies that set up manufacturing or operating sites abroad.

Publications: Export Tax Letter, quarterly; *FSC/DISC News,* quarterly; *FSC Leasing News,* quarterly.

**India Engineering Export Promotion Council
(International Trade) (IEEPC)**
333 N. Michigan Avenue, Suite 2014
Chicago, IL 60601

Description: Founded 1968. Has 6,000 members. Members manufacture engineering products in India.

Purpose: To promote sales of engineering products made in India.

Activities: Aids members in sales and product promotion, marketing research, advertising, and importing of engineering products into Canadian and U.S. markets. Helps U.S. importers select products manufactured in India.

Publications: Directory of Indian Engineering Exporters, triennial; *Indian Engineering Exporter,* quarterly; *Turnkey Offers from India,* biennial.

Inland International Trade Association (IITAI)
Center for International Trade Development
1787 Tribute Road, Suite A
Sacramento, CA 95815

Description: Founded 1979. Has 100 members interested in import and export trade in northern California and Nevada. Holds monthly meeting on the fourth Wednesday of the month.

Purpose: To promote export and import business in northern California and Nevada.

Activities: Disseminates information. Acts on issues concerning the import and export business. Provides social setting for interaction among members.

Publications: IITAI Newsletter, bimonthly.

International Trade Action Council
1225 19th Street, NW, Suite 210
Washington, DC 20036

Description: Founded 1978. Ad hoc trade coalition of industry trade associations and unions. No meeting is scheduled.

Purpose: To advocate changes in import trade laws.

Activities: Suggests changes in import trade laws. Focuses on multilateral trade negotiations, trade legislation, and subsidies code.

Publications: None.

International Trade Club of Chicago (ITCC)
203 Wabash Avenue, Suite 1102
Chicago, IL 60601

Description: Founded 1919. Has 500 members and three staff. Members are involved in import/export operations for their firms. Annual meeting at the Chicago World Trade Conference.

Purpose: To expand international business.

Activities: Works to remove barriers that may interfere with expansion and development of international trade. Members discuss problems and share their experience to promote a better understanding of U.S. foreign policy and its impact on international business. Has luncheons and dinner programs and special interest seminars. Works primarily through committees.

Publications: INTERCOM, monthly; *International Trade Club of Chicago— Membership Directory,* annual.

International Trade Council (ITC)
3144 Circle Hill Road
Alexandria, VA 22305

Description: Founded 1976. Has 850 members and 35 staff. Budget is $750,000. Members are companies and organizations that deal in importing and exporting. Holds an annual conference—1993, Singapore; 1994, Copenhagen, Denmark; 1995, Madrid, Spain. Also holds 11 meetings per year.

Purpose: To disseminate information regarding importing and exporting products.

Activities: Promotes free trade, removes trade barriers, facilitates research and marketing for members. Maintains legislative and educational services to develop world trade. Conducts management, technical, and educational programs. Conducts financial studies of export banking, insurance, and transportation costs to help exporters to be more competitive. Has speakers' bureau. Sponsors International Development Institute. Offers an opportunity/risk analysis service to help members find new overseas markets for their commodities. Maintains 4,700-volume library including technical books and overseas market surveys. Presents Exporter of the Year Award. Holds seminars.

Publications: Membership Directory, annual; *Research Report,* monthly; *World Agricultural Review,* quarterly; *World Agriculture Directory,* annual; *World Opportunity/Risk Review,* quarterly; *World Trade Directory,* periodic; *World Trade Review,* quarterly; *Worldbusiness Directory,* annual; *Worldbusiness Review,* quarterly; *Worldbusiness Weekly.*

International Traders Association (IT)
c/o The Mellinger Company
6100 Variel Avenue
Woodland Hills, CA 91367

Description: Founded 1947. Has 74,000 members and 50 staff. Members are involved in export/import business. Budget is $200,000. Holds annual conference and semiannual seminar.

Purpose: To promote international business.

Activities: Issues publications and makes personal visits to promote world trade and disseminates information about the trader's role in the marketplace. Sponsors seminars and trade shows. Bestows awards.

Publications: Trade Agreement Catalogs Book, semiannual; *Trade Opportunities Magazine,* monthly.

Joint Industry Group (International Trade) (JIG)
c/o James Clawson
818 Connecticut Avenue, NW, 12th Floor
Washington, DC 20006

Description: Founded 1976. Has 100 members, mostly trade associations and business firms. Budget is $40,000.

Purpose: To keep administration informed about customs and trade laws.

Activities: Informs the administration about customs and trade laws in order to facilitate trade.

Publications: None.

Labor-Industry Coalition for International Trade (LICIT)
c/o Alan Wolff
1775 Pennsylvania Avenue, NW
Washington, DC 20006

Description: Founded 1980. Has 16 members and 2 staff. Members are unions and multinational companies. Holds semiannual board meeting.

Purpose: To stay informed about trade issues.

Activities: Lobbies for reforms of international trade policy. Sponsors research. Tries to increase awareness of international trade issues.

Publications: Studies.

National Association of Export Companies
(International Trade) (NAXCO)
P.O. Box 1330
Murray Hill Station
New York, NY 10156

Description: Founded 1965. Has 100 members and one staff person. Members are independent export firms. Budget is less than $25,000. Holds annual trade show and quarterly meetings.

Purpose: To assist independent export firms.

Activities: Established independent export firms to act as representatives and distributors for manufacturers in the United States, export trading companies, and export management companies. Promotes expansion of U.S. trade. Encourages U.S. manufacturers to use export management and trading companies as export departments. Conducts educational programs. Maintains speakers' bureau and placement service.

Publications: News Alert, monthly.

**National Association of Foreign Trade Zones
(International Trade) (NAFTZ)**
1735 Eye Street, NW, Suite 506
Washington, DC 20006

Description: Founded 1973. Has 275 members and 2 staff. Members involved in foreign trade zone operations. Budget is $400,000. Holds annual conference.

Purpose: To promote and improve foreign trade zones.

Activities: Promotes use of foreign trade zones as valuable tools in the international commerce of the United States. Encourages establishment of foreign-trade zones to foster investment and the creation of new jobs in the United States.

Publications: Zones Report, periodic. Also publishes brochures, special reports, and handbook.

**National Customs Brokers and Forwarders Association
of America (International Trade) (NCBFAA)**
World Trade Center, Suite 1153
New York, NY 10048

Description: Founded 1892. Has 600 members and 5 staff. Thirty- three regional groups. Members are treasury-licensed customs brokers, licensed independent ocean freight forwarders, and registered air cargo agents and associate members. Holds annual meeting. Also holds annual Government Affairs Conference in Washington in September.

Purpose: To maintain high standards of business practice in the industry.

Activities: Monitors legislative and regulatory issues affecting customs brokers and forwarders. Holds seminars on new developments and techniques in the industry. Disseminates information among brokers and forwarders. Conducts educational programs. Bestows awards. Does some work through committees.

Publications: NCBFAA Bulletin, monthly; *NCBFAA Membership Directory,* annual.

National Foreign Trade Council (International Trade) (NFTC)
1270 Avenue of the Americas
New York, NY 10020

Description: Founded 1914. Has 550 members and 15 staff. Members include manufacturers, exporters, importers, banks, insurance, transportation lines, and investors. Holds periodic conference and seminars.

Purpose: To promote and protect U.S. foreign trade and investments.

Activities: Removes arbitrary barriers to expansion of international trade and investment. Makes government aware that this expansion is necessary to the economic growth of the United States. Seeks to form a consistent international economic policy. Holds conferences. Presents awards. Does some work through committees.

Publications: Bulletin, periodic; *Council Highlights,* monthly; *Noticias: Latin American Report,* 48 per year; also publishes memoranda and texts of laws, regulations, and treaties.

NCITD—The International Trade Facilitation Council
1800 Diagonal Road, Suite 220
Alexandria, VA 22314

Description: Founded 1967. Has 200 members including exporters, importers, custom brokers, insurance underwriters, and other people involved in exporting and importing. Budget is $400,000. Holds International Trade and Computerization Conference and Exhibition in June in Washington or New York City.

Purpose: To improve international trade documentation and procedures.

Activities: Disseminates information to help improve international trade. Maintains a library of research studies and implementation brochures. Conducts special education and research programs. Sponsors seminars and forums. Holds monthly committee meetings.

Publications: NCITD—The International Trade Facilitation Council Annual Report; NCITD—The International Trade Facilitation Council Members Newsletter, monthly; also publishes brochures, manuals, handbooks, and educational materials; makes available slide films.

New York Board of Trade (NYBT)
1328 Broadway, Suite 1033
New York, NY 10001

Description: Founded 1873. Has 580 members and 30 staff. Members include corporations and professional people interested in trade. Budget is $1,260,000. Holds annual meeting in New York City.

Purpose: To promote trade and commerce in the New York area.

Activities: Represents business before legislative and administrative and government agencies. Maintains foundation for educational and cultural programs. Conducts seminars. Works through several divisions.

Publications: New York Business Speaks, bimonthly.

**Overseas Sales and Marketing Association
of America (International Trade) (OSMA)**
P.O. Box 37
Lake Bluff, IL 60044

Description: Founded 1964. Has 35 members. Members include export management and trading companies. Has periodic meetings.

Purpose: To serve the interests of independent exporters.

Activities: Fosters high standards of professional conduct in the field. Serves as forum for exchange of views and concerns. Acts as a clearinghouse for contacts with manufacturers, overseas buyers, industry groups, and government agencies.

Publications: Directory, periodic; *Newsletter,* periodic.

**Representative of German Industry and Trade
(International Trade) (RGIT)**
1627 Eye Street, NW
Washington, DC 20006

Description: Staff of ten. Nonmembership.

Purpose: To promote U.S. trade with Germany.

Activities: Represents German corporations that trade in the United States. Disseminates information on German trade in the United States. Conducts seminars and workshops.

Publications: Report to Patrons, periodic. Also publishes government information materials and position papers.

**Sell Overseas America—The Association of American
Export (International Trade) (SOSA)**
2512 Artesia Boulevard
Redondo Beach, CA 90278

Description: Founded 1980.

Purpose: To promote U.S. export and international trade.

Activities: Works for greater participation in international trade. Assists, educates, and recruits. Supports U.S. companies involved in export that wish to expand overseas markets. Helps those just beginning exporting operations.

Publications: Showcase USA, quarterly; *Showcase USA Buyers Guide,* annual.

Services Group (International Trade) (SG)
2300 Clarendon Boulevard, Suite 1110
Arlington, VA 22201

Description: Founded 1980. Has staff of 14. Has two regional groups. Nonmembership. Budget is $1,000,000. No meeting is scheduled.

Purpose: To provide assistance to free trade zones, enterprise zones, and free ports.

Activities: Helps free trade zones, enterprise zones, and free ports to get started and operate. Offers workshops and technical services. Compiles statistics. Operates database on U.S. and international free zones. Maintains a 2,500-volume library on economic and community development.

Publications: Caribbean and Central American Free Zone, annual; *Free Zone Update,* quarterly; *TSG Review,* quarterly; also publishes source books on free zones, foreign trade zones, and enterprise zones; manuals on development; papers and monographs on free trade zones and economic development.

Trade Relations Council of the United States (International Trade) (TRC)
c/o Stewart Trade Data
1 Church Street, Suite 601
Rockville, MD 20850

Description: Founded 1885. Has 40 members and 2 staff. Includes members interested in manufacturing, mining, and agriculture, and trade associations. No meeting is scheduled.

Purpose: To promote a better understanding of factors involved in trade.

Activities: Researches factors involved in trade between nations. Sponsors educational programs to study effects of trade on U.S. labor, industry, and agriculture.

Publications: Employment, Outlook, and Foreign Trade of United States Manufacturing Industries, 1958-1984 (7th ed.); *TRC Study.*

U.S.A.–Republic of China Economic Council (International Trade) (USA–ROCEC)
815 Connecticut Avenue, NW, Suite 1202
Washington, DC 20006

Description: Founded 1976. Has 370 members and three staff. Includes people interested in trade with Taiwan. Budget is $325,000. Holds annual meeting.

Purpose: To promote trade between United States and Taiwan.

Activities: Aims to increase business between the countries. Holds conferences and seminars to develop better understanding of business climate, government policies, opportunities, and laws and regulations. Publishes conference papers. Acts to improve regulations. Helps develop business communications and contacts. Maintains file of information on Taiwan of importance to the United States.

Publications: Conference Report, annual; *Membership List,* periodic; *Progress Report,* annual; *Taiwan Economic News,* quarterly; also distributes material on the laws and regulations and Taiwan business publications.

**United States–China Business Council
(International Trade) (USCBC)**
1818 N Street, NW, Suite 500
Washington, DC 20036

Description: Founded 1973. Has 225 members and 20 staff. Members are interested in trading and investing in the People's Republic of China. Holds annual meeting in Washington, DC, in June.

Purpose: To promote trade between the People's Republic of China and United States.

Activities: Facilitates the development of commerce between the United States and China. Provides up-to-date information and assistance to members. Hosts delegations to and from PRC. Provides business advisory service. Sponsors conferences on Chinese trade. Conducts market research for member firms. Maintains offices in Washington, DC, and Beijing, China. Has many industry committees.

Publications: China Business Review, bimonthly.

**United States–New Zealand Council
(International Trade) (USNZC)**
1250 24th Street, NW, Suite 600
Washington, DC 20037

Description: Founded 1986. Has 55 members and 3 staff. Has five regional groups. Members are interested in the economic relationship between the United States and New Zealand. Budget is $150,000. No meeting is scheduled.

Purpose: To develop the economic relationship between United States and New Zealand.

Activities: Corporations, nonprofit organizations, and individuals work to strengthen and improve relationship between United States and New Zealand. The council enhances climate for trade, investment, research, and public understanding. Acts as a clearinghouse for information. Bestows awards and grants. Conducts research and educational programs. Sponsors meetings and social events. Compiles statistics. Operates speakers' bureau. Maintains Friends of New Zealand (subsidiary).

Publications: Economic Profits of New Zealand, quarterly.

U.S. Business Council for Southeastern Europe (USBCSEE)
P.O. Box 3635
Warrenton, VA 22186

Description: Founded 1974. Has 180 members and 2 staff. Members are interested in trade between the United States and Southeastern Europe. Budget is $173,000. Holds annual meeting in winter in New York and an annual briefing session.

Purpose: To develop trade between the United States and Yugoslavia.

Activities: Represents firms in the United States in development of trade and investment with Yugoslavia. Conducts meetings on current topics of interest.

Publications: U.S. Business Council for Southeastern Europe–Business News, monthly.

World Trade Center of New Orleans (International Trade) (WTCNO)
2 Canal Street, Suite 2900
New Orleans, LA 70130-1507

Description: Founded 1985. Has 3,300 members and 140 staff. Includes U.S. and foreign business leaders interested in international trade. Holds annual meeting.

Purpose: To promote international trade.

Activities: Offers programs for foreign VIPs. Sends trade and cultural and civic leaders abroad on business. Offers instruction in 16 languages. Presents annual awards. Maintains 10,000-volume library dealing with trade, travel, and international relations. Offers seminars and a quarterly import/export course.

Publications: Louisiana International Trade Directory, biennial; *Trade Winds,* periodic.

World Trade Centers Association (WTCA)
1 World Trade Center, Suite 7701
New York, NY 10048

Description: Founded 1968. Has 238 members and 14 staff. Members are involved in development of a world trade center. Holds annual general assembly.

Purpose: To develop and operate a world trade center.

Activities: Welcomes affiliate members such as chambers of commerce and organizations sponsoring world trade center clubs. Maintains libraries and exhibit facilities. Works to expand world trade. Encourages developing countries to participate in world trade. Maintains a world trade center network to offer low-cost message service. Plans to develop worldwide video-conferencing network. Works through several committees.

Publications: World Trade Centers Association—Proceedings of the General Assembly, annual; *World Traders Magazine,* quarterly; *WTCA Membership Directory,* semiannual; *WTCA News,* monthly; *WTCA Services Directory,* annual; also publishes brochures

International Organizations

Andean Trade Information Network (ATIN)
Apartado Postal 18-1177
Paseo de la Republica 3895
Lima 18, Peru

Description: Founded 1969. Has five members interested in trade of the Andean countries. Bolivia, Colombia, Ecuador, Peru, and Venezuela. Multinational. No meeting is scheduled.

Languages: Spanish.

Purpose: To disseminate information on trade.

Activities: Informs signatories of the Cartagena Agreement of events in international commerce and supply and demand patterns relating to Andean industries. Seeks to eliminate all internal customs tariffs between member countries. Operates educational programs. Compiles statistics and does research.

Publications: Boletin (in Spanish), biweekly. Also publishes market outlines.

Asociacion de Exportadores del Peru (Trade)
Avenida Salaverry 1910
Apartado 1806, Jesús Maria
Lima 11, Peru

Description: Founded 1973. Members are exporters and export service firms in Peru. No meeting is scheduled.

Languages: English and Spanish.

Purpose: To promote Peru's trade.

Activities: Promotes export of Peruvian goods.

Publications: Export Directory of Peru, annual.

Cardiff International Arena (CIA)
Harlech Court, Bute Terrace
Cardiff, Wales

Description: Members are businesses, professionals, and individuals interested in trade. National. No meeting is scheduled.

Purpose: To develop trade of Wales.

Activities: Develops national and international trade by providing traders and investors with information on new markets and products. Organizes trade missions to world trade centers. Contacts government agencies. Researches trade opportunities. Holds educational programs. Provides consumer and business assistance. Affiliated with World Trade Centers Association (parent).

Publications: None.

**Center Introducing Literature and Samples
of New Foreign Products (Trade) (CCPIT)**
6 Beisanhuan East Road
Beijing 100028, People's Republic of China

Description: Founded 1977. Has 30 members and 20 staff. Operates under auspices of the China Council for Promotion of International Trade. National. No meeting is scheduled.

Languages: Chinese and English.

Purpose: To promote international trade.

Activities: Introduces foreign product samples and information on products to Chinese consumers. Fosters economic, technical, and commercial cooperation between the People's Republic of China and other countries. Provides foreign firms ways to promote their products in

China. Organizes foreign trade shows in China. Offers translation and printing services. Maintains a 10,000-volume technical library.

Publications: None.

Central Board of Finnish Wholesale
and Retail Trade (CBFWRT)
Kasarmikatu 44, Pastilokero 160
SF-00131 Helsinki 13, Finland

Description: Founded 1972. Has five members and seven staff who are involved in wholesale and retail trade. National. No meeting is scheduled.

Languages: English.

Purpose: To promote wholesale and retail trade.

Activities: Tries to improve wholesale and retail trade in Finland. Meets with government agencies on economic policies, taxation, and matters of interest in the industry. Favors discussion on competition, consumer protection, and product liability. Tries to solve transportation and storage problems. Recommends improvements to transport authorities. Disseminates information on domestic trade. Has many working groups.

Publications: None.

China Council for Promotion of
International Trade (CCPIT)
1 Fu Xing Men Wai Street
P.O. Box 100860
Beijing, People's Republic of China

Description: Founded 1952. Has 10,000 members and 1,350 staff. Members are interested in trade. There are 47 local groups. National. Holds periodic meeting.

Languages: Arabic, Chinese, English, French, German, Japanese, Russian, Spanish.

Purpose: To develop China's trade with other countries.

Activities: Advocates reform in China's international trade policy. Introduces new technology. Looks for new sources of foreign funding. Plans visits abroad to develop friendly contact with countries not already having diplomatic relations. Seeks additional export and import markets. Acts as a liaison between China and foreign businesses. Offers consulting services. Sponsors international trade fairs in China and participates in trade fairs abroad. Maintains representative office in ten countries. Operates the China International Exhibition Center; Video and Photo Service for Economic Relations and Trade and Center Introducing Literature and Samples of New Foreign Products.

Publications: China Trade Promotion Review, weekly; *China's Exports* (in Chinese and English), bimonthly; *China's Foreign Trade* (in Chinese, English, French, and Spanish), monthly; *Directory of China's Foreign Trade* (in Chinese and English), annual; *Products and Technology Abroad* (in Chinese), bimonthly; also publishes *Directory of CCPIT Membership Enterprises,* and *CCPIT Annual Report.*

China International Trade Association (CITA)
2 E. Chang'an Avenue
Beijing 100731, People's Republic of China

Description: Founded 1981. Has 1,269 members. Members are international trade groups and individuals. National. No meeting is scheduled.

Purpose: To promote China's international trade.

Activities: Organizes research programs to develop international trade. Promotes technical and information dissemination. Offers educational programs and consulting service.

Publications: International Trade Forum (in Chinese), periodic.

China Materials Trade and Trust Association (CMTTA)
10 Hongju Tenth Lane
Guangan Menwai, Beijing 100055
People's Republic of China

Description: Founded 1991. Has 620 members interested in China's trade. National. No meeting is scheduled.

Purpose: To promote China's trade.

Activities: Fosters technological exchange with corporations in other countries. Conducts surveys on materials and equipment markets. Disseminates information. Offers consulting services.

Publications: None.

Confederation of International Trading Houses Associations (Trade) (CITHA)
Adriaan Geokooplaan 5
NL-2517 JX The Hague
Netherlands

Description: Founded 1955. Has 11 members and 2 staff. Members are interested in trading houses and international trade. Multinational. Holds annual conference.

Languages: English.

Purpose: To develop international trade.

Activities: Represents members' interests internationally. Studies problems affecting international trade. Disseminates information in order to solve international problems. Serves as coordinating body for national associations engaged in international trade. Justifies free trade and its existence and development. Conducts symposia.

Publications: None.

**Federation of German Wholesalers
and Foreign Traders (FGWFT)**
Karber-Friedrich-Strasse 13
Postfach 1349, W-5300 Bonn 1
Germany

Description: German industries interested in trade. No meeting is scheduled.

Purpose: To develop German trade.

Activities: Furnishes information on German industries for businesses that want to export products to Germany.

Publications: None.

Finnish Foreign Trade Association (FFTA)
Arkadiankatu 2
Postilokero 908
SF-00101 Helsinki, Finland

Description: Founded 1919. Has 800 members interested in export and import trade. National. No meeting is scheduled.

Languages: English, Finnish, Swedish.

Purpose: To develop Finnish export and import trade.

Activities: Promotes export trade in Finland. Disseminates information between manufacturers, exporters, importers, and foreign investors. Maintains library on foreign trade.

Publications: Design in Finland (in English, French, and German); *Finnish Trade Review* (in English); *Register of Finnish Exporters;* also publishes brochures.

Foreign Trade Association (FTA)
Mauritiussteinweg 1
50676 Cologne, Germany

Description: Founded 1977. Has 52 members and 4 staff. Members are retail trade associations and firms. Twelve national groups. Multinational. Holds biennial meetings.

Languages: English, French, German.

Purpose: To improve international trade conditions.

Activities: Advocates free world trade. Opposes nontariff barriers to trade and any practices that disrupt international trade. Seeks reduction of custom tariffs. Acts as a liaison between members and information service to facilitate foreign transactions in the commodity sector. Compiles statistics. Studies market conditions.

Publications: Annual Report; also publishes brochures and statements.

General Agreement on Tariffs and Trade (GATT)
Centre William Rappard
154, rue de Lausanne
CH-1211 Geneva 21, Switzerland

Description: Founded 1947. Has 100 members and 400 staff. Multinational. Holds annual session of contracting parties—always late November or early December in Geneva, Switzerland.

Languages: English, French, Spanish.

Purpose: To promote international trade.

Activities: Multilateral trade treaty embodying reciprocal rights and obligations for member states. Encourages expansion of world trade. Has a framework of rules for solving trade problems. Negotiates to reduce tariffs and barriers of trade. Holds training courses for government officials from developing countries. Maintains a 30,000-volume library on international trade and statistics. Works through many committees and divisions.

Publications: Basic Instruments and Selected Documents, annual; *GATT Activities,* annual; *International Market for Meat,* annual; *International Trade,* annual; *News of the Uruguay Round,* monthly; *Studies in International Trade,* periodic; *Trade in Natural Resources Products,* periodic; *Trade Policy Reviews,* periodic; *World Market for Dairy Products,* annual.

Ghana Export Promotion Council (Trade) (GEPC)
Republic House, Tudu Road
P.O. Box M146
Accra, Ghana

Description: Founded 1969. Has 57 members and 71 staff. Members are interested in exporting. Budget is Cd 2,000,000. National. Holds bimonthly forum.

Languages: English.

Purpose: To increase Ghana's overseas markets.

Activities: Studies export potential of Ghana's products. Locates overseas markets. Publicizes Ghanaian exports through trade fairs. Establishes links between exporters and foreign customers. Advises exporters on procedures regarding insurance shipping documentation and credit arrangements. Provides information to Ghanaian businessmen traveling abroad. Supports export incentive schemes such as corporate tax rebate, customs duty drawback, and duty exemption. Provides training programs. Sponsors educational programs. Disseminates market advisory services. Bestows National Award for Export Achievement. Maintains library on products, markets, and international trade. Compiles statistics. Has several working divisions.

Publications: Exporter (in English), quarterly; also publishes *GEPC at a Glance* and *Handicraft Catalog.*

Hong Kong Exporters Association (Trade) (HKEA)
Star House, Room 825
3 Salisbury Road
Kowloon, Hong Kong

Description: Founded 1955. Has 270 members and five staff interested in export trade. National. Holds annual meeting.

Languages: Cantonese, English.

Purpose: To develop Hong Kong's export trade.

Activities: Promotes export trade in Hong Kong. Offers information on quota exchange and quota reporting. Organizes seminars. Maintains library and speakers' bureau.

Publications: Annual Report; Exporters Bulletin, monthly; *Hong Kong Exporter's Association Members Directory,* annual.

Hong Kong Trade Development Council (HKTDC)
Office Tower, 36-39th Floors
Convention Plaza, 1 Harbour Road
Wanchai, Hong Kong

Description: Founded 1969. Has staff of 400. National. Holds periodic conferences.

Languages: English.

Purpose: To promote trade.

Activities: Participates in trade fairs worldwide. Promotes Hong Kong trade worldwide.

Publications: Hong Kong Apparel, semiannual; *Hong Kong for the Business Visitor,* annual; *Hong Kong Collection,* quarterly; *Hong Kong Electronics,* quarterly; *Hong Kong Enterprise,* monthly; *Hong Kong Gifts and Premiums,* semiannual; *Hong Kong Household,* semiannual; *Hong Kong Jewelry,* semiannual; *Hong Kong Toys,* semiannual; *Hong Kong Trades,* monthly; *Hong Kong Watches and Clocks,* semiannual.

Importers and Exporters Association of Taipei (Trade) (IEAT)
350 Sungkiang Road
Taipei 10477, Taiwan

Description: Founded 1947. Has 10,000 members and 60 staff interested in trade. National. Holds monthly directors meeting.

Languages: Chinese, English, Mandarin.

Purpose: To develop trade of Taiwan.

Activities: Organizes trade promotion groups. Holds receptions for foreign exporters and importers. Collects and disseminates trade information. Offers scholarships to students studying international trade. Maintains 3,000-volume library including domestic and foreign trade directories and periodicals. Sponsors competitions and bestows awards. Works through several committees.

Publications: Taiwan International Trade (in English) monthly; *Taiwan Trade Directory* (in English), annual; *Trade Weekly* (in Chinese). Also publishes brochures.

International Association of State Trading
Organizations for a Developing World (Trade) (ASTRO)
Dunajska Ceista 104
SLO–61000
Ljubljana, Slovenia

Description: Founded 1984. Has 54 members and 8 staff. Has $500,000 budget. Multinational. Holds periodic assemblies.

Languages: English, French, Spanish.

Purpose: To promote trade of developing countries.

Activities: Comprises state trading organizations (STOs) of 34 developing countries. Works to strengthen skills of STOs and managers. Exchanges trade information. Has consulting services. Promotes economic and technical cooperation among developing countries. Sponsors on-the-job training, seminars, and workshops. Participates in international and regional symposia, round tables, and conferences.

Publications: ASTRO Update (in English), quarterly; *Handbook of STOs in the Developing Countries,* annual; also publishes *Buy-Back Arrangements and Trade Expansion, Comprehensive Reference Service on Countertrade, Manual of Special Transactions,* and reports.

International Trade Centre
Palais des Nations
CH-1211 Geneva 10, Switzerland

Description: Founded 1964. Has 270 staff. Members are governments of the General Agreement on Tariffs and Trade and the United Nations Conference on Trade and Development. Multinational. Holds annual joint advisory meeting.

Languages: English, French, Spanish.

Purpose: To promote international trade.

Activities: Promotes technical cooperation in trade promotion for developing countries. Assists in development of trade institutions and promotion strategies. Establishes export and import services. Works to find markets for export products and promotes them on the world market. Adapts and develops products for export. Offers advice on importing materials. Offers export/import training. Has 6,000-volume library.

Publications: International Trade FORUM, quarterly; *World Directory of Trade Promotion Organizations,* annual; also publishes handbooks, bibliographies, market surveys, directories, monographs on trade functions, and training materials.

Islamic Centre for Development of Trade (ICDT)
Tours de Habous
Avenue des FAR
Boite Postale 13545
Casablanca, Morocco

Description: Founded 1981. Has 46 members, 23 staff, and a budget of $1,500,000. Multinational. Holds periodic meeting of general assembly.

Languages: Arabic, English, French.

Purpose: To develop trade of Islamic countries.

Activities: Assists member states in creating and maintaining national trade organizations. Gives advice concerning trade matters. Collects and disseminates information. Compiles foreign trade statistics for member countries. Does research to further regional trade to help economic development. Holds training seminars. Has a 3,000-volume library of statistical reports, periodicals, monographs, and press files.

Publications: Directory of Foreign Trade Operators in the Islamic Countries, periodic; *Directory of Trade Training Organizations,* periodic; *Inter-Islamic Trade* (in Arabic, English, and French), annual; *Intra-Communal Trade of Islamic Countries* (in Arabic, English, and French), periodic; *Tijaris: Magazine of International and Inter-Islamic Trade* (in English), bimonthly. Also publishes background notes for Islamic summits and ministerial conferences.

Jamaica Exporters Association (Trade) (JEA)
13 Dominica Drive
P.O. Box 9
Kingston 5, Jamaica

Description: Founded 1965. Its 250 members and 9 staff include Jamaican exporters. National. Holds periodic conferences.

Languages: English.

Purpose: To develop export products of Jamaica.

Activities: Does marketing research to help exporters. Offers secretarial and documentation services. Does photocopying and mailing. Organizes seminars and has charitable programs. Maintains database and speakers' bureau. Compiles statistics.

Publications: Jamaican Exporter, annual; *JEA Newsletter/Bulletin,* monthly; *Magazine and Membership Directory,* annual.

Japan External Trade Organization (JETRO)
2-5 Toranomon
2-chome, Minato-Ku
Tokyo 105, Japan

Description: Members interested in import trade. National.

Purpose: To develop import trade.

Activities: Works to develop import trade. Promotes and protects interest of members.

Publications: Importers of Japan.

Macao Exporters Association (Trade) (MEA)
Avenida Do Infante
D. Henrique 60-64
Andar 3, Macao

Description: Founded 1965. Has 200 members and 4 staff. National. Holds annual meeting in Macao.

Languages: Chinese, English, Portuguese.

Purpose: To develop the export trade of Macao.

Activities: Promotes trade with Macao. Develops new markets. Disseminates information with exporters. Maintains a small library.

Publications: Macao Export Directory (in English), every 2-3 years. Also publishes trade journals.

National Chamber of Exporters (Trade) (NCE)
Avenido Arce 2017
Apartado Postal 12145
La Paz, Bolivia

Description: Founded 1969. Has 450 members and six staff. Budget is $150,000. Three regional groups. National. Holds biweekly meeting.

Languages: English, Spanish, French.

Purpose: To develop Bolivian export.

Activities: Promotes export of Bolivian goods in an international market. Offers legal and technical assistance to members. Exchanges information on trade fairs, promotion techniques, and expositions. Compiles statistics. Bestows awards. Sponsors seminars and research programs. Has reference library.

Publications: Bolivia Yellow Pages (in Spanish), periodic; *Bulletin Exportemos* (in Spanish), monthly; *Exporters Directory* (in Spanish), annual;

News, biweekly. Also publishes *Bolivia: Insercion Internacional y Desarrollo de Exportaciones.*

**Ratmir Association for Business Cooperation
with Germany (Trade)**
Ulitsa Abel' manovskaya 2A, Building 1
SU-109147 Moscow, Russia

Description: Founded 1988. Has 75 members and 30 staff. National. No meeting is scheduled.

Languages: English, German, Russian.

Purpose: To help export-import trading companies.

Activities: Aids joint ventures in exporting and importing. Provides consultative services for international trade. Is developing a school of management. Has a 300-volume library.

Publications: Panorama, monthly. Also publishes informational bulletins.

Singapore Trade Development Board (STDB)
World Trade Center
1 Maritime Square, 10-40, Lobby D
Telok Blangah Road
Singapore 0409, Singapore

Description: Founded 1983. National. No meeting is scheduled.

Purpose: To develop overseas markets.

Activities: Encourages contact between local and overseas businesses. Maintains network of overseas centers. Conducts market research. Operates a trade information unit and offers a trade technical advisory service. Conducts field trips, seminars, conferences, and workshops. Has a small library.

Publications: Annual Report; Commodities Directory, periodic; *Electronics Manufacturers Directory,* periodic; *Fashionware Singapore,* periodic; *IC Producers—Singapore a Support Base,* periodic; *Industrial Machinery Directory,* periodic; *Jewelry Singapore,* periodic; *Major Supporting Industries in Singapore,* periodic; *Printing and Allied Services in Singapore,* periodic; *Singapore Exporters Directory,* periodic; *Singapore Food and Beverages,* periodic; *Singapore Garment and Textile Directory,* periodic; *Singapore Trade News* (in English and Japanese), bimonthly; *Timber Singapore,* periodic. Also publishes *International Trading Centre, Singapore: For Total Quality Procurement and Warehousing and Distribution.*

Tokyo Foreign Trade Association (TFTA)
c/o Tokyo Trade Center Building, 6th Floor
1-7-8, Kaigan, Minato-Ku
Tokyo 105, Japan

Description: Members interested in international trade. National.

Purpose: To develop international trade.

Activities: Manufacturers, exporters, importers, and government associations work with exhibitions, business shows, and trade shows in Tokyo. Promotes international trade with Japan.

Publications: Buyer's Guide of Tokyo (in English), annual.

**United Nations Conference on Trade
and Development (UNCTAD)**
Palais des Nations
CH-1211 Geneva 10, Switzerland

Description: Founded 1964. Has 166 members and 500 staff. Members are governments of independent nations. Budget is $35,000,000. Multinational. Holds quadrennial conference, next one scheduled for 1995.

Languages: Arabic, Chinese, English, French, Russian, Spanish.

Purpose: To help developing countries by promoting international trade.

Activities: Plans and carries out trade policies to help developing countries. Organizes transfer of technology from developed to developing countries. Encourages economic cooperation among developing nations. Provides technical assistance. Holds annual meetings of government experts on tungsten and iron ore. Compiles statistics. Does much work through committees, working groups, and permanent groups.

Publications: Commodity Price Bulletin, monthly; *Guide to UNCPAD Publications,* annual; *Handbook of International Trade and Development Statistics,* annual; *Least Developed Countries Report,* annual; *Quarterly Bulletin of the UNCTAD Committee on Tungsten,* quarterly; *Review of Marine Transport,* annual; *Trade and Development Report,* annual; *Trade and Development Review,* annual; *UNCTAD Bulletin,* six issues per year, *UNCTAD Commodity Yearbook,* annual; *UNCTAD Statistical Pocket Book,* periodic. Also publishes discussion papers, proceedings of meetings, and reprints of periodical articles.

**World Export Processing Zones Association
(Trade) (WEPZA)**
P.O. Box 986
Flagstaff, AZ 86002

Description: Founded 1978. Has 20 members. Budget is $100,000. Multinational. Holds annual fall conference with exhibits.

Languages: English.

Purpose: To develop export-processing zones.

Activities: EPZs bring in materials to assemble and process. Zones are customs-controlled, allowing for inexpensive production and export of goods. Disseminates information. Represents members' interests before international bodies. Trains EPZ staff. Conducts management programs. Sponsors conferences of managers and export zone users. Holds workshops. Maintains professional code of conduct. Compiles statistics.

Publications: Journal of the Flagstaff Institute, semiannual; *WEPZA Newsletter,* quarterly.

World Trade Centers

World Trade Centers Association (WTCA)
1 World Trade Center, Suite 7701
New York, NY 10048

Description: Founded 1968. Has 217 members and 8 staff involved in developing and operating a world trade center. Multinational. Holds annual general assembly with exhibits.

Languages: English.

Purpose: To develop and operate a world trade center.

Activities: Develops a world trade center. Affiliate members are chambers of commerce and organizations sponsoring world trade center clubs, libraries, and individuals involved in trade-related activities. Encourage expansion of world trade, promotes international business relations and Third World participation in world trade. Maintains WTC Network that provides low-cost message service. Identifies qualified prospects worldwide. Promotes subscribers' businesses in a select international community. Does much work through committees.

Publications: World Trade Centers Association—Proceedings of the General Assembly, annual; *World Traders Magazine,* quarterly; *WTCA News,* monthly; *WTCA Services Directory,* annual. Also publishes brochures.

Other world trade centers affiliated with the World Trade Centers
Association (parent):

China World Trade Center
No. 1 Jian Guo Men Wai Avenue
China World Tower, Level 4
Beijing 100004, People's Republic of China

Cyprus World Trade Center
Chamber Building
38 Grivas Dhigenis Avenue and 3 Deligiorgis Street
P.O. Box 1455
Nicosia, Cyprus

Guadalajara World Trade Center
Avenida de las Rosas 2965
44640 Guadalajara
Jalisco, Mexico

HEFEI World Trade Centre Club
Bank of China Hefei Building, 8th Floor
155 Chang Jiang Road, Jinzhai Road
Hefei, Anhui, People's Republic of China

International Club of Flanders
Sint-Pietersplein 11
B-9000 Ghent, Belgium

International Trade Center Curacao
Piscadera Bay, Postbus 6005
Curacao, Netherlands Antilles

Korea World Trade Center and
Korea Foreign Trade Association
159-1 Samsung-Dong
Kangnam-Ku
Seoul, Republic of Korea

Lyon Commerce International (Trade)
Lyon World Trade Center
16 rue de la Republique
F-69289 Lyon Cedex, France

Maisons du Commerce International de Strasbourg
Immeuble 'Le Concorde'
4, Quai Kleber
F-67056 Strasbourg Cedex, France

Putra World Trade Centre
PWTC-UMNO Complex, Level 3
41 Jalan Tun Ismail
50480 Kuala Lumpur, Malaysia

Sao Paulo World Trade Center
Rua Estados Unidos 1093
01427 Sao Paulo, Ceara, Brazil

Scandinavian World Trade Center
Massans Gata 18
Postfack 5253
S-402 25 Goteborg, Sweden

South African Foreign Trade Organization
P.O. Box 782706
Export House, 5th Floor
Corner of Moud and West Streets
Sandton Johannesburg 2146, South Africa

World Flower Trade Center
Postbus 104
NL-1430 BC Aalsmeer, Netherlands
World Trade Center of Abidjan
Boite Postale V 68
Abidjan, Cote d'Ivoire

World Trade Center Adelaide
c/o Harmony Corp. Pty. Ltd.
101 Pirie Street
Adelaide SA5000, Australia

World Trade Center Amsterdam Association
Strawinskylaan 515
NL-1077 X Amsterdam, Netherlands

World Trade Center Association of Antwerp
Korte Sint Annastraat 11
B-2000 Antwerp, Belgium

World Trade Center Association Brussels
162 Boulevard Emile Jacqmain Boite 12
B-1210 Brussels, Belgium

World Trade Center Bangkok
World Trade Center Complex, 7th Floor
Rajprasong Intersection
4 Rajdamri Road
Bangkok 10330, Thailand

World Trade Center Basel
Isteinerstrasse 53
CH-4021 Basel, Switzerland

World Trade Centre Beijing
2d Central Building, Room 409 4/F
Hualong Street, Nankeyan
East City District, Beijing, People's Republic of China

World Trade Center Bilbao
Alameda de Urquijo 10
E-48008 Bilbao, Spain

World Trade Center Bogota
Calle 98, Numero 9-03
Bogota, Colombia

World Trade Center Bombay
M. Visvesvaraya Industrial Research and Development Center
Centre 1, 31st Floor
Cuffe Parade
Bombay 400 005, India

World Trade Center Budapest
Hungarian Chamber of Commerce
Kossuth Lajos Ter 6-8
H-1055 Budapest, Hungary

World Trade Center Buenos Aires
Reconquista 656, 1st Floor
1091 Buenos Aires, Argentina

World Trade Center Cairo
1191 Cornich El-Nil
P.O. Box 2007
Cairo, Egypt

World Trade Center Caracas
Apartado Postal 64978
Caracas 1061, Venezuela

World Trade Center Edmonton
P.O. Box 1480
Edmonton, AB, Canada T5J 2N5

World Trade Center Geneva
10, Route de L'Aeroport
Boite Postale 306
CH-1215 Geneva 15, Switzerland

World Trade Center Grenoble
c/o GREX
Place Robert Schuman
Boite Postale 1509
F38025 Grenoble Cedex, France

World Trade Center Halifax
1800 Argyle Street, 8th Floor
P.O. Box 955
Halifax, NS, Canada B3J 2V9

World Trade Center Hamburg
Neuer Wall 50
20354 Hamburg, Germany

World Trade Center Israel
Industry House
29 Hamered Street
68125 Tel Aviv, Israel

World Trade Center Istanbul
Ataturk Hava Limani Yani
Cobancesme Kavsagi
P.O. Box 40, Havalimani
TR-3480 Istanbul, Turkey

World Trade Center Jakarta
Visma Metropolitan II, Level 16
Jalan Jendi, Sudirman Kav, 31
P.O. Box 8395/JKSMP/12803/J
12920 Jakarta, Indonesia

World Trade Center of Japan
P.O. Box 57
World Trade Center Building
4-1-2 Hamamatsu-cho, Minato-Ku
Tokyo 105, Japan

World Trade Center Leipzig
Grassistrasse 12
04107 Leipzig, Germany

World Trade Center Lille
58, Rue de l'Hôpital Militaire
Boite Postale 209
F-59029 Lille Cedex, France

World Trade Center Lima
Avenida de la Marina 2355
Lima 32, Peru

World Trade Center Lisbon
Avenida do Brasil 1
P-1700 Lisbon, Portugal

World Trade Center Ljubljana
Dunajska 160
SLO-61113 Ljubljana, Slovenia

World Trade Center Luxembourg
6-10 Place de la Gare
1616 Luxembourg, Luxembourg

World Trade Center Madrid
Paseo de la Habana 26-3
E-28036 Madrid, Spain

World Trade Center Malmo
Chamber of Commerce of Southern Sweden
Skeppsbron 2
S-211 20 Malmo, Sweden

World Trade Centre Martinique
c/o Chambre de Commerce et d'Industrie
50, Rue Ernest Deproge
Boite Postale 478
97241 Fort de France, Martinique

World Trade Center Metro Manila
Pacific Star Building, 5th Floor
Makati Avenue
Makati, Manila Metro
Philippines

World Trade Center Metz
10112 Avenue Foch
Boite Postale 330
F-57000 Metz Cedex 1, France

World Trade Center Mexico City
Montecito 38, Piso 34
Colonia Napoles
03810 Mexico City, DF, Mexico

World Trade Centre Montreal
1253 McGill College Avenue, Suite 404
Montreal, PQ, Canada H3B 2Y5

World Trade Center Moscow
SOVINCENTR
Krasnopresnenskaya 12 nab
SU-123610 Moscow, Russia

World Trade Centre Nantes
Centre Atlantique de Commerce International
16, Quai Ernest Renaud
Boite Postale 718
F-44027 Nantes Cedex, France

World Trade Center of Nigeria
Western House, 8th Floor
8-10 Broad Street
P.O. Box 4466
Lagos, Nigeria

World Trade Centre Ottawa
17 Sunset Boulevard
Ottawa, Ontario
Canada KIS 3G8

World Trade Center of Paris
Chamber of Commerce and Industry
2, Rue de Viarmes
F-75001 Paris, France

World Trade Centre Porto
Avenida da Boavista 1269/81
P-4100 Porto, Portugal

World Trade Center Rotterdam
Beursplein 37, Postbus 30055
NL-3001 DB Rotterdam, Netherlands

World Trade Center Ruhr Valley
Sparkassenstrasse 1
45879 Gelsenkirchen, Germany

World Trade Center Salzburg
c/o WTC Development Gesellschaft
Kohlmarkt 4
A-1010 Vienna, Austria

World Trade Centre Seville
Recinto de la Cartuja
E-41092 Seville, Spain

World Trade Centre Shanghai
33 Zong Shan Dong Yi Lu
Shanghai, People's Republic of China

World Trade Centre Shenzen
Block B, Suite 712
Sunshine Hotel
Shenzen, People's Republic of China

World Trade Centre Singapore
1 Maritime Square, No. 09-72
Singapore 0409, Singapore

World Trade Center Split
c/o Institute for Informatics and Telecommunications
Rudjera Boskovica 22
YU-58000 Split, Croatia

World Trade Center Stockholm
Box 70354
S-107 24 Stockholm, Sweden

World Trade Center Taichung
60 Tienpao Street
Taichung 40706, Taiwan

World Trade Center Tianjin
c/o Tainjin Leadar (Group) Corporation
3 Xinyuan, Kunming Road
Heping District
Tianjin 300050, People's Republic of China

World Trade Centre Toronto
60 Harbour Street
Toronto, Ontario
Canada M5J 1B7

World Trade Center Trinidad and Tobago
Airports Authority of Trinidad and Tobago
Airports Administration Centre
Caroni North Bank Road
Piarco, P.O. Box 1273
Port of Spain, Trinidad and Tobago

World Trade Centre Vancouver
Vancouver Board of Trade
999 Canada Place, Suite 400
Vancouver, British Columbia
Canada V6C 3C1

World Trade Center Vienna-Airport
World Trade Center Building
A-1300 Vienna, Austria

Organization Sources

Encyclopedia of Associations, Vol. 1, *National Organizations of the United States*, Detroit, MI: Gale Research, 1994.

Encyclopedia of Associations, Vol. 4, *International Organizations*. Detroit, MI: Gale Research, 1994.

Encyclopedia of Governmental Advisory Organizations, 1994–1995, 9th ed. Detroit, MI: Gale Research, 1994.

The United States Government Manual, 1994–1995. Washington, DC: U.S. Government Printing Office, 1994.

Bibliography 5

Although the United States has engaged in international trade since the early colonial period, only in recent years has trade played an important role in the nation's economy. Consequently, the literature has increased greatly. The trade studies vary from popular accounts to highly specialized technical papers. The selection of bibliographical items in this chapter provides a wide perspective on modern trade developments in the United States. The first section presents reference works, followed by annotated entries of books. The next portion lists journal articles and government publications, with a final section listing journals that publish articles on international trade.

Books

General

Anderson, Kym, and Richard Blackhurst. *The Greening of World Trade Issues*. Ann Arbor, MI: University of Michigan Press, 1992. 276 pp. ISBN 0-472-10349-0.

This book addresses the effects of environmental and trade policies on the environment and the effect of environmental concerns on the politics of trade policy. The problems for the world trading system of a public-choice approach to environmental policy formation is that there may be direct and indirect opportunities to create new barriers to trade. Each chapter has notes and references. Tables and figures illustrate the book.

Axtell, Roger E. *The Do's and Taboos of International Trade: A Small Business Primer.* New York: Wiley, 1989. 305 pp. ISBN 0-471-61637-0.

International commerce is extremely important to the economic well-being of our nation both in terms of the dollar value of commercial trade and the amount of foreign industrial investment that has come to the United States. Jobs depend on free trade. Agriculture, manufacturing, service industries, and finance rely on favorable conditions for the free flow of capital and commodities between the United States and other countries. This book discusses various aspects of international trade, such as exporting, importing, licensing, joint ventures, direct investment overseas, foreign investment in the United States, and barter and countertrade. The book lists international trade administration and U.S. and Foreign Commerical Service (FCS) district offices, international trade directors of the national association of state development agencies, directors of small business development centers, small business administration field offices, and county desk offices. The book also features an interesting short glossary of selected common international terms. The book is illustrated with a few tables and figures.

Bovard, James. *The Fair Trade Fraud.* New York: St. Martin's Press, 1991. 330 pp. ISBN 0-312-06193-5.

The author examines the U.S. tariff code, how the dumping law operates, import quotas, the U.S. International Trade Commission's role in unfair trade, political control of trade, and the morality of free trade. The U.S. trade policy is really a war against abundance. The fewer trade barriers the United States has, the more competitive its companies will be. Each chapter is well footnoted.

Brown, Michael Barratt. *Fair Trade: Reform and Realities in the International Trading System.* London: Zed Books, 1993. 226 pp. ISBN 1-85649-073-4.

In part one, the author discusses the development of unfair trade, showing the role played by markets and the effects on the middleman. In part two, he shows how trade can be made fairer by regulating and aiding the market. In the last chapter the author tells us what can be done to ensure fair trade. The book has an annexe that lists alternative trading organizations and a glossary of acronyms and technical trade terms.

Corden, W. Max. *International Trade Theory and Policy. Economists of the Twentieth Century.* Brookfield, VT: Edward Elgar Publishing Company, 1992. 560 pp. ISBN 1-85278-732-5.

This volume contains a selection of 23 articles on the theoretical international economies published by the author over the last 35 years. The articles are arranged in five parts. The volume begins with survey articles, followed by theory of trade policy, trade and growth, balance of payments theory, booming section economics and monetary integration, and international policy interaction. References accompany the chapters. Both an author and subject index are useful in using this book.

Findlay, Robert. *Trade Development and Political Economy: Selected Essays of Ronald Findlay. Economists of the Twentieth Century.* Brookfield, VT: Edward Elgar Publishing Company, 1993. ISBN 1-85278-982-4.

This volume collects 27 essays on topics ranging from capital, time and comparative advantage, tariffs and trade policy, oil shocks, employment and trade, wage differentials and economic development, primary exports and industrialization, North-South models, slavery, trade and history and political economy, and trade, justice, and the state. The book has a few figures and a page of bibliographical references.

Frazier, Michael. *Implementing State Government Export Programs.* Westport, CT: Praeger, 1992. 204 pp. ISBN 0-275-93850-6.

This volume compares the implementation experiences of selected state-supported export trade agencies in Michigan, Virginia, Indiana, and Arkansas. In order to increase exports from the United States, states have organized and funded export trade programs. The part played by each state is discussed in detail. Appendix A gives a list of interviewees. Appendix B lists people who have done important research in the implementation research. The book is well illustrated with tables and figures and has a lengthy bibliography.

Greenaway, David, ed. *Economic Development and International Trade.* New York: St. Martin's, 1988. 211 pp. ISBN 0-312-01588-7.

The relationship between economic development and international trade is the theme of this book. Issues investigated include alleged instability of primary commodity prices, the declining terms of trade of primary producers, the relative merits of export promotion, import substitution programs, trade strategies, export instability and growth, and export-processing zones in developing countries. Book is illustrated with many tables. There are several pages of endnotes for each chapter and many pages of references. Book also has an author index and a subject index.

Holtfrerich, Carl-Ludwig. *Interactions in the World Economy: Perspectives from International Economic History.* New York: New York University Press, 1989. 376 pp. ISBN 0-8147-3465-0.

This volume presents the broad trends in the growth and development of world trade since the eighteenth century and provides standard explanations for these developments. Part one surveys the theoretical literature on international trade and its relation to development economies. Part two discusses trade before the Industrial Revolution, the growth of trade between 1750 and World War I, the growth and stagnation of trade in the world economy between 1920 and 1960, and trends in world trade in recent decades. In the last part, emphasis is placed on the United States and the world economy, the importance of Latin American trade, and the place of the Third World in world trade. Notes and references are found at the end of the chapters. A few tables can be found. A list of contributors is found at the beginning of the volume.

Jackson, Tim. *The Next Battleground: Japan, America, and the New European Market.* Boston: Houghton Mifflin, 1993. 332 pp. ISBN 0-395-61594-1.

This interesting volume shows that Western Europe has organized to form a single market and will compete with the United States and Japan. It discusses the activities of U.S. and Japanese banking, automobile, computer, and electronics industries in the European market and the effect that they will have on international free trade. The book has several pages of notes covering each chapter.

Neff, Stephen C. *Friends but No Allies: Economic Liberalism and the Law of Nations.* The Political Economy of International Change. New York: Columbia University Press, 1990. 345 pp. ISBN 0-231-07142-6.

This volume examines the two basic forms of international cooperation, between states and between peoples. Diplomacy and treaty making are involved in dealing with states; dealing with peoples takes such economic forms as international trade or investment that is governed by private-law rules of property and contract. The "political" order is concerned with power and security, whereas the "economic" order is concerned with the unification of the peoples of the world. The book has several pages of notes and a lengthy bibliography.

Ostry, Sylvia. *Governments and Corporations in a Shrinking World: Trade and Innovation Policies in the United States, Europe, and Japan.* New York: Council on Foreign Relations, 1990. 123 pp. ISBN 0-87609-079-X.

This book grew out of a Council on Foreign Relations study group. The author, former Canadian ambassador to the Uruguay Round of multilateral trade negotiations, surveys the international economic order on trade and focuses on differences in the corporate-government interface in policymaking in the United States, European Community, and Japan. She foresees problems arising and offers solutions. Notes for each chapter are found at the end of the book. Book has a glossary of abbreviations and acronyms.

Usunier, Jean-Claude. *International Marketing: A Cultural Approach.* New York: Prentice-Hall, 1993. 494 pp. ISBN 0-13-194580-7.

This unique book considers two aspects of international trade that have received little attention. Two currents are investigated. One deals with marketing and market research, the other with culture and organizations. The literature on culture and organizations has grown rapidly in recent years. Its findings have, however, only slowly been recognized by the marketing theorists.

Countries that developed political and economic power have always become exporters of ideas. The dominant position of the United States in the post–World War II decade led to a dominance of management theories and techniques developed by the United States. More recently, other countries, such as Japan, have gained a strong position in world markets. Management and marketing are cultural artifacts and therefore should be studied cross-nationally. The book deserves attention, for it investigates relationships that were neglected in the past. References and notes are found at the end of each chapter. Book has an author index and a subject index.

Walmsley, John. *The Development of International Markets.* Boston, MA: Graham and Trotman, 1989. 222 pp. ISBN 1-85333-279-8.

Walmsley, an international businessman, wrote this book from personal experience. He analyzes world trading patterns, explains factors that can cause change, and shows ways to cope with the rules and regulations of trade. He also discusses trade incentives and risks; problems and advantages of international expansion; overseas partner selection; countertrade; technology transfers; management contracts; joint ventures; and financial decisions. Book has several figures and tables. References are found at the end of each chapter. A special table at the end of the book lists treaties and pacts with and by countries of the world.

Trade Policies

Dell, Sidney Samuel. *International Development Policies: Perspectives for Industrial Countries*. Durham, NC: Duke University Press, 1991. 378 pp. ISBN 0-8223-1079-1.

These nine essays address some of the major problems of international economics and development policy that have confronted the international community in recent years. Directed to readers in the industrial countries, the essays provide a rationale for a more positive and constructive approach to the prevailing problems of world development. The author suggests that international cooperation in achieving world development can be successful only if the developing countries themselves take the necessary steps for their own advancement. The book provides a list of abbreviations, several pages of notes and references, and an index.

De Melo, Jaime, and David Tarr. *A General Equilibrium Analysis of U.S. Foreign Trade Policy*. Cambridge, MA: MIT Press, 1992. 289 pp. ISBN 0-262-04122-7.

Applied general equilibrium methods are used to analyze recent issues in the conduct of U.S. foreign trade policy. The general equilibrium approach is often criticized for the opaqueness surrounding its model-generated results. Here, however, the authors carefully reveal the economic institutions behind each result.

This book begins with recent issues on U.S. foreign trade, next offers a trade policy analysis in a one-sector general equilibrium model with product differentiation, and then develops the basic general equilibrium trade model. Subsequent chapters deal with quota premium rates and rent capacity; welfare costs of U.S. quotas in textiles, apparel, automobiles, and steel; welfare cost of quantitative restrictions under different factor market assumptions; welfare costs of quantitative restriction with imperfect competition in automobiles and steel; and revenue raising taxes. The book demonstrates the cost per job protected and cost of quantitative restrictions, and provides a compilation of tariffs with a welfare cost equivalent. Tables and figures illustrate the book. Several pages of notes elaborate each chapter. A lengthy list of references is included. Name and subject indexes can be found at the end of the book.

Gill, William J. *Trade Wars against America: A History of United States Trade and Monetary Policy.* New York: Praeger, 1990. 324 pp. ISBN 0-275-93316-4.

This volume presents the history of trade and trade regulations in the United States from the late eighteenth century to the present. A wide assortment of topics are considered. The book is written from the viewpoint of the United States. The author believes that every nation in the world could ultimately benefit from a rejection of, and gradual withdrawal from, the subsidization of exports under the false barriers of free trade. He develops the notions that the present frenetic state of world trade is a conscienceless waste of the earth's resources and that subsidized trade is contributing substantially to the mounting threat to the planet's environment. The author adds that free trade has brought hardship to millions of people and communities, and indeed has disrupted the very infrastructure of society. He cites the 500,000 U.S. steelworkers whose jobs have disappeared since 1950. Several pages of notes and bibliography are found at the end of the book.

Heckscher, Eli F., and Bertil Ohlin. *Heckscher-Ohlin Trade Theory,* ed., trans., intro., Harry Flam and H. June Flanders. Cambridge, MA: MIT Press, 1991. 222 pp. ISBN 0-262-08201-2.

This book is considered a classic in the field. Flam and Flanders translate Heckscher's magnificent 1919 article on how differences in geographical factor endowments affect income distribution and determine regional specialization patterns and how trade in mobile goods serve as a substitute for mobility of factors in reducing factor-price differentials. Ohlin, a former student of Heckscher, rebuts many of his ideas. Between them, the two men revolutionized the theory of international trade. Ohlin's contribution in trade theory was to elaborate and expand the essential elements laid down by Heckscher. The book has tables, footnotes, and a few bibliographical references.

Howell, Thomas R., et al. *Conflict among Nations: Trade Policies in the 1990s. Economic Competition among Nations.* Boulder, CO: Westview Press, 1992. 633 pp. ISBN 0-8133-1255-8.

The book is the result of the study and experience of members of the International Trade Group of Dewey Ballantine, a group of lawyers, economists, and trade specialists headed by Alan William Wolff. The group provided legal, analytic, and economic services to U.S. and foreign clients. The conclusions are those of the authors, not of U.S. or foreign governments. The book deals with how major trading nations and the European Community participate in the open international trading system and their trade policies. The book is well footnoted and has a few tables.

Paliwoda, Stanley, ed. *New Perspectives on International Marketing.* New York: Routledge, 1991. 374 pp. ISBN 0-415-05344-7.

This interesting volume is divided into three parts. Part one discusses the economic importance of international trade. One author describes the findings of 50 empirical studies, another focuses on the international involvement of companies in the Unlisted Securities Market (USM). Part two deals with studies on marketing to China and Japan. Part three gives results of empirical studies of international marketing that are industry-specific. The chapters have bibliographical references and tables.

Trebilcock, Michael J., Marsha A. Chandler, and Robert Howse. *Trade and Transitions: A Comparative Analysis of Adjustment Policies.* New York: Routledge, 1990. 277 pp. ISBN 0-415-04977-6.

This book examines how a number of countries—Canada, the United States, the United Kingdom, France, West Germany, Japan, Sweden, and Australia—have, over the past several decades, solved adjustment pressures induced by competitive inroads of foreign imports such as steel, coal, automobiles, shipbuilding, textiles, clothing, and footwear. In many instances, economic adjustment pressures have become severe, as the international community has had to face the implications of newly industrialized countries emerging as major trading powers and has confronted worldwide recessions, increased energy costs, increased exchange rate volatility, and reallocation of corporate capital as capital markets have become increasingly globalized. In the analysis of trade relationships, the study adopts a comparative perspective in its empirical evaluation. The study does not confine its normative perspective to economic efficiency concerns, nor does it confine itself to a single class of policy response to adjustment pressures. Many tables and figures are found throughout the book, which also features a lengthy bibliography.

Wolman, Paul. *Most Favored Nation: The Republican Revisionists and U.S. Tariff Policy 1897–1912.* Chapel Hill, NC: University of North Carolina Press, 1992. 328 pp. ISBN 0-8078-2022-9.

This book studies the movement for tariff revision in the early twentieth century and the attempts to reshape U.S. commercial policy. The first part of the book studies the tariff under McKinley and Roosevelt; the second part deals with the Payne-Aldrich Tariff and revisionist policy; the third part concludes with revisionism in practice. The book includes several pages of notes and a bibliography.

Modelling

Dagenais, M. G., and P-A. Muet, eds. *International Trade Modelling. International Studies in Economic Modelling.* New York: Chapman & Hall, 1992. 357 pp. ISBN 0-412-45000-3.

The papers in this book were selected from the twenty-seventh Conference of the Applied Econometric Association on International Trade held in 1989 in Montreal. Traditional trade theory expressed comparative advantages as differences in labor productivity or in factors of production; this theory does not adequately describe a major part of the world's trade between developed industrial countries with similar labor productivity and other factors of production. The new theory elaborated in this collection asserts, first, that increasing returns lead to larger trade flows and larger potential gains from trade than those resulting from comparative advantages, and, second, that the imperfect competition resulting from increasing returns compromises the simple case for free trade.

The first two papers test the two central hypotheses of the new trade theory, namely, the role of imperfect competition and economies of scale in the determinations of commercial flows, and the impact of product differentiation in estimating export functions. Subsequent chapters address price discrimination and exchange rate pass-through, new protectionism, trade liberalization in perfect or imperfect competition models, evaluation of trade protectionism with CGE model, comparative advantages, import demand in industrialized and developing countries, and disequilibrium models of an open economy. The book features tables, figures, and author and subject indexes. References are placed at the end of chapters.

Lord, Montague J. *Imperfect Competition and International Commodity Trade: Theory, Dynamics, and Policy Modelling.* New York: Oxford University Press, 1991. 419 pp. ISBN 0-19-828347-4.

This book offers a unified treatment of the theory, econometric modelling, and policy evaluation of international commodity trade. This technique has been made possible by the progress in the specification of consumer preferences for differential products and in the determination of equilibrium conditions in markets with imperfect competition. Strategies for model selection have been devised and ways of using time-series analysis to represent dynamic behavior have been developed. Finally, greater recognition has been given to the importance of the dynamics underlying adjustment processes in international trade. The goal of this book is to present a useful treatment of the theory, dynamics, and policy modelling of international commodity trade with imperfect competition. This technique will provide a useful framework for analyzing trade in goods. This book has many tables and figures throughout and features a list of abbreviations and symbols, author and subject indexes, four appendixes, and several pages of references.

Export Controls

Alexandrides, Costas G., and Barbara L. Bowers. *Countertrade: Practices, Strategies, and Tactics. Wiley Professional Banking and Finance Series.* New York: Wiley, 1987. 235 pp. ISBN 0-471-84711-9.

Countertrade, that is, accepting goods as part or complete payment for sales, accounts for about 20 percent of world trade. Many governments prefer this method of payment. Countertrade can help solve our trade deficit problem, for corporations can enter inaccessible markets, increase market share, and create new business through trading. The book traces postwar economic and trade developments that led to countertrade, then examines countertrade practices, and finally cites examples of world countertrade practices. A directory of selected countertrade service organizations is included as an appendix. The book provides a selected bibliography and a list of abbreviations used in the book.

Boltuck, Richard, and Robert E. Litan, eds. *Down in the Dumps. Administration of the Unfair Trade Laws.* Washington, DC: Brookings Institution, 1991. 350 pp. ISBN 0-8157-1019-4.

This book draws from papers presented at a conference held at the Brookings Institution in November 1990. The editors and a team of attorneys and economists with experience in "unfair trade" practice investigations made a study of the Department of Commerce to show and critique its discharge of its statutory mission. The book focuses on the antidumping and countervailing duty statutes, that is, provisions allowing the United States to impose offset duties on imports that are sold here at prices below those charged by producers in their home countries or that benefit from subsidies provided by foreign governments encouraging exports. The book features many explanatory footnotes and tables and provides a list of contributors.

Greenaway, David, et al. *Global Protectionism*. New York: St. Martin's, 1991. 310 pp. ISBN 0-312-06158-7.

This book contains the proceedings of a two-day conference on protectionism held in 1991 at Lehigh University. Important topics discussed included protection of U.S. manufacturers; restructuring the Japanese economy; agricultural protection in industrial countries; international trade in services; reasons for negotiating trade-related investment measures (TRIMS); export restraints; protection in the European Community before and after 1992; and agricultural trade, the GATT, and less developed countries (LDCs). Each paper is accompanied by a critique of its good and bad points and by explanatory figures. The book has a lengthy bibliography. Notes on the contributors are found at the beginning of the book.

Grieco, Joseph M. *Cooperation among Nations: Europe, America, and Nontariff Barriers to Trade. Cornell Studies in Political Economy*. Ithaca, NY: Cornell University Press, 1990. 255 pp. ISBN 0-8014-2414-3.

This book examines the notion of international cooperation as the basis for world peace and order. Although there is a recognition that international anarchy makes cooperation among nations difficult, there is considerable disagreement about how and why international anarchy constrains the willingness of states to work together. Two theories—modern realism and the newest liberal institutionalism—dominate the contemporary debate on that crucial question. The goal of this book is to examine these two competing theories and to determine which one best explains the problem of international cooperation. The first chapter outlines the major theoretical perspectives. The next chapter presents the argument that realism has a stronger legal grasp of the implications of anarchy for states than does neoliberal institutionalism. Subsequent chapters test the two theories by applying them to the Uruguay Round of GATT and summarize the present and outlines future research. There are four appendixes, and many tables illustrate the book. Chapters are well footnoted.

Ito, Takatoshi, and Anne Krueger, eds. *Trade and Protectionism. NBER–East Asia Seminar on Economics*. Vol. 2. Chicago, IL: University of Chicago Press for The National Bureau of Economic Research, 1993. 449 pp. ISBN 0-226-38668-6.

This book examines a number of viewpoints of the world trade system from World War II to the present. For the thirty years after World War II, the increasingly open, multilateral international trading system served the entire world economy well. Successive GATT agreements, unilateral liberalization of trade on the part of the European countries, and falling costs of transport increasingly integrated the world economy. The 1980s brought some evidence that liberalization of trade was reversing. In the Uruguay Round of trade negotiations under GATT, a satisfactory outcome on the planned timetable of liberalization of trade policies was not reached. The protectionist policies of some industrial countries appeared to strengthen, and certain countries developed regional trading arrangements such as the United States–Canada Free Trade Agreement and the European Common Market.

The first two papers of this book establish the context of East Asia trading relations with the United States. The second set of papers focuses on sensitive sectoral issues that have led to friction, such as agriculture and high-tech products. Next, the aspects of international economic selection among Asian countries is considered. Finally, the political economy between the United States and Asian countries is examined. The book contains many tables and figures. A list of references follows each chapter. Contributors are listed, and the book provides author and subject indexes.

Jain, Subhash C. *Export Strategy.* New York: Quorum, 1989. 253 pp. ISBN 0-89930-276-9.

The author bases his book on seminars and workshops he held on export strategy, and he thus provides a unique perspective on global trade. International trade, although pursued for hundreds of years, is now an issue of intense interest. The book begins with an excellent chapter on international trade, then takes up such topics as foreign trade issues, export strategy, ways to identify export markets, pricing, promotion, and export organization. The book has tables, a glossary of trade terms, and a bibliography.

Kemme, David M., ed. *Technology Markets and Export Controls in the 1990s.* New York: New York University Press, 1991. 139 pp. ISBN 0-8147-4617-9.

This book is the result of a colloquium held in New York, September 14, 1990, on technology transfer issues in the 1990s. Participants represented academia, government, and business. The members discussed restrictions on the exports of certain Western high-technology items to Eastern Europe and the Soviet Union. They addressed such issues as the current and future role of the Coordinating Committee for Multilateral Export Controls; the question of whether the negative consequences of technology control outweigh the positive; and the form post–Cold War export control plans should take. The book lists participants and provides information about the authors.

Law, Patrick, ed. *International Trade and the Environment.* World Bank Discussion Papers 159. Washington, DC: World Bank, 1992. 365 pp. ISBN 9-8213-2115-3.

There is widespread agreement that governments must act to prevent environmental degradation. This book is primarily concerned with the international aspects of environmental policy and the relationship between environmental concerns and nations' use of the standard tools of international economic policy. There is a distinctly different case of demand for intergovernmental action because world economies are integrated through trade and capital mobility. This economic intergration is the main focus of the book, which investigates the two major pressures for governmental action to control trade. First, many industries that have increased costs due to environmental regulations want control of imports from countries where few environmental regulations provide an unfair trade competition. Second, there is concern that the threatened migration of polluting activities will undermine the political will to impose necessary environmental controls on domestic industry. The text is interspersed throughout with tables and figures and is followed by a lengthy bibliography.

McDaniel, Douglas E. *United States Technology Export Control: An Assessment.* Westport, CT: Praeger, 1993. 290 pp. ISBN 0-275-94164-7.

This volume deals with the controversy and assesses the costs and benefits to the United States of a policy that controls the export of high technology. Chapter 1 discusses the West's embargo of the Soviet Bloc and gives a brief history of the Coordinating Committee for Multilateral Export Controls (COCOM). Chapter 2 examines views and policies within the Atlantic Alliance as they affected embargoes of the former U.S.S.R. and its allies and trading with Moscow and Eastern Europe. Chapter 3 gives a strategic evaluation of U.S. high-technology export control policy. It addresses the implications or restrictions on scientific information, communication, and exchanges. Chapter 4 blames the poor performance of U.S. business overseas on restrictions. Chapter 5 concludes with an exploration of the options the United States might consider. Recommendations are given to improve U.S. COCOM policy. The book is illustrated with a few figures. There are several appendixes and many pages of bibliographical references.

Nivola, Pistro S. *Regulating Unfair Trade.* Washington, DC: Brookings Institution, 1993. 190 pp. ISBN 0-8157-6090-6.

Complaints by the United States about foreign commercial unfairness have multiplied over the past dozen years. In response, the U.S. government has devised elaborate programs to combat these unwelcome business practices. The subject of this book is how to "level the playing field" of international trade. The book sounds an important cautionary note: trade regulations now bear too much of the burden for remedying perceived economic failings. Although the book recognizes the need for a sound commercial policy, it concludes that the policy must be based on realistic expectations and ought to complement, not take precedence over, a more basic agenda. Improvements in the national rate of saving and investment, better preparation of the work force, and containment of health-care costs, for instance, are likely to be far more consequential than trade activism for the nation's long-term competitiveness and living standards. Many tables and notes follow each chapter.

Ramadas, Ganga. *U.S. Export Incentives and Investment Behavior.* Boulder, CO: Westview, 1991. 146 pp. ISBN 0-8133-8129-0.

This study examines the effects of tax-deferred incentives on the investment behavior of U.S. manufacturing firms. In U.S. international export, policy objectives are accomplished by export regulations, customer benefits, and tax incentives. Export regulations cover export-licensing procedures, antidiversion measures to decide the flow of U.S. exports to legally authorized destinations, antiboycott procedures, broad principles under the antitrust laws that prohibit price-fixing agreements, monopolization of markets by competitors, and certain group boycotts. The second tool of export policy, custom benefits, includes the reimbursement of taxes paid on international goods imported into the United States. The third instrument of export policy is the use of special commercial assistance tax programs. The book is illustrated with many tables and figures, and it includes bibliographical references and appendixes.

Ray, Edward John. *U.S. Protectionism and the World Debt Crisis.* New York: Quorum, 1989. 245 pp. ISBN 0-89930-367-6.
This book presents a comprehensive analysis of U.S. protectionism and the world debt. Two major policies are presented on the political economy of protectionism. These policies are based on the concept that the product of a weighted consensus of constituent demand remains stable and predictable over time, unless those weights are disturbed by

substantial and persistent shifts in the underlying political and/or economic interests of the parties vying for political favors.

The book raises the question of whether or not U.S. trade concessions to developing countries in general and to Argentina, Brazil, Indonesia, Korea, Mexico, Philippines, and Venezuela in particular contribute positively to their efforts to meet their debt obligations. Emphasis is placed on U.S. trade policy throughout the post–World War II period, with particular emphasis on how that policy affected developing countries. The book examines changes in tariffs that have been implemented under GATT, the U.S. Generalized System of Preferences, the world debt problem in 1987, U.S. imports, and the preferential aspects of the Caribbean Basin initiatives. The conclusion provides an analysis of the role current legislation can play in providing severely indebted nations access to U.S. markets in order to alleviate debt problems, a discussion of the politics of changing the interest of preferential trade legislation, and, finally, an assessment of the relevance of preferential trade agreements to the critical role of GATT in world trade negotiations. The book contains both tables and figures. Each chapter concludes with notes and references. Additional information can be found in the four appendixes.

Waverman, Leonard, ed. *Negotiating and Implementing a North American Free Trade Agreement.* Toronto: Fraser Institute, Center for International Studies, 1992. 152 pp. ISBN 0-88975-139-0.

This book contains studies of institutions and procedures that affect North American economic integration, including legal institutions that either facilitate or hamper free trade in North America. Several papers provide a historical outline of North American trade negotiations and assess issues involved in moving toward a trilateral free trade agreement. Two additional chapters treat subsidy and countervailing duty issues in the context of North American economic integration and the nontariff barriers implicit in a Trilateral Free Trade Agreement. This volume provides insightful analyses of the problems of trade liberalization and the obstacles to free trade and liberalization. The book provides bibliographic references and a few tables.

Environment

Anderson, Terry L., ed. *NAFTA and the Environment.* Studies on the Economic Future of North America. San Francisco: Pacific Research Institute for Public Policy, 1993. 107 pp. ISBN 0-936488-73-5.

This small volume contains a wealth of information. It provides an overview of NAFTA and its relation to the environment, argues that

NAFTA means more to the Mexicans than simply the prospect of access to U.S. markets, and then examines the provisions of NAFTA, concluding that the treaty will improve environmental conditions in North America. Subsequent chapters center on environmental areas where trade liberalization can have positive environmental effects. The last chapter deals with bootleggers and Baptists—environmentalists and Protectionists—old reasons for new coalitions. Each chapter has notes and references.

Bognanno, Mario F., and Kathryn J. Ready, eds. *The North American Free Trade Agreement: Labor, Industry, and Government Perspectives.* Westport, CT: Quorum, 1993. 255 pp. ISBN 0-89930-849-X.

Part one is a short comparison of the three NAFTA countries, a summary of their reasons for supporting NAFTA, and a characterization of controversies about NAFTA that arose between environmental and labor groups at the conference, November 19–20, 1991, held at the Minneapolis Convention Center. This conference brought together leaders from labor, industry, and government from the United States, Canada, and Mexico. The second part of the book is a collection of papers and recorded remarks presented at the convention. The book has a few tables, a bibliography, and information about the contributors.

Free Trade

Batra, Ravi. *The Myth of Free Trade: A Plan for America's Economic Revival.* New York: Macmillan, 1993. 274 pp. ISBN 0-684-19592-5.

Batra challenges the gospel of free trade and says the opposite of free trade is protectionism, that is, domestic industries should be protected from foreign competition through barriers such as tariffs and quotas. The book argues for a return to protectionism, a ban on mergers, greater government funding for research and development, and other regulatory changes to increase U.S. competitiveness. Chapter notes are found in back of book; tables and figures are found throughout the book.

O'Driscoll, Gerald P., Jr., ed. *Free Trade within North America: Expanding Trade for Prosperity.* Norwell, MA: Kluwer Academic Publishers, 1991. 224 pp. ISBN 0-7923-9291-4.

The chapters of this volume were presented at the fourth annual Southwest Conference sponsored by the Federal Reserve Bank of Dallas. It presents a use for tree trade on a world basis. As countries around the globe were discovering political freedom, free trade was frequently neglected. The speaker at this conference believes that free trade will become a preeminent, competitive force in the twenty-first century, for the world is becoming one interdependent marketplace. No longer are there domestic and foreign firms. Decisionmakers go anywhere via computerization and telecommunications. The five-part book examines expanding trade for prosperity, the North-South connection, the hemisphere and beyond, obstacles to commerce, and important issues for the U.S. Southwest. Tables and charts illustrate the book. Bibliographical references are included.

Oxley, Alan. *The Challenge of Free Trade.* New York: St. Martin's, 1990. 254 pp. ISBN 0-312-05675-3.

This book describes the historical development and prospects of GATT and the Uruguay Round. The purpose of the book is to analyze what is at stake in the Uruguay Round negotiations. Over 100 governments and hundreds of individuals are involved and its outcome could affect every facet of economic activity in the world. The international trade meeting took place in September 1986 at Punta del Este, a South American resort east of Montevideo. Participants discussed the possibility of placing barriers against imports into the United States to keep the U.S. trade deficit from increasing further, which would ultimately destroy the economy of most countries in the world. The chronology of the Uruguay Round is given in an appendix. Other appendixes offer a businessman's guide to GATT and a glossary of Uruguay Round terminology and trivia.

Schott, Jeffrey J., and Murray G. Smith, eds. *Free Trade Agreement: The Global Impact.* Washington, DC, and Montreal, Canada: Institute for International Economics and Institute for Research on Public Policy, 1988. 202 pp. ISBN 0-88132-073-0.

This book gives the perspectives of Canada and the United States on the Free Trade Agreement. Comments are made on the auto pact between the United States and Canada and on the implications of the energy provisions, services, and investment. One chapter is devoted to implications of the Uruguay Round. An appendix lists conference participants. The book is illustrated with several tables.

GATT

GATT Activities, 1991. An Annual Review of the Work of GATT. Geneva: General Agreement on Tariffs and Trade, 1992. 161 pp. No ISBN.

This annual publication discusses trends, issues, and policies for world trade in 1991. One section relates the origin and development of the

Uruguay Round. Another section discusses the GATT framework for international trade, commenting on disputes. Tokyo Round agreements and arrangements occupy several pages. Five appendixes supply GATT membership and officers, chairman's concluding remarks in GATT meetings, 1991 chairmen of Uruguay Round, legal status of Tokyo Round agreements, and a list of new publications.

Globerman, Steven, and Michael Walker, eds. *Assessing NAFTA: A Trinational Analysis.* Vancouver, British Columbia: Fraser Institute, 1993. 314 pp. ISBN 0-88975-156-0.

The book delineates the perspectives of the United States, Mexico, and Canada on the North American Free Trade Agreement. Such trade agreements as NAFTA benefit competitive producers by assuring them access to markets in countries participating in the agreement. The book also describes the impact on automobiles, textiles, agriculture, energy, and financial services that was discussed in the negotiations, as well as environmental impact. Footnotes, tables, and references are included.

Golt, Sidney. *The GATT Negotiations 1986–1990: Origins, Issues, and Prospects.* London: British–North American Committee, 1989. 116 pp. ISBN 0-902594-48-6.

This short work discusses the Uruguay Round and the origin and development of GATT. A chapter discusses GATT negotiations, detailing the rounds that led to the Uruguay Round, 1982–1986. Several pages are devoted to topics for negotiation. The last few pages discuss the conclusions reached. Book has ten appendixes.

Jerome, Robert W., ed. *World Trade at the Crossroads: The Uruguay Round, GATT, and Beyond.* Lanham, MD: University Press of America, 1992. 275 pp. ISBN 0-8191-8495-0.

This book contains articles written by members of the Economic Strategy Institute, founded in 1990, examining a new U.S. trade policy and describing the outlines for this policy. The book is divided into three parts. The first part addresses various aspects of the Uruguay Round. Part two addresses the relationship of the United States to GATT and the world trading system. Part three outlines a future trade order, reminding readers that trade policy cannot be a substitute for a strong U.S. economy. The stronger the United States is economically, the more freedom of action it will have. References are limited to a few footnotes.

Nau, Henry R., ed. *Domestic Trade Politics and the Uruguay Round.* New York: Columbia University Press, 1989. 216 pp. ISBN 0-231-06822-0.

This book develops the viewpoint that international trade is mostly a matter of domestic politics. This perspective is based on the concept that trade flows originate in domestic price structures, which depend on the organization of production and government policies in individual countries. Production and policy in turn depend upon political choices, the accumulated decisions of past decades, but they also present choices that influence the domestic organization of economic life within each society and the international economic relationship between different societies. When societies are organized differently, they are unable to trade extensively with one another.

The chapters develop the viewpoints presented at the Uruguay Round of GATT. They consider such aspects as domestic trade policies and the Uruguay Round trade policies of Mexico, China, West Germany, India, Japan, Korea, and the United States. The book includes tables, bibliographies, and index. A list of contributors is found at the end of the book.

Randall, Stephen J., Herman Konrad, and Sheldon Silverman, eds. *North America without Borders?* Calgary, Alberta: University of Calgary Press, 1992. 328 pp. ISBN 1-895176-18-2.

This book is a compilation of the writings of several authors who attended a conference at the University of Calgary in May 1991. It is divided into six parts. The authors in part one discuss diplomatic perspectives. In part two, the economic perspectives on free trade are discussed. Part three examines the politics of North American integration. Part four deals with borderlands, industry labor, and immigration. Energy and the environment are discussed in part five; public policy and culture inform the last part. The book has a few tables and figures, a list of other papers presented at the conference, and notes on the contributors.

Robinson, Peter, Karl P. Sauvant, and Vishwas P. Govritrikar, eds. *Electronic Highways for World Trade: Issues in Telecommunication and Data Services.* The Atwater Series on the World Information Economy. Boulder, CO: Westview, 1989. 367 pp. ISBN 0- 8133-7764-1.

In September 1986, ministers from 92 countries met in Punta del Este, Uruguay, and agreed to inaugurate a new round of multilateral trade negotiations: the Uruguay Round. For the first time, they agreed that in addition to the customary negotiations on trade in goods, there should be "parallel-track" negotiations on trade and services. This book addresses some of the fundamental issues raised by the discussion on an international framework for trade in services and, in particular, examines those issues in the context of a core section in international service transactions: telecommunications and data services. Chapters include trade in telecommunications and data services, participation of developing countries, global trade in services, appropriate regulation, market access and telecommunications services, international network competition, and legal rights of access to transnational data. The book has four appendixes. The bibliography is quite long.

United States–Canada Free Trade Agreement

Crookell, Harold. *Canadian-American Trade and Investment under the Free Trade Agreement.* New York: Quorum, 1990. 218 pp. ISBN 0-89930-481-8.

This book focuses on a major North American response to globalization: the United States–Canada Free Trade Agreement and how it is likely to affect parent companies and subsidiaries in the United States and Canada. The agreement seeks mutual economic benefits without the surrender of political independence. Each partner, then, remains a distinct identity. This voluntary cooperation is expected to provide benefits to both countries. The author analyzes the basic problems facing the two nations in the implementation of the treaty. Figures and tables illustrate the book. Appendix A gives Maclean's/Decima Poll and Appendix B summarizes the trade agreement. Bibliographic notes conclude each chapter. The book ends with a bibliographic essay.

Diebold, William, Jr., ed. *Bilateralism, Multilateralism, and Canada in the U.S. Trade Policy.* Council on Foreign Relations Series on International Trade. Cambridge, MA: Ballinger, 1988. 206 pp. ISBN 0-88730-287-4.

This book is basically a study of U.S. foreign trade policy, giving the history and the evolution of the international trading system. A chapter analyzes Canadian aims and the decision to propose a free trade area. GATT requirements for a free trade area and some of the uncertain areas that are important to the U.S.–Canadian agreement are examined. Ways to cope with some vital problems are suggested. A Mexican viewpoint of the agreement between Canada and the United States is analyzed. The book concludes with recommendations for the agreement. There are two appendixes, a glossary of acronyms, and a list of abbreviations. Bibliographical notes accompany each chapter.

Rugman, Alan M. *Multinationals and Canada–United States Free Trade. Critical Issues Facing the Multinationals Enterprise.* Columbia, SC: University of South Carolina Press, 1990. 193 pp. ISBN 0-87249-652-2.

The largest trading relationship in the world is between Canada and the United States, and any changes in the relationship would have economic, political, and social consequences reaching beyond these two countries. The early chapters of this timely book discuss the relationship between trade and investment, showing that trade and direct investment complement rather than replace one another. The book illustrates how Canada and the United States would benefit from trade liberalization. Many figures illustrate the book, which also features bibliographical references, a name index, and a company index.

NAFTA

Dobell, Rodney, and Michael Neufeld. *Beyond NAFTA: The Western Hemisphere Interface.* Lantzville, British Columbia: Oolichan Books, 1993. 234 pp. ISBN 0-88982-131-3.

This book is the product of a forum sponsored by the North American Institute in Queretaro, Mexico, May 28–30, 1993. Sixty influential representatives of the public and private sectors of North, Central, and South America attended the meeting. The main topic of discussion was economic integration in the Western Hemisphere in the post-NAFTA era. They also discussed ways to bring the developing countries of Latin America more effectively into the trading system, concluding that the plight of the poor and destitute in developing countries can only be addressed through global economic welfare.

Fatemi, Khosrow, ed. *North American Free Trade Agreement: Opportunities and Challenges.* New York: St. Martin's, 1993. 301 pp. ISBN 0-312-09976-2.

This multiauthor volume is divided into five parts and 23 chapters. Part one provides a general overview of the NAFTA debate. Part two raises the macroeconomic issues involved in implementation of NAFTA. Part three deals with national perspectives and bilateral issues. Part four is devoted to industry-specific and cross-border issues. Part five discusses environmental issues. The chapters have notes and references, and the book is illustrated with a few figures and tables and contains bibliographic references.

Garber, Peter M. *The Mexico–U.S. Free Trade Agreement.* Cambridge, MA: MIT Press, 1993. 317 pp. ISBN 0-262-07152-5.

Papers in this book were prepared for a conference held at Brown University on October 18–19, 1991, and examine the impact of a free trade agreement with Mexico on the U.S. economy. The first part of the book considers how sources of comparative advantage may affect the outcome. The second part deals with locational effects on U.S. production of an agreement. The last part deals with effects of free trade on specific industries such as agriculture, autos, and financial services. The book has many tables and figures. Each chapter has notes and references.

Grinspun, Ricardo, and Maxwell A. Cameron, eds. *The Political Economy of North American Free Trade*. New York: St. Martin's, 1993. 348 pp. ISBN 0-312-07599-5.

This book is written in five parts. Part one gives the framework of discussion. Parts two and three discuss the political economy of Canadian and Mexican integration. Part four deals with NAFTA, the United States, and new continental relations. The last part examines the North American auto and petroleum industry and shows how the countries are affected. The book has a list of acronyms and a glossary of trade terms. Each chapter includes references.

Lawrence, Robert Z., and Charles L. Schultze, eds. *The American Trade Strategy: Options for the 1990s*. Washington, DC: Brookings Institution, 1990. 234 pp. ISBN 0-8157-5179-6.

After World War II, the United States was the leader in promoting liberalization of world trade and negotiating multilateral agreements establishing the rules of the game for trade. The U.S. trade deficits of the 1980s and industries' fear for the future competitiveness of U.S. high-technology industries pressured Congress to retaliate against countries that practiced unfair trade. Economists have developed theories or refined existing ones to show how a nation can enrich itself by using active trade policies to expand markets in high-technology industries. The United States, for example, made bilateral trade agreements with Israel and Canada and is considering others. This book contains versions and critiques of papers presented at a conference on U.S. trade strategy. The book includes tables, index, and bibliographical references.

Lich, Glen E., Joseph A. McKinney, et al., eds. *Region North America: Canada, United States, Mexico*. Waco, TX: Baylor University Regional Studies, 1990. 175 pp. ISBN 1-878804-02-2.

This book collects the papers presented at the Region North America symposium at Baylor University, 1987–1988. The material brings several related academic disciplines to bear on the question of how regions form amd how regional boundaries can be discussed from multidisciplinary perspectives. The 22 chapters are divided into six parts: emerging concepts of trade regions, the United States–Canada Free Trade Agreement, history, impacts, lessons for the future, Mexico in a North American free trade area, impacts of a North American free trade area on the borderlands, perspectives on a North American free trade area, and North American free trade in a global economy. This interesting volume has bibliographical notes, a list of acronyms, and information about the contributors.

Lustig, Nora, Barry P. Bosworth, and Robert Z. Lawrence, eds. *North American Free Trade: Assessing the Impact.* Washington, DC: Brookings Institution, 1992. 274 pp. ISBN 0-8157-5316-0.

This book is the result of a conference held at the Brookings Institution in April 1992. The editors give an overview of the main issues and summarize the papers at the beginning of the book. The aim of the conference was to discuss how NAFTA would reduce and ultimately eliminate barriers to trade and investment among Canada, Mexico, and the United States. NAFTA is also perceived as a model for expanding trade between the United States and all of Latin America, a way to unite countries that are at different stages of economic development. The book has many tables, notes for each paper, and a list of principal contributors, discussants, and panelists.

Riggs, A. R., and Tom Velk, eds. *Beyond NAFTA: An Economic, Political, and Sociological Perspective.* Vancouver, BC: Fraser Institute, 1993. 272 pp. ISBN 0-88975-162-5.

This book is based on papers presented at a conference held at McGill University in March 1993. It contains the opinions, predictions, and analyses of economists, business leaders, historians, political scientists, politicians, legal experts, and diplomats. The book begins by giving the background and prospects of NAFTA. Section two discusses what's in it for Canada. Section three discusses the perquisites of the United States. Section four considers the effects NAFTA will have on the business community. Section five discusses the likely advantages for Mexico and the rest of the hemisphere. The final section discusses law and dispute settlement. Most papers have footnotes. Information is given about the contributors.

Rugman, Alan M., ed. *Foreign Investment and NAFTA.* Columbia, SC: University of South Carolina Press, 1994. 340 pp. ISBN 0-87249-993-6.

This compilation by several authors is divided into five parts. In part one, the authors discuss the politics and economics of NAFTA. Part two examines the motives and expectations of countries involved in NAFTA. Part three discusses the impact of NAFTA on the forest products industry and the energy sector, and explains why the impact of NAFTA will be neutral for large U.S. and Canadian multinationals. Part four examines the impact NAFTA will have on outsiders—Japan and Latin America—and the prospects for extending NAFTA to the rest of the Western Hemisphere. Part five concludes with the changes NAFTA may herald. The book has both tables and figures, an addendum to chapter 2 concerning the politics of NAFTA, and a list of contributors. Each chapter has many notes.

Which Way for the Americas: Analysis of NAFTA Proposals and the Impact on Canada. Ottawa, Ontario: Canadian Centre for Policy Alternatives in Cooperation with Common Frontiers and Action Canada Network, 1992. 130 pp. ISBN 0-88627-132-0.

The book theorizes that NAFTA will govern relations between Canada, Mexico, and the United States. The NAFTA text contains a clause that can integrate and lock other important countries of the Americas into a bloc dominated by the United States. The Canadians feel they were falsely promised much in the original free trade agreement with the United States: jobs, prosperity, protection. Now they are not much interested in the future development. The book leaves the reader feeling that Canadians and Mexicans are told there is no alternative. The book has no bibliography or tables.

Russia

Cullen, Robert, ed. *The Post-Containment Handbook: Key Issues in U.S.–Soviet Economic Relations.* Boulder, CO: Westview, 1990. 227 pp. ISBN 0-8133-7978-4.

In response to the changing political and economic relationship between the United States and the Soviet Union, there was a need for the United States to review a large number of existing laws, regulations, and bureaucratic practices. This book presents an analysis and explanation of the various issues, addressing the development of an export control regime appropriate to the new Soviet economy, the cooperation with allies in the erection and operation of such a regime, and the institutional mechanism best suited for encouraging rapid integration of the Russian economy into the larger economy. A few tables illustrate the book.

Developing World

Bakan, Abigail B., David Cox, and Colin Leys, eds. *Imperial Power and Regional Trade: The Caribbean Basin Initiative.* Waterloo, Ontario: Wilfrid Laurier University Press, 1993. 268 pp. ISBN 0-88920-220-6.

This book studies the power of the United States in the Caribbean since 1980. The U.S. policy directly affected the Caribbean nations and their hard-won and still precarious regional organization, and indirectly affected other industrial powers with significant interests in the Caribbean, notably Canada and Britain. The authors explore such topics as the political logic of the Caribbean Basin Initiative, philosophy and development prospects, the political impact on the Caribbean islands, and the CBI and the Caribbean Community. Many tables are found throughout the book, and notes covering each chapter can be found in the back of the book.

Brown, Janet Welsh, ed. *In the U.S. Interest: Resources Growth and Security in the Developing World.* Boulder, CO: Westview, 1990. 228 pp. ISBN 0-8133-1053-9.

The basic question investigated in this study is how important developing countries are to broad U.S. interests and how important resource management and population growth are to these nations' economic and political future. The four countries analyzed are Mexico, Philippines, Egypt, and Kenya. Although all these countries are important in their region, each faces ominous trends in environmental degradation and in population growth that are undermining long-term development projects. Between 1983 and 1988, the World Resources Institute brought together policymakers to build understanding of the need for north-south cooperation on population, resource, and environmental challenges. This book is the product of these meetings. The book is illustrated with figures and tables. References are found at the end of each chapter. Members of a public forum in the U.S. interest and participants in the WRI colloquium in the U.S. interest are listed.

Krueger, Anne O. *Economic Policies at Cross-Purposes: The United States and Developing Countries.* Washington, DC: Brookings Institution, 1993. 253 pp. ISBN 0-8157-5054-4.

In the early postwar years, U.S. economic policy toward developing countries consisted almost entirely of foreign aid. Over time, developing

countries have become increasingly differentiated, and U.S. policies regarding international trade, capital flows, debt forgiveness, and the
multilateral institutions have assumed greater importance. Unfortu-
nately, the programs and policies are not always coordinated. This
book analyzes the development of U.S. policies, showing how they
have evolved at cross purposes. Special emphasis is placed on the U.S.
international economic policies for the Caribbean Basin Initiative and
Korea, and on the impact of U.S. trade policies for developing countries. Many tables illustrate the book. Several pages of bibliographical
notes are included for each chapter.

Madeley, John. *Trade and the Poor: The Impact of International Trade on
Developing Countries.* New York: St. Martin's, 1993. 209 pp. ISBN 0-312-
09236-9.

The problems of international trade for most developing countries are
analyzed in this book. For most developing countries, international
trade in goods and services is a paradoxical mix of potentially higher
living standards and current low returns. Developing countries currently earn about 15 times more from this trade than they receive in development aid. Yet this trade has brought few benefits for most poor
countries. Despite its shortcomings, few countries have opted out of
the international trading system. This book investigates such questions as, Why do the underdeveloped countries pin their future on international trade? Are they so locked into the system that they cannot
leave it even if they wish? Do they really want to trade, when the system seems so unfavorable and shows few signs of changing, or does
poverty grant them little option? Are reforms possible? Can developing countries act together to get a better deal from the system? The
book contains three appendixes, several pages of notes for the chapters, and a lengthy bibliography.

Iron and Steel Industry

Lima, Jose Guilherme de Heraclito. *Restructuring the U.S. Steel Industry:
Semi-Finished Steel Imports, International Integration, and U.S. Adaptation.*
Boulder, CO: Westview, 1991. 182 pp. ISBN 0-8133-8043-X.

Dr. Lima was employed by Siberbras, Brazil's government-owned steel
company, when he wrote this book showing that the production of
high-quality raw steel for flat-rolling is more expensive in the United
States than in foreign countries. Brazil, Venezuela, and South Korea can
supply U.S. mills for slabs needed to produce finished rolled products
at a low cost. Importing of slabs may increase employment in the steel
industry. The changing economics of steelmaking has made steel

production move closer to raw materials and farther from markets. The book has four appendixes detailing the financial situation of U.S. producers, the closures of steel capacity, capacity balance equations, and cost estimation procedures. Each chapter has many explanatory tables, and bibliographical references are included.

Textiles

Friman, H. Richard. *Patchwork Protectionism: Textile Trade Policy in the United States, Japan, and West Germany*. Cornell Studies in Political Economy. Ithaca, NY: Cornell University Press, 1990. 209 pp. ISBN 0-8014-2423-2.

The author points out that since World War II, protectionism has become a patchwork of applied tariffs, unilateral and nonunilateral quotas, state subsidies, administrative restrictions, and production cartels. Each in its way has been successful in disrupting import flows and has caused retaliation in international economic relations. Friman discusses in depth the textile trade policy of the United States, Japan, and West Germany and the rationales for protectionist policies. The book has an appendix on operationalization and is well footnoted.

Agriculture

Carter, Colin Andre, and Walter H. Gardiner, eds. *Elasticities in International Trade: Agricultural Trade*. Westview Special Studies in International Economics and Business. Boulder, CO: Westview, 1988. 316 pp. ISBN 0-8133-7563-0.

These collected papers were presented at the 1987 Symposium on Elasticities in International Agricultural Trade in Dearborn, Michigan. The book is an outgrowth of renewed interest by researchers, policy-makers, traders, and others in quantifying the factors that affect international trade of agricultural products. The papers consider issues related to the estimation, interpretation, and application of elasticities in international agricultural trade, including elasticities in international trade, estimated U.S. agricultural export demand elasticities, the role of exchange rates, macroeconomic shocks, market share models, and imperfect price transmission and implied trade elasticities. References are found at the end of each chapter. Many tables illustrate the book. Contributors are listed.

Carter, Colin, Alex F. McCalla, and Jerry A. Sharples. *Imperfect Competition and Political Economy: The New Trade Theory in Agricultural Trade Research*. Boulder, CO: Westview, 1990. 270 pp. ISBN 0-8133-7993-8.

Papers in the book were presented at a symposium in Montreal sponsored by the International Agricultural Trade Research Consortium (IATRC) in July 1989. The theory is that countries will export goods that use the country's abundant factor most intensively and it will import goods that do not—a country might, for example, export wheat and import automobiles. Thus the trade position is characterized by interindustry trade. Intraindustry trade exists when countries export and import similar products. For example, the United States exports and imports beef. Trade economists study why trade takes place between nations and what commodities are traded. Part one discusses imperfect competition and trade. Part two discusses the political economy of trade. Each paper has a discussant. There are notes, references, and a few tables.

Helmuth, John W., and Don F. Hadwiger, eds. *International Agricultural Trade and Market Development Policy in the 1990s*. Contributions in Economics and Economic History. Westport, CT: Greenwood, 1993. 217 pp. ISBN 0-313-28614-0.

In this book, the potential impact of policy reforms is discussed in terms of the success or failure of GATT. International agricultural trade development is evaluated along with new opportunities and initiatives for international agricultural trade and market development. Chapters have references and a selected bibliography. Information is given about the editors and contributors. Tables and figures are also used.

Hillman, Jimmye S. *Technical Barriers to Agricultural Trade*. Boulder, CO: Westview, 1991. 199 pp. ISBN 0-8133-8130-4.

This interesting book examines the use of nontariff measures in agricultural trade, protection in historical perspective, and nontariff barriers to trade in meat, livestock, and poultry industries. Different types of nontariff measures in agricultural trade are discussed. One chapter examines the future prospects for technical trade barriers in agriculture. Five appendixes, a bibliography, chapter notes, and many tables augment the book.

Lerner, George, and K. K. Klein, eds. *Canadian Agricultural Trade: Disputes Actions and Prospects*. Calgary, Alberta: University of Calgary Press, 1990. 250 pp. ISBN 0-91983-90-9.

Many authors compiled this book. The first section examines agricultural trade disputes and their resolution. The United States–Canada

Free Trade Agreement (FTA) came into effect January 1, 1989, amidst the hope that the bilateral agreement would be a model for change in the GATT and make countries reduce their trade barriers. One entire chapter is devoted to solving disputes in the United States–Canada Free Trade Agreement. The second section of the book deals with countervailing duty and dumping cases for agricultural products. The last section contains four chapters on prospects for Canadian agricultural trade in a better trading environment. Tables are found throughout the book. References are found at the end of each chapter.

Michelmann, Hans J., Jack C. Stabler, and Garey E. Storey, eds. *The Political Economy of Agricultural Trade and Policy: Toward a New Order for Europe and North America*. Boulder, CO: Westview, 1990. 242 pp. ISBN 0-8133-7992-X.

This book contains papers presented at the Political Economy of European–North American Agricultural Policy and Trade Conference, held March 7–9, 1990, in Saskatoon, Saskatchewan, Canada. The perplexing issue of rationalization of international agricultural trade among the European Community, the United States, and Canada was the main topic for discussion. This issue is the core of GATT negotiations and needs to be resolved so as not to impede other trade issues. Political and economic factors are considered. The book has many figures and tables to illustrate points considered at the meeting. Papers have notes and references.

Schmitz, Andrew. *Free Trade and Agricultural Diversification: Canada and the United States*. Westview Special Studies in Agricultural Science and Policy. Boulder, CO: Westview, 1989. 368 pp. ISBN 0-8133-7851-6.

The findings of this book are primarily the results of a study undertaken by the Economic Council of Canada on the future of the prairie grain region of Canada as a response to the 1988 Free Trade Agreement between the United States and Canada. One area of emphasis is the diversification of prairie agriculture and how it is affected by various policies, primarily the United States–Canada Free Trade Agreement. Other agricultural issues considered include growth and development of value-added activities, irrigation of prairie agriculture, farm enterprise size and diversification, effects of U.S. farm programs on Canadian agricultural diversification, and agricultural subsidies in Canada. The studies collected here recognize that U.S. and Canadian agriculture are highly interconnected and that trade problems in those areas where Canada and the United States compete directly abroad can be resolved by forming stronger relationships with each other. The book is illustrated with tables and figures. Each chapter ends with notes and references. A summary concludes most chapters.

Arms

Ferrari, Paul L., Jeffrey W. Knopf, and Raul L. Madrid. U.S. *Arms Exports: Policies and Contractors.* Washington, DC: Investor Responsibility Research Center, 1988. 342 pp. ISBN 0-931035-12-0.

The book begins with a global view of arms exports. It was written to illuminate the debate over exportation of weapons and gives enough information to help people form intelligent opinions on U.S. policy in arms sales. The nine chapters of part one concentrate mainly on U.S. military exports to the Third World. Part two profiles 20 of the largest U.S. arms exporters: what they sell to whom. Part three lists the orders placed with the 20 companies by foreign governments for military supplies. Many figures and charts illustrate the book.

Laurance, Edward J. *The International Arms Trade.* New York: Lexington, 1992. 245 pp. ISBN 0-669-19928-1.

This book was written at the time of the disintegration of the Soviet Union to show that Russia and the Ukraine will not be able to fill the gap in international arms trade, causing a decline in arms trade and a change in the nature of that trade. The book also sets forth the legal and illegal means used to import military capability in the Persian Gulf War. The author describes and compares four historical international arms trade systems. This comprehensive book is illustrated with many tables and figures and supported by several pages of notes and bibliographical references.

National Research Council. Committee on Japan. Office of Japan Affairs. *U.S.-Japan Strategic Alliances in the Semiconductor Industry: Technology Transfer, Competition, and Public Policy.* Washington, DC: National Academy, 1992. 118 pp. ISBN 0-309-04779-X.

This report was undertaken by a group of experts from the National Research Council's Committee on Japan to examine technology linkages between Japan and the United States in 1991. Companies from the United States must build and carry out strategies to increase the benefits received from the Japanese alliance so that the United States will remain the leader in research, design, manufacturing, and marketing. In other words, the United States should adopt policies favorable to U.S. industry building and competitiveness. Costs and benefits in terms of U.S. competitiveness must be considered. Four appendixes provide case studies of U.S.-Japanese technology and Japanese acquisitions and investments in U.S. semiconductor companies and equipment and materials companies. The agenda and participants in the workshops are given. The book has a few tables and figures.

Reference Sources

American Export Register, 1994. 2 vols. New York: Thomas International Company, 1993.

American Export Register, 1993. 2 vols. New York: Thomas International Publishing Company, 1992.

American Export Register, 1992. 2 vols. New York: Thomas International Publishing Company, 1991.

Ancel, B. "How To Use External On-line Databases for Trade Promotion." *International Trade Forum* 23 (April–June 1987): 26–38.

Bednarzik, Robert W. "An Analysis of U.S. Industries Sensitive to Foreign Trade, 1982–87." *Monthly Labor Review* 116 (February 1993): 15–31.

Cobb, C. E. "Export Trading Companies: Five Years of Bringing U.S. Exporters Together." *Business America* 10 (October 12, 1987): 2–13.

Coughlin, C. C., and T. B. Mandelbaum, "Measuring State Exports: Is There a Better Way?" *Federal Reserve Bank of St. Louis Review* 73 (July–August 1991): 65–79.

Czinkota, M. R., and M. Ursic. "Classification of Exporting Firms According to Sales and Growth into a Share Matrix." *Journal of Business Research* 22 (May 1991): 243–253.

Estell, Kenneth, ed. *World Trade Resources Guide: A Guide to Resources on Importing from and Exporting to the Major Trading Nations of the World.* Detroit, MI: Gale Research Company, 1992. 891 pp.

The Export Yellow Pages, 1993. Englewood, CO: Delphos International, 1993. 855 pp.

Graboyes, R. F. "International Trade and Payments Data: An Introduction." *Federal Reserve Bank of Richmond Economic Review* 77 (September–October 1991): 20–31.

"Import-Export Freight [Special Report]." *Traffic World* 224 (October 22, 1990): 19–35.

Kennedy, Mark W., ed. *Exporters' Encyclopaedia, 1991.* Toronto, Ont.: Dun's Marketing Services, 1991. 1580 pp.

Kennedy, Nancy. "Overseas Opportunities: New Jersey Firms in a Variety of Industries Are Finding That in Order To Draw Jobs and Money into the State, They Must Ship Their Products Out." *Business Journal of New Jersey* 9 (November–December 1991): 34–38+.

Kishaba, Aileen M., ed. *Exporter's Guide to Federal Resources for Small Business.* Rev. ed. Washington, DC: U.S. Small Business Administration, Office of International Trade, 1992. 122 pp.

Miller, E. Willard, and Ruby M. Miller. *United States Trade—Legislation and Policy: A Bibliography.* Public Administration Series: Bibl. no. P 3060. Monticello, IL: Vance Bibliographies, 1991. 22 pp.

Organization for Economic Co-operation and Development. Statistics Directorate. *Foreign Trade by Commodities, 1992.* 5 vols. Paris, France, 1994.

"Reading Lists in International Trade." *American Economist* 31 (Spring 1987): 72–84.

Ryans, C. C. "Resources [Literature for Small Business Entering Global Markets]." *Journal of Small Business Management* 31 (January 1993): 83–93.

Tuller, Lawrence W. *The McGraw-Hill Handbook of Global Trade and Investment Financing.* New York: McGraw-Hill Book Company, 1992. 535 pp.

U.S. Bureau of the Census Foreign Trade Division. *Guide to Foreign Trade Statistics, 1991.* Washington, DC, 1991 (looseleaf).

U.S. Congress. House. Committee on Ways and Means. *Overview and Compilation of U.S. Trade Statutes: September 18, 1989.* 101st Cong., 1st sess. Washington, DC: GPO, 1989. 898 pp.

U.S. Department of Commerce. International Trade Administration. *Caribbean Basin Exporter's Guide.* Washington, DC, 1992. 84 pp.

———. *Destination Japan: A Business Guide for the 90s.* Washington, DC, 1991. 67 pp.

Washington Researchers. *Asian Markets: A Guide to Company and Industry Information Sources, 1991–1992.* 20th ed. Washington, DC: Washington Researchers Publishing, 1991. 410 pp.

———. *European Markets: A Guide to Company and Industry Information Sources, 1992–1993.* 4th ed. Washington, DC: Washington Researchers Publishing, 1992. 598 pp.

World Trade Annual, 1989. 5 vols. New York: Walker and Company, 1993.

Dictionaries

Gipson, Carolyn R. *The McGraw-Hill Dictionary of International Trade and Finance.* New York: McGraw-Hill, 1994. 419 pp.

Rosenberg, Jerry M. *Dictionary of International Trade.* Business Directory Series. Somerset, NJ: Wiley, 1994. 314 pp.

Directories

Directory of United States Exporters, 1992. Phillipsburg, NJ: Journal of Commerce, 1992. 1680 pp.

Directory of United States Importers, 1993. Phillipsburg, NJ: Journal of Commerce, 1993. 1408 pp.

Directory of United States Importers, 1992. Phillipsburg, NJ: Journal of Commerce, 1992. 1376 pp.

"Global Trade Computer Directory [Preview of Computer Systems and Programs for Import-Export Industry]." *Global Trade* 107 (November 1987): 7–25.

Irvin, Linda, ed. *World Trade Centers Association World Business Directory, 1994: Detailed Information on More Than 140,000 Businesses Involved in International Trade.* 4 vols. 2d ed. Detroit, MI: Gale Research Company, 1994.

Made in New Hampshire, 1991: A Directory of Manufacturers, Manufactured Products and Export Directory. 25th ed. Concord, NH:

New Hampshire Department of Resources and Economic Development, Office of Business and Industrial Development, 1991. 323 pp.

Memberships Directory and Yearbook, 1993. Frankfurt/Main, Germany: American Chamber of Commerce in Germany, 1993. 324 pp.

National Membership Directory, 1993–1994. New York: French-American Chamber of Commerce, 1993. 327 pp.

New Hampshire. Department of Resources and Economic Development. Office of Business and Industrial Development. *Made in New Hampshire, 1991: A Directory of Manufacturers, Manufactured Products, and Export Directory.* Concord, NH: 1991. 323 pp.

Ragogna, Ilda M., ed. *United States–Italy Trade Directory, 1992.* New York: Italy-America Chamber of Commerce, Inc. 1992. 368 pp.

U.S. Small Business Administration. Office of International Trade. *International Trade: State and Local Resource Directory.* Washington, DC, 1991. 184 pp.

———. *International Trade: State and Local Resource Directory: Texas, 1990–1991.* Washington, DC: 1991. 184 pp.

———. *International Trade: State and Local Resource Directory: Washington, 1990–1991.* Washington, DC, 1991. 120 pp.

Washington Researchers. *Asian Markets: A Guide to Company and Industry Information Sources, 1993–1994.* 3d ed. Washington, DC, 1993. 498 pp.

Journal Articles and Government Documents

Trade—General

Aggarwal, Raj, et al. "The Export of High Value-Added Products: The Role of International Port and Carrier Services." *Journal of Global Marketing* 2, 4 (1989): 65–80.

Arbogast, K., and A. Ochlis. "Import and Export Price Gains Ease in 1989." *Monthly Labor Review* 113 (June 1990): 3–25.

Bailey, Victor B., and Joanne Tucker. *U.S. Foreign Trade Highlights, 1989.* Washington, DC: U.S. Department of Commerce, International Trade Administration, Office of Trade and Investment Analysis, 1990. 291 pp.

Bayne, Nicholas. "In the Balance: The Uruguay Round of International Trade Negotiations." *Government and Opposition* 26 (Summer 1991): 302–315.

Bernstein, A., et al. "The Global Economy: Who Gets Hurt [Free Trade Fueling Income Inequality]." *Business Week* (August 10, 1992): 48–53.

Blecker, R. A. "The Consumption Binge Is a Myth." *Challenge* 33 (May–June 1990): 22–30.

Butler, Alison, "The Trade-Related Aspects of Intellectual Property Rights: What Is at Stake?" *Federal Reserve Bank of St. Louis Review* 72 (November–December 1990): 36–46.

Calingaert, M. "What Europe 1992 Means for U.S. Business." *Business Economics* 24 (October 1989): 30–36.

Catoline, J., and J. Chopoorian. "The European Market in 1992: Strategies for U.S. Companies." *Advanced Management Journal* 55 (Spring 1990): 33–41.

Clark, D. B. "Regulation of International Trade in the United States: The Tokyo Round." *Journal of Business* 60 (April 1987): 297–306.

Coughlin, C. C., and T. B. Mandelbaum. "Accounting for Changes in Manufactured Exports at the State Level: 1976–86." *Federal Reserve Bank of St. Louis Review* 72 (September–October 1990): 3–14.

Culpan, R. "Export Behavior of Firms: Relevance of Firm Size." *Journal of Business Research* 18 (May 1989): 207–218.

Deyak, T. A., et al. "An Empirical Examination of the Structural Stability of Disaggregated U.S. Import Demand." *Review of Economics and Statistics* 71 (May 1989): 337–341.

Driessen, P. A. "Net Imports and the U.S. Corporate Tax Base." *National Tax Journal* 44 (September 1991): 315–324.

Emmerij, L. "Globalization, Regionalization and World Trade." *Columbia Journal of World Business* 27 (Summer 1992): 6–13.

Faltermayer, E. "Is Made in U.S.A. Fading Away? [America Losing Markets and Selling Off Pieces of Its Economy To Pay Its Import Binge]." *Fortune* 122 (September 24, 1990): 62–65+.

Farrell, C., et al. "What's Wrong? Why the Industrialized Nations Are Stalled." *Business Week* (August 2, 1993): 54–59.

Fieleke, N. S. "The Terms on Which Nations Trade." *New England Economic Review* (November–December 1989): 3–12.

Franko, L. G. "Global Corporate Competition II: Is the Large American Firm an Endangered Species?" *Business Horizons* 34 (November–December 1991): 14–22.

Gilmer, R. W., et al. "The Service Sector in a Hierarchy of Rural Places: Potential for Export Activity," *Land Economics* 65 (August 1989): 217–227.

Global New York: The World of New Yorks Exports: 1992 Fact Book. Albany, NY: New York (State) Department of Economic Development, 1993. 7 pp.

Green, R. T., and T. L. Larsen. "Changing Patterns of U.S. Trade: 1985–1989." *Business Horizons* 34 (November–December 1991): 7–13.

Greif, A. "Institutions and International Trade: Lessons from the Commercial Revolution." *American Economic Review* 82 (May 1992): 128–133.

Hickok, S. "The Shifting Composition of U.S. Manufactured Goods Trade." *Federal Reserve Bank of New York Quarterly Review* 16 (Spring 1991): 27–37.

Hickok, S., and J. Orr. "Shifting Patterns of U.S. Trade with Selected Developing Asian Economies [Taiwan, S. Korea, Malaysia, and Thailand]." *Federal Reserve Bank of New York Quarterly Review* 14 (Winter 1989–1950): 36–47.

Hilton, R. S. "Capacity Constraints and the Prospects for External Adjustments and Economic Growth: 1989–90." *Federal Reserve Bank of New York Quarterly Review* 13 (Winter–Spring 1989): 52–68.

Hipple, F. S. "The Measurement of International Trade Related to Multinational Companies." *American Economic Review* 80 (December 1990): 1263–1270.

Inikori, J. E. "Slavery and Atlantic Commerce, 1650–1800." *American Economic Review* 82 (May 1992): 151–157.

Kowalczyk, C. "Trade Negotiations and World Welfare." *American Economic Review* 79 (June 1989): 552–559.

Krugman, P. "Rethinking International Trade." *Business Economics* 23 (April 1988): 7–12.

Levinson, M. "Is Strategic Trade Fair Trade?" *Across the Board* 25 (June 1988): 46–51.

Macchiarola, Frank J., ed. "International Trade: The Changing Role of the United States." *Proceedings of the Academy of Political Science* 37, 4 (1990): 1–206.

McDonough, William J. "The Global Derivatives Market." *Federal Reserve Bank of New York Quarterly Review* 18 (Autumn 1993): 1–5.

McFaul, Francis G. *U.S. Foreign Trade Highlights, 1992.* Washington, DC: U.S. Department of Commerce, International Trade Administration, Office of Trade and Economic Analysis, 1993. 207 pp.

Magnusson, Paul, and Blanca Riemer. "Carla Hills, Trade Warrior: She Must Battle Japan and Europe—and Keep U.S. Protectionists at Bay." *Business Week* (January 22, 1990): 50–55.

Niskanen, William A. "The Bully of World Trade." *Orbis* 33 (Fall 1989): 531–538.

Nolle, D. E. "An Empirical Analysis of Market Structure and Import and Export Performance for U.S. Manufacturing Industries." *Quarterly Review of Economics and Business* 31 (Winter 1991): 59–78.

Preeg, Ernest H. "The U.S. Leadership Role in World Trade: Past, Present, and Future" *Washington Quarterly* 15 (Spring 1992): 81–91.

Reich, Robert B. "Trade with Whom? For What? A Citizen's Guide to the Trade Debate." *Journal of Policy Analysis and Management* 9 (Summer 1990): 391–399.

Riley, Tony. "The Collapse of the GATT Uruguay Round: The Start of a U.S.-EC Trade War? Protectionism Is Usually Unleashed by an Economic Downturn or Other Shock to the System: The Deadlock in the Uruguay Round—Coming at the Peak of the 1980s' Long Boom—Bodes Ill for the Future of the World Trading System." *Journal of European Business* 2 (March–April 1991): 5–10.

Schott, Jeffrey J. "Trading Blocs and the World Trading System." *World Economics* 14 (March 1991): 1–17

Sharma, S. C., et al. "Exports and Economic Growth in Industrialized Countries." *Applied Economics* 23, 4A (April 1991): 697–707.

Sigalla, Fiona D., and Beverly Fox. "Investing for Growth: Thriving in the World Marketplace." *Federal Reserve Bank of Dallas Economic Review* (2d Quarter 1993): 53–64.

Stekler, L. "U.S. International Transactions in 1990." *Federal Reserve Bulletin* 77 (May 1991): 287–296.

Terpstra, Vern, and Chwo-Ming Joseph Yu. "Export Trading Companies: An American Trade Failure?" *Journal of Global Marketing* 6, 2 (1992): 29–54.

Thursby, J. G. "Evaluation of Coefficients in Misspecified Regressions with Application to Import Demand." *Review of Economics and Statistics* 70 (November 1988): 690–695.

Tully, Shawn. "What Eastern Europe Offers: Though Troubled, East Germany and Czechoslovakia Have the Strongest Economies: There's Opportunity in Consumer Goods, Capital Equipment, and Telecommunications." *Fortune* 121 (March 12, 1990): 52–55.

U.S. Congress. Senate. Committee on Finance. *Europe-92 Trade Program: Hearing, May 10, 1989.* 101st Cong., 1st sess. Washington, DC: GPO, 1989. 94 pp.

U.S. Department of Commerce. *International Trade Administration. United States Trade Performance in 1988.* Washington, DC: GPO, 1989. 92 pp.

U.S. General Accounting Office. *International Trade: Rumanian Trade Data: Report to the Chairman, Committee on Finance, U.S. Senate.* Gaithersburg, MD: 1992. 25 pp.

———. *International Trade: U.S.-Albanian Trade Data: Report to the Chairman, Committee on Finance, U.S. Senate.* Gaithersburg, MD: 1992. 12 pp.

Warner, Andrew. "The Secret behind American Export Success." *Regulation* (Cato Institute) 16 (Winter 1993): 52–60.

Young, A. "Learning by Doing and the Dynamic Effects of International Trade." *Quarterly Journal of Economics* 106 (May 1991): 369–405.

Young, J. A. "An American Giant Rethinks Globalization [Views of Hewlett-Packard CEO]." *Information Strategy* 6 (Spring 1990): 5–10.

Trade Theory

Adams, J. "Trade and Payments as Instituted Process: The Institutional Theory of the External Sector." *Journal of Economic Issues* 21 (December 1987): 1839–1860.

Albers, N. D., and V. Kumar. "International Direct Marketing Efforts: Are They Useful to Small Businesses in Establishing Consistent Patterns of Exporting?" *Journal of Direct Marketing* 5 (Autumn 1991): 29–38.

Bagwell, K., and R. W. Staiger. "A Theory of Managed Trade." *American Economic Review* 80 (September 1990): 779–795.

Bergstrand, J. H. "The Generalized Gravity Equation, Monopolistic Competition and the Factor-Proportions Theory in International Trade." *Review of Economics and Statistics* 71 (February 1989): 143–153.

Dellas, H., and B.-Z. Zilberfarb. "Real Exchange Rate Volatility and International Trade: A Reexamination of the Theory." *Southern Economic Journal* 59 (April 1993): 641–647.

Fosu, A. K. "Influences of International Factors on U.S. Prices: A Theoretical and Empirical Analysis." *Applied Economics* 23 (March 1991): 517–524.

Krauss, Ellis S., and Simon Reich. "Ideology, Interests, and the American Executive: Toward a Theory of Foreign Competition and Manufacturing Trade Policy." *International Organization* 46 (Autumn 1992): 857–897.

United Nations. Centre on Transnational Corporations. *The Impact of Trade-Related Investment Measures on Trade and Development: Theory, Evidence, and Policy Implications.* New York: U.N. Agent, 1991. 104 pp.

Models

Anania, G., and A. F. McCalla. "Does Arbitraging Matter? Spatial Trade Models and Discriminatory Trade Policies [Analysis of 1980 U.S. Embargo to USSR]." *American Journal of Agricultural Economics* 73 (February 1991): 103–117.

Hummels, D., and J. Levinsohn. "Product Differentiation as a Source of Comparative Advantage?" *American Economic Review* 83 (May 1993): 445–449.

Lim, J. S., et al. "An Empirical Test of an Export Adoption Model." *Management International Review* 31, 1 (1991): 51–62.

Marin, D. "Is the Export-Led Growth Hypothesis Valid for Industrialized Countries?" *Review of Economics and Statistics* 74 (November 1992): 677–688.

Perry, A. C. "The Evolution of the U.S. International Trade Intermediary in the 1980s: A Dynamic Model." *Journal of International Business Studies* 21, 1 (1990): 133–153.

Walters, P. G. P., and S. Samill. "A Model for Assessing Performance in Small U.S. Exporting Firms." *Entrepreneurship Theory and Practice* 15 (Winter 1990): 33–50.

Trade Competition

Dentzer, Susan. "The Coming Global Boom: The Cold War Is Over, Japan Is Forging Vast New Markets and Europe Is Awash in Europhoria: The Expansion of the 1980s Will Surge Forward into the 1990s: Yet the U.S. May Well Miss the Boat." *U.S. News* 109 (July 16, 1990): 22–26+.

Ferguson, Charles H. "Computers and the Coming of the U.S. Keiretsu: U.S. and European Information Technology Companies Face a Stark Choice: Cooperate or Become Vassals of Their Japanese Competitors—Hang Together or Hang Separately." *Harvard Business Review* 68 (July–August 1990): 55–70.

"The High-Tech Debate: Can America Keep Pace?" *Management Review* 78 (December 1989): 30–36.

Hillman, Arye L. "Protectionist Policies as the Regulation of International Industry." *Public Choice* 67 (November 1990): 101–110.

"Japan and the United States." *Washington Quarterly* 13 (Summer 1990): 55–120.

Johnson, Chalmers. "Economics and the Classroom: How Japan Measures Up." *Forum for Applied Research and Public Policy* 4 (Winter 1989): 48–56.

Kline, John M. "Trade Competitiveness and Corporate Nationality." *Columbia Journal of World Business* 24 (Fall 1989): 25–32.

Kwaczek, Adrienne S., and William A. Kerr. "Canadian Exports of Electricity to the U.S.: International Competitiveness or International Risk Bearing?" *World Competition* 13 (September 1989): 19–28.

Lambright, Henry W., and Dianne Rahm, eds. "Symposium on Technology and American Competitiveness." *Policy Studies Journal* 18 (Fall 1989): 87–212.

Lawrence, Robert. *Manufacturing in the 1990s: The Adjustment Challenge.* Working Paper 124. St. Louis, MO: Center for the Study of American Business, Washington University, 1989. 30 pp.

Lipsey, Robert E., et al. *Measures of Prices and Price Competitiveness in International Trade in Manufactured Goods.* Cambridge, MA: National Bureau of Economic Research, 1990. 72 pp.

McKenzie, R. B. "American Competitiveness—Do We Really Need To Worry?" *Public Interest* 90 (Winter 1988): 66–80.

Marshall, Patrick G. "Photonics Next U.S. High-Tech Surrender? Photonics—Technologies That Use Light Instead of Electricity to Process and Transmit Information—Are Expected To Lead to an Industry Worth More Than $100 Billion in the Near Future: The United States Is Currently Ahead of the Rest of the World in Many Types of Photonics Research, Particularly in Areas Relating to Optical Fibers for Telecommunications." *Editorial Research Reports* (January 12, 1990): 18–31.

National Research Council. Committee on Competitiveness of the Minerals and Metals Industry. *Competitiveness of the U.S. Minerals and Metals Industry.* Washington, DC: National Academy Press, 1990. 140 pp.

Reich, Robert B. "Who Is Us? Across the United States You Can Hear Calls for Us To Revitalize Our National Competitiveness." *Harvard Business Review* 68 (January–February 1990): 53–64.

"Special Issue [U.S. International Competitiveness]." *Business Horizons* 34 (November–December 1991): 3–100.

Steingraber, Fred G. "Managing in the 1990s: Competitiveness Will Not Vanish in the Next Decade; To Confront the Issue, Management Will Need to Manage Both the Present and the Future." *Business Horizons* 33 (January–February 1990): 50–61.

U.S. Congress. *U.S. Wood Products Competitiveness: Timber, Taxes and Trade: Joint Hearing, July 8, 1989, Before the Subcommittee on Regulation, Business Opportunities, and Energy of the Committee on Small Business. House of Representatives, and the Subcommittee on Conservation and Forestry of the Committee on Agriculture, Nutrition, and Forestry, United States Senate.* 101st Cong., 1st sess. Washington, DC: GPO, 1989. 288 pp.

U.S. Congress. House. Committee on Armed Services. Procurement and Military Nuclear Systems Subcommittee. *Competitive Strategies: Hearings, March 2–3, 1989.* 101st Cong., 1st sess. Washington, DC: GPO, 1989. 114 pp.

U.S. Congress. House. Committee on Banking, Finance, and Urban Affairs. *Role of the Financial Services Sector: Hearing, April 24, 1990, Before the Subcommittee on Financial Institutions Supervision, Regulation, and Insurance Task Force on the International Competitiveness of U.S. Financial Institutions.* 101st Cong., 2d sess. Washington, DC: GPO, 1990. 31 pp.

U.S. Congress. House. Committee on Science, Space, and Technology. *Europe 1992 and Its Effects on U.S. Science, Technology, and Competitiveness: Hearings, May 16–17, 1989.* 101st Cong., 1st sess. Washington, DC: GPO, 1989. 815 pp.

———. Subcommittee on International Science Cooperation. *High Definition Television: The International HDTV Standard-Setting Process and the Role of International Standards on U.S. Competitiveness: Hearing, May 31, 1989.* 101st Cong., 1st sess. Washington, DC: GPO, 1989. 157 pp.

————. Subcommittee on Science, Research, and Technology. *The Government Role in Joint Production Ventures: Hearing, September 19, 1989.* 101st Cong., 1st sess. Washington, DC: GPO, 1989. 266 pp.

————. *U.S. Supercomputer Industry: Hearing, June 20, 1989.* 101st Cong., 1st sess. Washington, DC: GPO, 1989. 140 pp.

U.S. Congress. House. Committee on Small Business. Subcommittee on Exports, Tax Policy, and Special Problems. *Critical Issues Facing Small American Manufacturers: Hearing, October 2, 1989.* 101st Cong., 1st sess. Washington, DC: GPO, 1990. 187 pp.

U.S. Congress. House. Committee on Ways and Means. Subcommittee on Trade. *Conditions of Competition between the United States and Canadian Durum Wheat Industries: Hearing, December 7, 1989.* 101st Cong., 1st sess. Washington, DC: GPO, 1990. 111 pp.

U.S. Congress. Joint Economic Committee. *Japan's Economic Challenge: Study Papers.* 101st Cong., 2d sess. Washington, DC: GPO, 1990. 498 pp.

U.S. Congress. Senate. Committee on Banking, Housing, and Urban Affairs. *Oversight Hearings on the Condition of U.S. Financial and Industrial Base: Hearings, July 11–15, 1989, on the Competitiveness of Many of Our Most Important Industries and More Generally about the Ability of the United States To Compete Effectively in the International Marketplace During the 1990's.* 101st Cong., 1st sess. Washington, DC: GPO, 1990. 475 pp.

————. Subcommittee on International Finance and Monetary Policy. *Treasury Department's Report on International Economic and Exchange Rate Policy: Hearing, May 16, 1991, on the Outlook for International Cooperation To Strengthen Economic Growth and To Review Findings of Countries Who Manipulate Their Currency To Gain a Competitive Advantage in International Trade.* 102d Cong., 1st sess. Washington, DC: GPO, 1991. 88 pp.

U.S. Congress. Senate. Committee on Commerce, Science, and Transportation. *Commercialization of New Technologies: Hearing, May 9, 1989, on Industry-Government Cooperation to Speed Commercialization of New Technologies.* 101st Cong., 1st sess. Washington, DC: GPO, 1990. 64 pp.

————. Subcommittee on Foreign Commerce and Tourism. *Competitiveness in the Glassware Industry: Hearing, October 30, 1989, on*

Competitiveness in Glassware and Commercial Chinaware Industry. 101st Cong., 1st sess. Washington, DC: GPO, 1990. 70 pp.

———. *Japanese Space Industry—An American Challenge: Hearing, October 4, 1989.* 101st Cong., 1st sess. Washington, DC: GPO, 1989. 55 pp.

———. Subcommittee on Science, Technology, and Space. *Comparative Assessment of U.S. Space Program: Hearing, July 19, 1989.* 101st Cong., 1st sess. Washington, DC: GPO, 1989. 83 pp.

U.S. Congress. Senate. Committee on Energy and Natural Resources. *Competition to Serve Northeast Natural Gas Markets: Hearing, May 3, 1990.* 101st Cong., 2d sess. Washington, DC: GPO, 1990. 314 pp.

———. Subcommittee on Energy Research and Development. *Establishing Three Centers for Metal Casting Competitiveness Research: Hearing, September 21, 1989, on S.775.* 101st Cong., 1st sess. Washington, DC: GPO, 1989. 120 pp.

U.S. Department of Commerce. International Trade Administration. *The Competitive Status of the U.S. Electronics Sector from Materials to Systems.* Washington, DC: GPO, 1990. 221 pp.

U.S. International Trade Commission. *Coumarin from the People's Republic of China.* USITC Publication 2733. Washington, DC, 1994. 5 pp.

———. Office of Economics. *The Economic Effects of Significant U.S. Import Restraints.* USITC Publication 2699. Washington, DC, 1993. 95 pp.

U.S. Office of Technology Assessment. *Arming Our Allies: Cooperation and Competition in Defense Technology.* Washington, DC: GPO, 1990. 113 pp.

———. *Competition in Coastal Seas: An Evaluation of Foreign Maritime Activities in the 200-Mile EEZ; Background Paper.* Washington, DC: GPO, 1989. 34 pp.

———. *Helping America Compete: The Role of Federal Scientific and Technical Information.* Washington, DC: GPO, 1990. 61 pp.

———. *Magnesium from Canada.* USITC Publication 2696. Washington, DC, 1993. 23 pp.

———. *Magnesium from the People's Republic of China, Russia, and the Ukraine.* USITC Publication 2775. Washington, DC, 1994. 5 pp.

———. *Making Things Better: Competing in Manufacturing.* Washington, DC: GPO, 1990. 241 pp.

———. *Softwood Lumber from Canada.* USITC Publication 2689. Washington, DC, 1993. 45 pp.

———. *Stainless Steel from Brazil, India, Italy, Japan and Spain.* USITC Publication 2734. Washington, DC, 1994. 5 pp.

———. *Worker Training: Competing in the New International Economy.* Washington, DC, 1990. 282 pp.

Trade Development

Ali, A., and P. M. Swiercz. "Firm Size and Export Behavior: Lessons from the Midwest." *Journal of Small Business Management* 29 (April 1991): 71–78.

André, Raymond. *Financing Exports to Developing Countries.* Paris, France: Organization for Economic Cooperation and Development, 1992. 116 pp.

Baker, Stephen, et al. "Mini-Nationals Are Making Maximum Impact: These Little Giants Are Emerging as a Boon to American Jobs and Exports." *Business Week* (September 6, 1993): 66–69.

Coughlin, Cletus C., and Thomas B. Mandelbaum. "Accounting for Changes in Manufactured Exports at the State Level: 1976–86." *Federal Reserve Bank of St. Louis Review* 72 (September–October 1990): 3–14.

———. "Measuring State Exports: Is There a Better Way?" *Federal Reserve Bank of St. Louis Review* 73 (July–August 1991): 65–79.

DeJong, Jan J. *New Jersey Manufacturing Exports: Destinations, Trends, and Opportunities.* Trenton, NJ: Department of Labor Market and Demographic Research, 1990. 45 pp.

Devine, P. G. "Fostering Trade in a Hostile International Environment." *American Journal of Agricultural Economics* 70 (November 1988): 767–778.

Eaton, J., and G. M. Grossman. "Optimal Trade and Industrial Policy under Oligopoly." *Quarterly Journal of Economics* 101 (May 1986): 383–406. Discussion. 103 (August 1988): 599–607.

Fieleke, Norman S. "Commerce with the Newly Liberalizing Countries: Promised Land, Quicksand, or What?" *New England Economic Review* (May–June 1990): 19–33.

"50 Firms Share Export Techniques [Views of Exporters Special Report]." *Business America* 109 (September 12, 1988): 16–36.

Freeman, Michael A., and Khi V. Thai. "Export Development: Local Initiatives." *Management Information Service Report* 24 (April 1992): 1–16.

Goldin, Ian, et al. *Trade Liberalisation: Global Economic Implications.* Paris, France: Organisation for Economic Cooperation and Development, 1993. 217 pp.

Green, R. T., and A. K. Kohli. "Export Market Identification: The Role of Economic Size and Socioeconomic Development." *Management International Review* 31, 1 (1991): 37–50.

Hickok, S. "The Shifting Composition of U.S. Manufactured Goods Trade." *Federal Reserve Bank of New York Quarterly Review* 16 (Spring 1991): 27–37.

Holden, A. C. "How To Locate and Communicate with Overseas Customers [Computer Messaging System NETWORK Designed To Address Communications Need of Small Exporting Firms]." *Industrial Marketing Management* 20 (August 1991): 161–168.

Koh, A. C., and R. A. Robicheaux. "Variations in Export Performance Due to Differences in Export Marketing Strategy: Implications for Industrial Marketers." *Journal of Business Research* 17 (November 1988): 249–258.

Kotabe, Masaaki, and Michael R. Czinkota. "State Government Promotion of Manufacturing Exports: A Gap Analysis." *Journal of International Business Studies* 23, 4 (1992): 637–658.

Kravis, Irving B., and Robert E. Lipsey. *Technological Characteristics of Industries and the Competitiveness of the U.S. and Its Multinational Firms.* NBER Working Paper no. 2933. Cambridge, MA: National Bureau of Economic Research, 1989. 31 pp.

Lawrence, Robert. *Manufacturing in the 1990s: The Adjustment Challenge.* Working Paper 124. St. Louis, MO: Center for the Study of American Business, Washington University, 1989. 30 pp.

Lovett, W. A. "Solving the U.S. Trade Deficit and Competitiveness Problem." *Journal of Economic Issues* 22 (June 1988): 459–467.

Lunn, J. "An Empirical Investigation of the Effects of Foreign Trade on the Measurement of Industrial Concentration." *Review of Business and Economic Research* 23 (Spring 1988): 51–62.

McFaul, Francis G. *U.S. Foreign Trade Highlights, 1992.* Washington, DC: U.S. Department of Commerce, International Trade Administration, Office of Trade and Economic Analysis, 1993. 207 pp.

Masek, M. A. "The Advantage of Developing U.S. Technology by a U.S. Person through a Foreign Corporation." *Journal of Corporate Taxation* 17 (Summer 1980): 138–168.

———. "Using Royalties To Avoid the Manufacturing Source Rules [Licensing Foreign Sales Rights to a Controlled Foreign Corporation]." *Taxes* 68 (October 1990): 730–735.

Moini, A. H. "Europe 1992: A Challenge to Small Exporters [Problems Faced by U.S. Manufacturers]." *Journal of Small Business Management* 30 (January 1992): 11–20.

Moran, Theodore H. "The Impact of TRIMS [Trade-Related Investment Measures] on Trade and Development." *Transnational Corps* (UN) 1 (February 1992): 55–65.

Murphy, P., et al. "A Contemporary Perspective of International Port Operations." *Transportation Journal* 28 (Winter 1988): 28–42.

Niskanen, William A. "The Bully of World Trade." *Orbis* 33 (Fall 1989): 531–538.

Nunnenkamp, Peter. *The World Trading System at the Crossroads: Multilateral Trade Negotiations in the Era of Regionalism.* Kiel, Germany: Institut für Weltwirtschaft, Universitat Kiel, 1993. 20 pp.

Organization for Economic Cooperation and Development. Centre for Co-operation with the Economies in Transition. *Integrating Emerging Market Economies into the International Trading System.* Paris, France, 1994. 99 pp.

Ott, M. "Have U.S. Exports Been Larger Than Reported?" *Federal Reserve Bank of St. Louis Review* 70 (September–October 1988): 3–23.

Persky, Joseph, et al. "Import Substitution and Local Economic Development." *Economic Development Quarterly* 7 (February 1993): 18–29.

Rill, James F. "Statement of Japanese Competition Policies and the U.S. Response before the U.S. Senate Committee on Judiciary, 29 July 1992." *World Competition* 16 (September 1992): 143–169.

Schott, Jeffrey J. "Trading Blocs and the World Trading System." *World Economy* 14 (March 1991) 1–17.

Stokes, Bruce. "End of the Boom: Rising Export Sales Have Kept America out of a Recession, But the Outbound Traffic Has Been Slowing Lately, and the Worldwide Rise in Oil Prices Will Make Things Worse." *National Journal* 22 (October 13, 1990): 2457–2460.

Torre, Augusto de la, and Margaret R. Kelly. *Regional Trade Agreements.* Occasional Paper no. 93. Washington, DC: International Monetary Fund, 1992. 54 pp.

U.S. Congress. House. Committee on Foreign Affairs. Subcommittee on Economic Policy, Trade, and Environment. *State of U.S. Export Promotion Programs: Hearing, March 15, 1993.* 103d Cong., 1st sess. Washington, DC: GPO, 1994. 53 pp.

U.S. Department of Defense. *Selling to the Allies: A Guide for U.S. Firms.* Washington, DC: GPO, 1990. 128 pp.

U.S. General Accounting Office. *International Trade: U.S. Business Access to Certain Foreign State-of-the-Art Technology: Report to the Honorable Lloyd Bentsen, U.S. Senate.* Gaithersburg, MD, 1991. 50 pp.

Wright, P. C. "The Personal and Personnel Adjustment and Costs to Small Businesses Entering the International Market Place." *Journal of Small Business Management* 31 (January 1993): 83–93.

Yang, Y. S., et al. "A Market Expansion Ability Approach To Identify Potential Exporters." *Journal of Marketing* 56 (January 1992): 84–96.

Young, A. "Learning by Doing and the Dynamic Effects of International Trade." *Quarterly Journal of Economics* 106 (May 1991): 369–405.

Trade Forecasting

Ashley, Gregory A., and James E. Epperson. *An Analysis of Potential International Market Penetration of U.S. Vegetables: Foreign Importers' Perspective.* Research Bulletin 380. Athens, GA: Agriculture Experiment Stations, 1989. 34 pp.

Bellégo, Alain. "Towards Paperless International Trade: EDI and EDIFACT: Paper Documents Are Being Replaced by Electronic Systems for Relaying Trade Data between the Buyer and the Seller." *International Trade Forum* (July–September 1991): 10–15+.

Cesal, L., et al. "Effects of Altering the Structure of U.S. Trade." *American Journal of Agricultural Economics* 71 (December 1989): 219–230.

Chittum, J. M. "How Do I Go International?" *Journal of Management Consulting* 7 (Fall 1992): 30–35.

Cushman, D. O. "U.S. Bilateral Trade Equations: Forecasts and Structural Stability." *Applied Economics* 22 (August 1990): 1093–1102.

Ernst, Maurice. "U.S. Exports in the 1990s: The Outlook for Exporters Is Bright, as More Markets Open around the World." *Business Horizons* 33 (January–February 1990): 44–49.

Hervey, Jack L. "Changing U.S. Trade Patterns: U.S. Foreign Trade Has Grown Ten-fold in Twenty Years—Much of the Increase Has Flowed to and from Japan and Emerging Southeast Asia." *Economic Perspectives* 14 (March–April 1990): 2–12.

Kupfer, A. "How American Industry Stacks Up [Global Market Share Ratings with Japan, W. Europe]." *Fortune* 125 (March 9, 1992): 30–34+.

"Managing U.S. Economic Destiny [Interview with R. Kuttner]." *Challenge* 34 (January–February 1991): 18–26.

Menes, J. C., and S. Carson. "1991 U.S. Industrial Outlook Predicts Major Role for Exports." *Business America* 112 (January 14, 1991): 2–9.

Orr, J. "The Performance of the U.S. Capital Goods Industry: Implications for Trade Adjustment." *Federal Reserve Bank of New York Quarterly Review* 13 (Winter–Spring 1989): 69–82.

Ostry, S. "Governments and Corporations in a Shrinking World: Trade and Innovation Policies in the United States, Europe, and Japan." *Columbia Journal of World Business* 25 (Spring–Summer 1990): 10–16.

"World Trade Outlook 1992 [Special Report]." *Traffic World* 229 (January 20, 1992): 21–36.

"World Trade Outlook 1991 [Special Report]." *Business America* 112 (April 22, 1991): 2–48.

"World Trade Outlook 1990." *Business America* 111 (April 23, 1990): 2–48.

Yang, Y. S., et al. "A Market Expansion Ability Approach To Identify Potential Exporters." *Journal of Marketing* 56 (January 1992): 84–96.

Trade Policy

Bagwell, K. "Optimal Export Policy for a New-Product Monopoly [Subsidy Impact on Quality Pricing]." *American Economic Review* 81 (December 1991): 1156–1169.

Baneth, Jean. *"Fortress Europe" and Other Myths about Trade: Policies toward Merchandise Imports in the EC and Other Major Industrial Economies (and What They Mean for Developing Countries).* World Bank Discussion Papers 225. Washington, DC: International Bank for Reconstruction and Development, 1993. 35 pp.

Beladi, H., and A. K. Parai. "Sluggish Intersectoral Factor Movements and Alternative Trade Policies." *Southern Economic Journal* 59 (April 1993): 760–767.

Bhagwati, Jagdish N. "United States Trade Policy at the Crossroads." *World Economy* (London) 12 (December 1989): 439–479.

Cheng, L. K. "Assisting Domestic Industries under International Oligopoly: The Relevance of the Nature of Competition to Optimal Policies." *American Economic Report* 78 (September 1988): 746–758.

"The Clinton Administration's International Economic Policy." *Foreign Policy Bulletin* 3 (May–June 1993): 2–16.

Cranford, John R. "Trade and Foreign Policy: The Ties That Bind: Congress Wants To Boost Competitiveness But Can't Let Go of Strings on Trade." *Congressional Quarterly Weekly Report* 48 (June 9, 1990): 1773–1778.

DiFilippo, Anthony. "Reindustrialization Politics: U.S. Industrial Policy at a Comparative Disadvantage." Pp. 269–289 in *Research in Politics and Society*, edited by Michael Wallace and Joyce Rothschild. Greenwich, CT: JAI Press, 1988.

"Diplomacy Focuses on Business." *Foreign Service Journal* 71 (March 1994): 32–41.

Dryden, Steve. "Untangling America's Technology Strategy: U.S. Export Control Policy Needs an Overhaul—and That May Be About To Happen." *International Economy* 4 (February–March, 1990): 40–46.

Feenstra, Robert C., et al. *Designing Policies To Open Trade.* NBER Working Paper no. 3258. Cambridge, MA: National Bureau of Economic Research, 1990. 26 pp.

Gardner, Bruce. *The Political Economy of U.S. Export Subsidies for Wheat.* NBER Working Paper no. 4747. Cambridge, MA: National Bureau of Economic Research, 1994. 75 pp.

Goldsborough, James O. "California's Foreign Policy." *Foreign Affairs* 72 (Spring 1993): 88–96.

Hillman, A. L., and H. W. Ursprung. "Domestic Politics, Foreign Interests, and International Trade Policy." *American Economic Review* 78 (September 1988): 729–745.

Irwin, D. A. "Strategic Trade Policy and Mercantilist Trade Rivalries." *American Economic Review* 82 (May 1992): 134–139.

Kahn, G. A. "Policy Implications of Trade and Currency Zones: A Summary of the Bank's 1991 Symposium [Federal Reserve Bank of Kansas City]." *Economic Review* 76 (November–December 1991): 37–51.

Kenety, William H. "Who Owns the Past? The Need for Legal Reform and Reciprocity in the International Art Trade." *Cornell International Law Journal* 23 (Winter 1990): 1–46.

Knetter, M. M. "International Comparisons of Pricing-to-Market Behavior [Price Discrimination Associated with Exchange-Rate Changes]." *American Economic Review* 83 (June 1993): 473–486.

Kumcu, M. E., and E. Kumcu. "Exchange Rate Policy Impact on Export Performance: What We Can Learn from the Turkish Experience." *Journal of Business Research* 23 (September 1991): 129–143.

Kurdila, Julianne. "The Introduction of Exotic Species into the United States: There Goes the Neighborhood." *Boston College Environmental Affairs Law Review* 16 (Fall 1988): 95–118.

Kuznets, Paul W. "Trade, Policy, and Korea–United States Relations." *Journal of Northeast Asian Studies* 8 (Winter 1989): 24–42.

Lenway, S. A., et al. "To Lobby or To Petition: The Political Environment of U.S. Trade Policy." *Journal of Management* 16 (March 1990): 119–134.

Marshall, Patrick G. "U.S. Trade Policy: Will Clinton Get Tough with America's Trading Partners?" *CQ Researcher* 3 (January 29, 1993): 75–95.

Monahan, Katherine E. "U.S. Sugar Policy: Domestic and International Repercussions of Sour Law." *Hastings International and Comparative Law Review* 15 (Winter 1992): 325–362.

Nelson, Douglas. "Domestic Political Preconditions of U.S. Trade Policy: Liberal Structure and Protectionist Dynamics." *Journal of Public Policy* 9 (January–March 1989): 83–108.

Ostry, S. "Governments and Corporations in a Shrinking World: Trade and Innovation Policies in the United States, Europe, and Japan." *Columbia Journal of World Business* 25 (Spring–Summer 1990): 10–16.

Rugman, Alan M., and Alan Verbeke. "Trade Policy and Global Corporate Strategy." *Global Marketing* 2, 3 (1989): 1–17.

Staiger, R. W., and G. Tabellini. "Discretionary Trade Policy and Excessive Protection." *American Economic Review* 77 (December 1987): 823–837.

Tilton, John E. "Mineral Endowment, Public Policy and Competitiveness: A Survey of Issues." *Resources Policy* 18 (December 1992): 237–249.

Torre, Fernando Castillo de la. "The EEC New Instrument of Trade Policy: Some Comments in the Light of the Latest Developments." *Common Market Law Review* 30 (August 1993): 687–719.

U.S. Congress. House. Committee on Foreign Affairs. *Chinese Forced Labor Exports to the United States: Hearings, September 23 and December 5, 1991, Before the Subcommittee on Human Rights and International Organizations, and on International Economic Policy and Trade.* 102d Cong., 1st sess. Washington, DC: GPO, 1992. 237 pp.

————. Subcommittee on International Economic Policy and Trade. *Technology Transfer to China: Hearing, July 8, 1987.* 100th Cong., 1st sess, Washington, DC: GPO, 1989. 95 pp.

U.S. Congress. House. Committee on Ways and Means. Subcommittee on Trade. *National Trade Policy Agenda: Hearings, February 28 and April 26, 1989.* 101st Cong., 1st sess. Washington, DC: GPO, 1989. 127 pp.

U.S. Congress. Senate. Committee on Finance. *Renewal of Fast-Track Authority and the Generalized System of Preferences Program: Hearing, May 20, 1993.* 103d Cong., 1st sess. Washington, DC: GPO, 1993. 98 pp.

Free Trade

"Asia's Environmental Offer to the West: You Free Trade, We'll Save Forests." *Far Eastern Economic Review* (June 4, 1992): 60–65.

Baer, Herbert L. "Foreign Competition in U.S. Banking Markets: Foreign Penetration of U.S. Wholesale Banking Already Exceeds That of Most Other Industry Groups; Unless Market Capitalization Ratios for U.S. Banks Go Up—or Down for Foreign Banks—This Trend Is Likely To Continue." *Economic Perspectives* 14 (May–June 1990): 22–29.

Blomstrom, Magnus, and Robert E. Lipsey. "The Export Performance of U.S. and Swedish Multinationals." *Review of Income and Wealth* 35 (September 1989): 245–264.

Bovenberg, A. L. "The Effects of Capital Income Taxation on International Competitiveness and Trade Flows." *American Economic Review* 79 (December 1989): 1045–1064.

Brand, Diana. "Regional Bloc Formation and World Trade." *Intereconomics* 27 (November–December 1992): 274–281.

Carter, Colin A. "The Economics of a Single North American Barley Market." *Canadian Journal of Agricultural Economics* 41 (November 1993): 243–255.

Christoforou, Theofanis. "Greek Law on Competition: An Analysis of Twelve Years' Case Law." *World Competition* 14 (September 1990): 49–77.

"Comparative Legal Aspects of the Environment for Innovation in Canada-U.S. Context: Proceedings of the Canada–United States Law Institute Conference, Cleveland, Ohio, April 14–16, 1989." *Canada–United States Law Journal* 15 (1989): 3–326.

Fieleke, Norman S. "One Trading World, or Many: The Issue of Regional Trading Blocs." *New England Economic Review* (May–June 1992): 1–20.

Friman, H. Richard. "From Policy Beliefs to Policy Choices: Resurgence of Tariff Retaliation in the U.S. Pursuit of Fair Trade." *Journal of Public Policy* 13 (April–June 1993): 163–182.

Gould, David, Graeme L. Woodbridge, and Roy J. Ruffin. "The Theory and Practice of Free Trade." *Federal Reserve Bank of Dallas Economic Review* (4th Quarter 1993): 1–16.

Hickok, Susan. "Recent Trade Liberalization in Developing Countries: The Effects on Global Trade and Output. *Federal Reserve Bank of New York Quarterly Review* 18 (Autumn 1993): 6–19.

Irwin, D. A. "Retrospectives: Challenges to Free Trade." *Journal of Economic Perspectives* 5 (Spring 1991): 1–8.

Kittichaisaree, Kriangsak. "Using Trade Sanctions and Subsidies To Achieve Environmental Objectives in the Pacific Rim." *Colorado Journal of International Environmental Law and Policy* 4 (Summer 1993): 296–322.

Krueger, Anne. *Free Trade Agreements as Protectionist Devices: Rules of Origin.* NBER Working Paper no. 4352. Cambridge, MA: National Bureau of Economic Research, 1993. 25 pp.

Krugman, P. R. "The Narrow and Broad Arguments for Free Trade." *American Economic Review* 83 (May 1993): 362–366.

Kulessa, Margaret E. "Free Trade and the Protection of the Environment: Is the GATT in Need of Reform? The GATT Negotiations under the Uruguay Round Have Almost Run Their Course; However, Consultations Are Certain To Continue, as Critics Regard the GATT

Rules on Environmental Protection as Inadequate." *Intereconomics* 27 (July–August 1992): 165–173.

Lloyd, Peter J. "Regionalism and World Trade." OECD (Organization for Economic Cooperation and Development) *Economic Studies* (Spring 1992): 7–43.

Miller, Randy E., and Jessica A. Wasserman. "Trade Relations between the European Community and the United States: An Overview of Current Issues and Trade Policy Institutions." *Boston College International and Comparative Law Review* 15 (Summer 1992): 339–342.

Mussa, M. "Making the Practical Case for Free Trade." *American Economic Review* 83 (May 1993): 372–376.

Nogués, Julio. "Less Than Fair Trade Cases against Latin American Countries." *World Economics* 14 (December 1991): 475–491.

"North American Energy Markets after Free Trade." *Energy Journal* 14, 3 (1993): 1–248.

Organization for Economic Cooperation and Development. *Assessing the Effects of the Uruguay Round.* Trade Policy Issues 2. Washington, DC, 1993. 38 pp.

Pastor, Robert A. "NAFTA's Green Opportunity: The Proposed North American Free Trade Agreement Can Make Possible Environmental Progress in All Three Countries." *Science and Technology* 9 (Summer 1993): 47–54.

Ramesh, M. "Explaining Cross-Industry Variations in Trade Protection: Textiles, Clothing and Footwear in Canada." *Review of International Studies* 20 (January 1994): 75–96.

Rayner, A. J., et al. "Agriculture in the Uruguay Round: An Assessment." *Economic Journal* 103 (November 1993): 1513–1527.

Rodrik, Dani. *The Rush to Free Trade in the Developing World: Why So Late? Why Now? Will It Last?* NBER Working Paper no. 3947. Cambridge, MA: National Bureau of Economic Research, 1992. 46 pp.

Staaf, Robert J. "The Law and Economics of the International Gray Market: Quality Assurance, Free-Riding and Passing Off." *Intellectual Property Journal* 4 (December 1988): 191–235.

U.S. Congress. House. Committee on Ways and Means. Subcommittee on Trade. *United States–China Trade Relations: Hearing, June 8, 1993.* 103d Cong., 1st sess. Washington, DC: GPO, 1993. 195 pp.

U.S. Custom Services. *The North American Free Trade Agreement: A Guide to Custom Procedures.* Customs Publication no. 571. Washington, DC: GPO, 1993. 44 pp.

Weintraub, Sidney, ed. "Free Trade in the Western Hemisphere." *Annals of the American Academy of Political and Social Science* 526 (March 1993): 9–194.

"Will Free Trade Link North and South?" *New Perspectives Quarterly* 10 (Fall 1993): 30–49.

"Will the Trade Blocs Affect Sustainable Development Positively?" *OPEC* (Organization of Petroleum Exporting Countries) *Bulletin* 24 (July–August 1993): 7–11.

Yoffie, D. B., and H. V. Milner. "An Alternative to Free Trade or Protectionism: Why Corporations Seek Strategic Trade Policy." *California Management Review* 31 (Summer 1989): 111–131.

General Agreement on Tariffs and Trade

Bethune, B. "Is There a Future for the GATT in the New World Economic Order?" *Business Economics* 27 (October 1992): 51–56.

Broadman, Harry G., and Carol Balassa. "Liberalizing International Trade in Telecommunication Services." *Columbia Journal of World Business* 4 (Winter 1993): 30–37.

Butler, Alison. "The Trade-Related Aspects of Intellectual Property Rights: What Is at Stake?" *Federal Reserve Bank of St. Louis Review* 72 (November–December 1990): 34–46.

Cloud, David S. "The GATT Battleground Shifts from Geneva to Capitol Hill: Anti-Dumping Rules Pit Domestic Producers against Large Exporters, While Congress Worries About How To Pay for the Agreement." *Congressional Quarterly Weekly Report* 52 (April 2, 1994): 792–795.

Emmert, Frank. "Intellectual Property in the Uruguay Round: Negotiating Strategies of the Western Industrialized Countries." *Michigan Journal of International Law* 11 (Summer 1990): 1317–1390.

Fisher, E. O'N., and H. de Gorter. "The International Effects of U.S. Farm Subsidies [Exports of Corn, Cotton, Rice, and Wheat]." *American Journal of Agricultural Economics* 74 (May 1992): 258–267.

"GATT Members Gear Up for Intense Phase of Negotiations [Special Report]." *Business America* 111 (September 10, 1990): 2–21.

Gavin, J. G., 3d. "Environmental Protection and the GATT: A Business View." *Columbia Journal of World Business* 27 (Fall–Winter 1992): 74–83.

"General Agreement on Tariffs and Trade—Multilateral Trade Negotiations (the Uruguay Round): Final Act Embodying the Results of the Uruguay Round of Trade Negotiations (December 15, 1993)." *International Legal Materials* 33 (January 1994): 1–152.

"International Energy Trade." *Journal of Energy and Natural Resources Law* 12 (February 1994): 4–185.

Junz, H. B., and C. Boonekamp. "What Is at Stake in the Uruguay Round?" *Finance and Development* 28 (June 1991): 10–15.

Just, R. E., and G. C. Rausser. "Environmental and Agricultural Policy Linkages and Reforms in the United States under GATT." *American Journal of Agricultural Economics* 74 (August 1992): 766–774.

Kulessa, Margaret E. "Free Trade and Protection of the Environment: Is the GATT in Need of Reform? The GATT Negotiations under the Uruguay Round Have Almost Run Their Course: However, Consultations Are Certain To Continue, as Critics Regard the GATT Rules on Environmental Protection as Inadequate." *Intereconomics* 27 (July–August 1992): 165–173.

Langguth, Gerd. "Will the GATT System Survive?" *Aussenpolitik* (Hamburg) 43, 3 (1992): 220–229.

Levinson, M. "Unfettering Trade in Services [Attempts to Bring Service Industries under GATT]." *Across the Board* 24 (April 1987): 24–31.

"NAFTA, APEC, GATT: Top Priority to Global Economics." *Foreign Policy Bulletin* 4 (January–April 1994): 59–86.

Prestowitz, C. V., Jr. "Life after GATT: More Trade Is Better Than Free Trade." *Technology Review* 94 (April 1991): 22–29.

Prestowitz, C. V., Jr., et al. "The Last Gasp of GATTism [Collapse of the Four-Year-Long Uruguay Round]." *Harvard Business Review* 69 (March–April 1991): 130–138.

Rayner, A. J., et al. "Agriculture in the Uruguay Round: An Assessment." *Economic Journal* 103 (November 1993): 1513–1527.

Riley, Tony. "Collapse of the GATT Uruguay Round: The Start of a U.S.-EC Trade War? Protectionism Is Usually Unleashed by an Economic Downturn or Other Shock to the System: The Deadlock in the Uruguay Round—Coming at the Peak of the 1980's Long Boom—Bodes Ill for the Future of the World Trading System." *Journal of European Business* 2 (March–April 1991): 5–10+.

Rivera-Batiz, L. A., and D. Xie. "GATT, Trade, and Growth." *American Economic Review* 82 (May 1992): 422–427.

Sills, C. F. "Draft-Horse, Not Dragon: Observations on Trade and the Environment [Uruguay Round of GATT]." *Columbia Journal of World Business* 27 (Fall–Winter 1992): 84–89.

U.S. Congress. House. Committee on Ways and Means. Subcommittee on Trade. *Uruguay Round of Multilateral Trade Negotiations: Hearing, April 11, 1989.* 101st Cong., 1st sess. Washington, DC: GPO, 1989. 86 pp.

United States–Canada Free Trade Agreement

Adams, Roy J., and Jerry P. White. "Labor and the Canada-U.S. Free Trade Agreement." *ILR* (Industrial and Labor Relations) *Report* 27 (Fall 1989): 15–21.

Buchanan, W. W. "The U.S. and Canada: Two Bottom Lines [Differences in Accounting Practices]." *Financial Executive* 4 (September–October 1988): 38–43.

Button, Kenneth R. "The United States–Canada Free Trade Agreement: An Overview and an Assessment for the U.S. Non-ferrous Metals and Forest Products Industries." *Law and Policy in International Business* 20, 4 (1989): 765–793.

"The Canada–United States Free Trade Agreement and Its Implications for Small Business." *Journal of Small Business Management* 28 (April 1990): 64–69.

Chandra, Satish. "An Examination of Free Trade Agreement between the United States and Canada." *Tennessee's Business* 1 (Spring 1990): 15–19.

Cohen, Marshall A., and Stephen Blank, eds. "The Challenge of the Canada–United States Free Trade Agreement: An Assessment from Many Perspectives." *American Review of Canadian Studies* 21 (Summer–Autumn 1991): 141–351.

"Comparative Legal Aspects of the Environment for Innovation in the Canada-U.S. Context: Proceedings of the Canada–United States Law Institute Conference, Cleveland, Ohio, April 14–16, 1989." *Canada-U.S. Law Journal* 15 (1989): 3–326.

Crawford, Michael. "Who's Abusing Whom? It's Not Hard To Find Canadian Companies That Feel Burned by the Free Trade Agreements; But Americans Insist That We're Not Playing Fair: Are They Bullies or Are We Just Chronic Complainers?" *Canadian Business* 65 (August 1992): 32–36+.

Daly, D. J. "Canadian Manufacturers Can't Compete." *Business Quarterly* 56 (Winter 1992): 76–80.

Drover, Glenn. "Free Trade and Social Policy: The Canadian Debate." *Social Policy and Administration* 29 (August 1989): 128–141.

Frenzel, K. A., and Douglas J. McCready. "Canada–United States Free Trade: Concern over Social Problems." *American Journal of Economics and Sociology* 51 (July 1992): 349–357.

Globerman, Steven, and Peter Booth. "The Canada-U.S. Free Trade Agreement and the Telecommunications Industry." *Telecommunications Policy* 13 (December 1989): 319–328.

Harrington, James W., Jr. "Implications of the Canada–United States Free Trade Agreement for Regional Provision of Producer Services." *Economic Geography* 65 (October 1989): 314–328.

Langille, Brian A. "Canadian Labour Law Reform and Free Trade." *Ottawa Law Review* 6, 3 (1991): 581–622.

Liesch, P. W. "International Trade in an Imperfectly Competitive Environment: Mandated Counter-trade." *International Journal of Technology Management* 5, 4 (1990): 423–430.

Reynolds, Stephen E., and James E. Seidelman. "Structural Impacts of the U.S.-Canadian Free Trade Agreement." *Canadian Public Policy* 19 (March 1993): 86–92.

"U.S.-Canada Free Trade Agreement." *Department of State Bulletin* 89 (October 1989): 1–16.

U.S. Congress. House. Committee on Small Business. *The Free Trade Agreement: Hearing, October 4, 1989.* 101st Cong., 1st sess. Washington, DC: GPO, 1990. 135 pp.

———. *What Is Next for the United States–Canada Free Trade Agreement? Hearings, September 4 and October 1, 1991.* 102d Cong., 1st sess. Washington, DC: GPO, 1992. 229 pp.

U.S. Congress. House. Committee on Ways and Means. *Customs' Enforcement of the Rules-of-Origin Provisions of the United States–Canada Free-Trade Agreement: Hearing, October 16, 1991, Before the Subcommittee on Trade, and the Subcommittee on Oversight.* 102d Cong., 1st Sess. Washington, DC: GPO, 1992. 141 pp.

U.S. Congress. Senate. Committee on Finance. Subcommittee on International Trade. *Bilateral Trade Agreements: Hearing, March 13, 1989.* 101st Cong., 1st sess. Washington, DC: GPO, 1989. 97 pp.

———. *Oversight of the United States–Canada Free Trade Agreement: Hearing, April 7, 1989.* 101st Cong., 1st sess. Washington, DC: GPO, 1989. 96 pp.

U.S. Congress. Senate. Committee on the Judiciary. *United States–Canada Free Trade Agreement: Hearing, May 20, 1988, on the Constitutionality of Establishing a Binational Panel to Resolve Disputes in Antidumping and Countervailing Duty Cases.* 100th Cong, 2d sess. Washington, DC: GPO, 1990. 283 pp.

Whalley, John. "CUSTA [Canada-U.S. Trade Agreement] and NAFTA [North American Free Trade Agreement]: Can WHFTA [Western Hemisphere Free Trade Area] Be Far Behind?" *Journal of Common Market Studies* 30 (June 1992): 125–141.

North American Free Trade Agreement

"All Wet on NAFTA." *International Economics* 7 (July–August 1993): 5–18.

Arden-Clarke, Charles. "South-North Terms of Trade, Environmental Protection, and Sustainable Development." *International Environmental Affairs* 4 (Spring 1992): 122–138.

Barkema, Alan. "The North American Free Trade Agreement: What Is at Stake for U.S. Agriculture?" *Federal Reserve Bank of Kansas City Economic Review* 77, 3 (1992): 5–20.

Brown, Drusilla K., et al. "North American Integration." *Economic Journal* 102 (November 1992): 1507–1518.

Castañeda, Jorge G. "Can NAFTA Change Mexico?" *Foreign Affairs* 72 (September–October 1993): 66–80.

Cloud, David S. "Free-Trade Pact Buffeted By Election-Year Forces: Hill Debate Mirrors Presidential Campaign Jockeying; Blows This Year May Shape NAFTA's Fate." *Congressional Quarterly Weekly Report* 50 (September 12, 1992): 2699–2701.

————. "Sound and Fury over NAFTA Overshadows the Debate: Actual Terms of the Agreement Seem To Have Little To Do with Emotional Arguments over Trade Accord's Effect." *Congressional Quarterly Weekly Report* 51 (October 16, 1993): 2791–2796.

"Debating NAFTA." *Foreign Policy* (Winter 1993–1994): 91–114.

Fisher, Robert C. "NAFTA: A U.S. Perspective." *SAIS* (School of Advanced International Studies) *Review* 12 (Winter–Spring 1992): 43–55.

Fraser, D. "NAFTA Strategies for Canadian Manufacturers." *Business Quarterly* 57 (Summer 1993): 84–92.

Friedman, Sheldon. "NAFTA as Social Dumping." *Challenge* 35 (September–October 1992): 27–32.

Galbraith, James K. "A New Picture of the American Economy." *American Prospect* (Fall 1991): 24–36.

Gantz, David A. "A Preliminary Assessment of the North American Free Trade Agreement." *Bulletin of International Fiscal Documentation* 46 (September 1992): 424–429.

Glasmeier, Amy, et al. "Tequila Sunset? NAFTA and the U.S. Apparel Industry." *Challenge* 36 (November–December 1993): 37–45.

Godwin, Stephen R. "The North American Free Trade Agreement: Implications for Transportation." *Government Finance Review* 9 (June 1993) 11–14.

Gooding, Elmer, and Jose Mendez. "The North American Free Trade Agreement." *Arizona Business* 39 (November 1992): 1–7.

Grennes, Thomas, and Barry Krissoff. "Agricultural Trade in a North American Free Trade Agreement." *World Economics* 16 (July 1993): 483–502.

Grossman, Gene M., and Alan B. Krueger. *Environmental Impacts of a North American Free Trade Agreement.* NBER Working Paper no. 3914. Cambridge, MA: National Bureau of Economic Research, 1991. 55 pp.

Gruben, William C., and John H. Welch. "Is NAFTA Economic Integration?" *Federal Reserve Bank of Dallas Economic Review* (2d Quarter 1994): 35–51.

Hummels, David, and Robert M. Stern. "Evolving Patterns of North American Merchandise Trade and Foreign Direct Investment, 1960–1990." *World Economy* 17 (January 1994): 5–29.

Kim, John J., and James P. Cargas. "The Environmental Side Agreement to the North American Free Trade Agreement: Background and Analysis." *Environmental Law Reporter* 23 (December 1993): 10720–10733.

Lapp, David, and Nadav Sadio. "NAFTA: Tracking the Border." *Multinational Monitor* 14 (May 1993): 8–13.

Lederman, Alan S., and Bobbe Hirsh. "U.S.-Mexico Tax Treaty Complements NAFTA." *Journal of Taxation* 79 (August 1993): 100–107.

Marshall, Patrick G. "North American Trade Pact: A Good Idea? The U.S.-Canada Free-Trade Pact, Which Took Effect Early This Year, May Serve as a Model for Future Bilateral Pacts with Mexico, the Caribbean and Central America." *Editorial Research Reports* (December 8, 1989): 682–695.

"Mini Symposium: Modelling North American Free Trade." *World Economics* 15 (January 1992): 1–100.

"NAFTA Crucible: Undecided Members Weigh Voter Fears as Trade Pact Showdown Approaches." *Congressional Quarterly Weekly Report* 51 (November 6, 1993): 3011–3022.

"NAFTA—What If It Loses?" *Business Week* (November 22, 1993): 32–43.

"North American Free Trade Agreement Debate: Where Domestic and Foreign Policy Meet." *Foreign Policy Bulletin* 3 (November–December 1992): 24–43.

"North American Free Trade Agreement: Pros & Cons." *Congressional Digest* 72 (November 1993): 257–288.

Owens, Ray, and Russ Parrish. "NAFTA's Impact on the District." Richmond, VA: *Federal Reserve Bank of Richmond Cross Sections* 10 (Winter 1993–1994): 1–5.

"Remarks at a Signing Ceremony for the North American Free Trade Agreement Supplemental Agreements, September 14, 1993." *Weekly Compilation of Presidential Documents* 29 (September 20, 1993): 1754–1759.

Ros, Jaime. "Free Trade Area or Common Capital Market? Notes on Mexico-U.S. Economic Integration and Current NAFTA Negotiations." *Journal of Interamerican Studies and World Affairs* 34 (Summer 1992): 53–91.

Rugman, A. M. "Investing in the U.S. after NAFTA [Canadian Business]." *Business Quarterly* 57 (Summer 1993): 26–31.

Sczudlo, Raymond S. "NAFTA Opportunities Abound for U.S. and Canadian Financial Institutions." *Bankers Magazine* (Boston) 176 (July–August 1993): 28–33.

"The Social Charter Implications of the NAFTA." *Canada-U.S. Outlook* 3 (August 1992): 3–59.

"Special Issues: The Case against NAFTA." *Multinational Monitor* 14 (October 1993): 5–33.

Stokes, Bruce. "A Hard Sell: The Clinton Administration Is Shooting for a Mid-November House Vote on the North American Free Trade Agreement." *National Journal* 25 (October 16, 1993): 2472–2476.

––––––. "In Your Face: Early On, U.S. Trade Representative Mickey Kantor's Penchant for Confrontation Raised Eyebrows: He's Toned Down His Rhetoric—and Produced Results; But He'll Be Tested as Never Before in the Coming Debate over the North American Free Trade Agreement." *National Journal* 25 (August 21, 1993): 2068–2072.

––––––. "Mexican Roulette: For Most Capitol Hill Lawmakers, the North American Free Trade Agreement Is a No-Win Proposition: NAFTA Would Open Up New Markets for U.S. Products in Mexico, But It Would Also Give U.S. Companies Incentives To Set Up Shop There: Voters Are Divided on the Issue, But with Ross Perot on the Warpath, NAFTA Is in Deep Trouble." *National Journal* 25 (May 15, 1993): 1160–1164.

––––––. "On the Brink: Last Year a Broad North American Trade Agreement Appeared To Be a Done Deal: But with Polls Showing Many Americans Worried about Losing Jobs to Mexico—and with a Bitter Presidential Campaign Brewing—Odds Are Growing That the Pact Will Be Shelved for a Year." *National Journal* 24 (February 29, 1992): 504–509.

"Symposium on the North American Free Trade Agreement." *Harvard International Law Journal* 34 (Spring 1993): 305–443.

U.S. Congress. House. Committee on Agriculture. Subcommittee on General Farm Commodities. *Impact of Canadian Grain Imports on United States Producers and Markets: Hearings, June 11–12, 1993.* 103d Cong., 1st sess. Washington, DC: GPO, 1993. 295 pp.

U.S. Congress. House. Committee on Energy and Commerce. Subcommittee on Commerce, Consumer Protection and Competitiveness. *North American Free Trade Agreement: Hearings, March 20–May 15, 1991.* 102d Cong., 1st sess. Washington, DC: GPO, 1991. 355 pp.

U.S. Congress. House. Committee on Foreign Affairs. *The North American Free Trade Agreement: Environment and Labor Agreements: Joint Hearings, February 24, 1993, Before the Subcommittee on Economic Policy, Trade and Environment and Western Hemisphere Affairs.* 103d Cong., 1st sess. Washington, DC: GPO, 1993. 132 pp.

————. *The North American Free Trade Agreement: Hearing, March 6–April 16, 1991, Before the Subcommittee on International Economic Policy and Trade on Western Hemisphere Affairs.* 102d Cong., 1st sess. Washington, DC: GPO, 1991. 312 pp.

U.S. Congress. House. Committee on Government Operations. Commerce, Consumer, and Monetary Affairs Subcommittee. *The North American Free Trade Agreement (NAFTA) and Its Impact on the Textile/Apparel/Fiber and Auto and Auto Parts Industries, Hearing, May 4, 1993.* 103d Cong., 1st sess. Washington, DC: GPO, 1993. 233 pp.

U.S. Congress. House. Committee on Small Business. *The North American Free Trade Agreement: Hearing, March 24, 1993.* 103d Cong., 1st sess. Washington, DC: GPO, 1993. 100 pp.

U.S. Congress. Senate. Committee on Banking, Housing, and Urban Affairs. *The Impact of the North American Free Trade Agreement on U.S. Jobs and Wages: Hearing, April 22, 1993.* 103d Cong., 1st sess. Washington, DC: GPO, 1993. 151 pp.

U.S. Congress. Senate. Committee on Commerce, Science, and Transportation. *Surface Transportation Implications of NAFTA: Hearing, May 4, 1993.* 103d Cong., 1st sess. Washington, DC: GPO, 1993. 101 pp.

U.S. Department of Commerce. International Trade Administration. *North American Free Trade Agreement Opportunities for U.S. Industries: NAFTA Industry Sector Reports.* Washington, DC, 1993. Various paging.

U.S. General Accounting Office. *North American Free Trade Agreement: U.S. Mexican Trade and Investment Data: Report to the Honorable Richard A. Gephardt, Majority Leader, and to the Honorable Sander Levin, House of Representatives.* Report B-250299. Gaithersburg, MD, 1992. 119 pp.

Valiante, Marcia, and Paul Muldoon. "Annual Review of Canada–United States Environmental Relations, 1992." *International Environmental Affairs* 5 (Summer 1993): 200–218.

Vaznauh, Richard. "Extraterritorial Jurisdiction: Environmental Muscle for the North American Free Trade Agreement." *Hastings International and Comparative Law Review* 17 (Fall 1993): 207–240.

Vialet, Joyce C. "The North American Free Trade Agreement and Immigration." *Migration World Magazine* 21, 2/3 (1993): 23–36.

"Will Free Trade Link North and South?" *New Perspectives Quarterly* 10 (Fall 1993) 30–49.

Trade Regulations

Trade Barriers

Adams, Paul H. "Suspension of Generalized System of Preferences from Chile: The Proper Use of a Trade Provision?" *George Washington Journal of International Law and Economics* 23, 2 (1989): 501–530.

Calvo, G. A. "Costly Trade Liberalization: Durable Goods and Capital Mobility." *International Monetary Fund Staff Papers* 35 (September 1988): 461–473.

Coughlin, Cletus C., et al. "Protectionist Trade Policies: A Survey of Theory, Evidence and Rationale. *Federal Reserve Bank of St. Louis Review* 70 (January–February 1988): 12–26.

Coughlin, Cletus C., and Geoffrey E. Wood. "An Introduction to Non-tariff Barriers in Trade." *Federal Reserve Bank of St. Louis Review* 71 (January–February 1989): 32–46.

Crook, Olive. "Nothing To Lose But Its Chains: A Survey of World Trade." *Economist* (London) 316 (September 22, 1990): 60 ff. (40 pp.).

European Communities Commission. *Report on United States Trade Barriers and Unfair Practices, 1991: Problems of Doing Business with the U.S.* Brussels, Belgium: Directorate General for External Relations, 1992. 87 pp.

Finger, J. Michael, and Tracy Murray. "Policing Unfair Imports: The United States Example." *Journal of World Trade* 24 (August 1990): 39–50.

Goehle, Donna G. "The Buy American Act: Is It Irrelevant in a World of Multinational Corporations?" *Columbia Journal of World Business* 24 (Winter 1989): 10–15.

Grossman, G. M., and H. Horn. "Infant-Industry Protection Reconsidered: The Case of Informational Barriers to Entry." *Quarterly Journal of Economics* 103 (November 1988): 767–787.

Hillman, Arye L. "Protectionist Policies as the Regulation of International Industry." *Public Choice* 67 (November 1990): 101–110.

Lawrence, R. Z., and R. E. Litan. "The Protectionist Prescription: Errors in Diagnosis and Cure." *Brookings Papers on Economic Activity* no. 1 (1987): 289–310.

Livingston, L. A., and S. Richards. "U.S. Import and Export Prices Continued To Register Sizable Gains in 1988." *Monthly Labor Review* 112 (May 1989): 11–33.

Ohno, K. "Export Pricing Behavior of Manufacturing: A U.S.-Japan Comparison." *International Monetary Fund Staff Papers* 36 (September 1989): 550–579.

Orr, J. "The Performance of the U.S. Capital Goods Industry: Implications for Trade Adjustments." *Federal Reserve Bank of New York Quarterly Review* 13 (Winter–Spring 1989): 69–82.

Pasquero, J. "Bilateral Protectionism: Lessons from a Cause Célèbre [Subway Car Sale by Bombardier of Montreal to New York City]." *California Management Review* 30 (Winter 1988): 124–141.

Pursell, Garry. "Industrial Sickness, Primary and Secondary: The Effects of Exit Constraints on Industrial Performance." *World Bank Economic Review* 4 (January 1990): 103–114.

Rabino, S., and J. Zif. "How To Counter the Onslaught of Imports." *Journal of Business Strategy* 8 (Summer 1987): 58–64.

Raina, H. K. "Techniques for Monitoring and Administering Import Contracts." *International Trade Forum* 27 (April–June 1991): 20–25.

Tornell, A. "Time Inconsistency of Protectionist Programs." *Quarterly Journal of Economics* 106 (August 1991): 963–974.

U.S. Congress. House. Committee on Energy and Commerce. Subcommittee on Oversight and Investigations. *Unfair Foreign Trade Practices: Hearings, March 1–2, 1989.* 101st Cong., 1st sess. Washington, DC: GPO, 1989. 403 pp.

U.S. Congress. House. Committee on Ways and Means. *American Jobs and Manufacturing Preservation Act of 1991: Hearing, October 3, 1991, on H.R. 2889 To Amend the Internal Revenue Code of 1986 To End Deferral for*

United States Shareholders on Income of Controlled Foreign Corporations Attributable to Property Imported into the United States. 102d Cong., 1st sess. Washington, DC: GPO, 1991. 186 pp.

U.S. Office of the U.S. Trade Representative. *National Trade Estimate Report on Foreign Trade Barriers, 1993.* Washington, DC: GPO, 1993. 275 pp.

————. *National Trade Estimate Report on Foreign Trade Barriers, 1992.* Washington, DC: GPO, 1992. 267 pp.

————. *National Trade Estimate Report on Foreign Trade Barriers, 1990.* Washington, DC: GPO, 1990. 216 pp.

Weimer, G. A. "World Trade: Is the Playing Field Level?" *Industry Week* 241 (May 18, 1992): 21–42.

Winkler, G. M. "Intermediation under Trade Restrictions." *Quarterly Journal of Economics* 104 (May 1989): 299–324.

Gray Markets

Cavusgil, S. T., and E. Sikora. "How Multinationals Can Counter Gray Market Imports." *Columbia Journal of World Business* 23 (Winter 1988): 75–85.

Cespedes, F. V., et al. "Gray Markets: Causes and Cures." *Harvard Business Review* 66 (July–August 1988): 75–82.

Duhan, D. F., and M. J. Sheffet. "Gray Markets and the Legal Status of Parallel Importation." *Journal of Marketing* 52 (July 1988): 75–83.

Hopp, R. Richard. "K Mart v. Cartier: The Supreme Court Decides the Gray Market Problem." *Maryland Journal of International Law and Trade* 14 (Spring 1990): 21–41.

Inman, J. E. "Gray Marketing of Imported Trademarked Goods: Tariffs and Trademark Issues." *American Business Law Journal* 31 (May 1993): 59–116.

Kaikati, Jack G. "Gray Marketers: A Growing Conflict in International Channels of Distribution." *Journal of Managerial Issues* 1 (Winter 1989): 192–204

Labor and International Trade

Abowd, John M., and Richard B. Freeman. *The Internationalization of the U.S. Labor Market.* NBER Working Paper no. 3321. Cambridge, MA: National Bureau of Economic Research, 1990. 41 pp.

Armah, Bartholomew K. "Impact of Trade on Service Sector Employment: Implications for Women and Minorities." *Contemporary Economic Policy* 12 (January 1994): 67–68.

Bernstein, Aaron. "The Global Economy: Who Gets Hurt; Free Trade Is a Net Plus—But Not for Everyone." *Business Week* (August 10, 1992): 48–53.

Charnovitz, Steve. "Environmental and Labour Standards in Trade." *World Economics* 15 (May 1992): 335–356.

Hunter, Linda C. "U.S. Trade Protection: Effects on the Industrial and Regional Composition of Employment." *Federal Reserve Bank of Dallas Economic Review* (January 1990): 1–13.

Karier, T. "Unions and the U.S. Comparative Advantage." *Industrial Relations* 30 (Winter 1991): 1–19.

Leamer, Edward E. *Wage Effects of a U.S.-Mexican Free Trade Agreement.* NBER Working Paper no. 3991. Cambridge, MA: National Bureau of Economic Research, 1992. 88 pp.

Mehl, Georg. *U.S. Manufactured Exports & Export-Related Employment: Profiles of the 50 States and 49 Selected Metropolitan Areas for 1986.* Washington, DC: United States Department of Commerce, International Trade Administration, Office of Trade and Investment Analysis, 1990. 118 pp.

Revenga, A. L. "Exporting Jobs? The Impact of Import Competition on Employment and Wages in U.S. Manufacturing [Import Prices]." *Quarterly Journal of Economics* 107 (February 1992): 255–284.

Simcox, David E. "Immigration and Free Trade with Mexico: Protecting American Workers against Double Jeopardy." *Population and Environment* 14 (November 1992): 159–175.

Stokes, Bruce. "Protection for a Price: Congress Is Warning the U.S. Auto Industry That If It Wants To Be Protected against Japanese Car

Imports It Will Have To Show What It Is Willing To Do for Itself." *National Journal* 24 (April 4, 1992): 794–799.

U.S. Congress. House. Committee on Government Operations. Employment, Housing, and Aviation Subcommittee. *Trade Adjustment Assistance: A Failure for Displaced Workers: Hearing, October 19, 1993.* 103d Cong., 1st sess. Washington, DC: GPO, 1993. 204 pp.

U.S. Congress. House. Committee on the Budget. Task Force on Urgent Fiscal Issues. *Loss of Manufacturing Jobs: Impact on Our Future Ability to Compete in the Global Market: Hearing, September 24, 1992.* 102d Cong., 2d sess. Washington, DC: GPO, 1992. 125 pp.

U.S. Congress. Senate. Committee on Finance. *Trade Adjustment Assistance for Dislocated Workers: Hearing, October 3, 1991.* 102d Cong., 1st sess. Washington, DC: GPO, 1992. 89 pp.

U.S. Department of Commerce. Trade Promotion Co-ordinating Committee. *Toward a National Export Strategy: U.S. Exports—U.S. Jobs: Report to the U.S. Congress, September 30, 1993.* Washington, DC: GPO, 1993. 104 pp.

U.S. Department of Labor. Bureau of International Labor Affairs. *Labor Standards and Development in the Global Economy.* Washington, DC: GPO, 1990. 265 pp.

International Competition

Ahijado, Manuel, et al. "The Competitiveness of Spanish Industry." *National Economic Review* (November 1993): 90–104.

"American Economic Competitiveness." *Congressional Digest* 71 (December 1992): 289–314.

Armey, Dick. "An Economic Strategy for the U.S.: Why the Market Works Best." *Strategic Review* 22 (Winter 1994): 25–33.

Barnet, Richard J., and John Cavanagh. "Creating a Level Playing Field." *Technology Review* 97 (May–June 1994): 46–53.

Carbaugh, Robert, and Darwin Wassink. "Environmental Standards and International Competitiveness." *World Competition* 16 (September 1992): 81–91.

"Competitiveness of the North American Auto Industry." *UMTRI* (University of Michigan Transportation Research Institute) *Research Review* 23 (November–December 1992): 1–16.

"Conference Proceedings: An Industrial Policy for North America/Canada/U.S.: Legal and Economic Considerations." *Canada–United States Law Journal* 19 (1993): 1–401.

Cox, James D., and Gary Lynch, eds. "International Regulatory Competition and the Securities Law." *Law and Contemporary Problems* 55 (Autumn 1992): 1–424.

"Industrial Policy: Investing in America." *Stanford Law and Policy Review* 5 (Fall 1993): 11–151.

Marshall, Patrick G. "U.S. Trade Policy: Will Clinton Get Tough with America's Trading Partners?" *CQ Researcher* 3 (January 29, 1993): 75–95.

Neto, Alfredo Lopes da Silva. "The International Effects of Mining Projects: The Case of Carajas Iron Ore." *Resources Policy* 19 (June 1993): 124–130.

"Playing by the Rules: A Guide to Competition Law around the World." *International Financial Law Review* (May 1993): 55-page supplement.

Rehder, Robert R. "Is Saturn Competitive? GMs Innovative Offspring Has a Mixed Record, Depending upon One's Criteria for Effectiveness." *Business Horizons* 37 (March–April 1994): 7–15.

Rill, James F. "Statement of Japanese Competition Policies and the U.S. Response before the U.S. Senate Committee on Judiciary, 29 July 1992." *World Competition* 16 (September 1992): 143–149.

"Special Issue: Global Competition and New Forms of International Cooperation." *International Spectator* 28 (April–June 1993): 3–105.

Stevens, Candice. "Do Environmental Policies Affect Competitiveness?" *OECD* (Organization for Economic Cooperation and Development) *Observer* (August–September 1993): 22–25.

Sullivan, Patrick. "Antidumping Law and the Dumping of Services." *New York University Journal of International Law and Politics* 24 (Summer 1992): 1677–1709.

Taylor, Alex, III. "The New Golden Age of Autos." *Fortune* 129 (April 4, 1994): 50–57+.

———. "U.S. Cars Come Back." *Fortune* 126 (November 16, 1992): 52–59+.

Taylor, Charles R., and J. Henisz Witold. *U.S. Manufacturers in the Global Marketplace: A Research Report.* Report no. 1058-94-RR. New York: Conference Board, 1994. 39 pp.

United Nations. Trade and Development Board. *Concentration of Market Power, Through Mergers, Takeovers, Joint Ventures and Other Acquisitions of Control, and Its Effects on International Markets, in Particular the Markets of Developing Countries.* New York, 1993. 72 pp.

U.S. Congress. House. Committee on Energy and Commerce. Subcommittee on Telecommunications and Finance. *Corporate Governance: Hearing, April 21, 1993.* 103d Cong., 1st sess. Washington, DC: GPO, 1994. 58 pp.

U.S. Congress. House. Committee on Science, Space, and Technology. *Biotechnology: Hearing, November 8, 1993.* 103d Cong., 1st sess. Washington, DC: GPO, 1994, 105 pp.

U.S. Congress. House. Committee on the Judiciary. Subcommittee on Economics and Commercial Law. *International Competition in the Steel Industry: Hearing, September 30, 1993.* 103d Cong., 1st sess. Washington, DC: GPO, 1993. 78 pp.

U.S. Congress. House. Committee on Ways and Means. Subcommittee on Trade. *U.S. International Trade Performance and Outlook: Competitive Position in the Automotive, Aerospace, and Chemical and Pharmaceutical Sectors: Hearing, March 11–April 7, 1992.* 102d Cong., 2d sess. Washington, DC: GPO, 1992. 669 pp.

U.S. Congress. Senate. Committee on Banking, Housing, and Urban Affairs. *The Fair Trade in Financial Services Act of 1993—S. 1527: Hearing, October 26, 1993, on S. 1527 Is Designed To Give U.S. Negotiators New Leverage To Obtain Same Quality of Competitive Opportunity for U.S. Financial Firms Operating in Foreign Markets That We Extend to Foreign Firms in Our Markets.* 103d Cong., 1st sess. Washington, DC: GPO, 1994. 87 pp.

U.S. Congress. Senate. Committee on Finance. Subcommittee on International Trade. *Renewing `Super 301': Hearing, June 14, 1993.* 103d Cong., 1st sess. Washington, DC: GPO, 1993. 80 pp.

U.S. Congress. Senate. Committee on Finance. Subcommittee on Taxation. *Alternative Minimum Tax: Hearing, February 19, 1992.* 102d Cong., 2d sess. Washington, DC: GPO, 1992. 90 pp.

U.S. Congress. Senate. Committee on the Judiciary. *Unfair Trade Practices: Hearings, January 10–27, 1992, on S. 986, a Bill To Amend Title 28 of the United States Code To Expand the Original Jurisdiction of Federal District Courts in Certain Civil Actions.* 102d Cong., 2d sess. Washington, DC: GPO, 1992. 443 pp.

Export-Import Bank

Carmichael, C. M. "The Interdependence of Firm and Government Behavior: Boeing and Eximbank [Game Theory Applied to Firm's Strategy in Setting Trade Policy]." *Applied Economics* 23, 1A (January 1991): 107–112.

Carnevale, Francesca, and Jack Lowenstein. "Exim [Export-Import Bank of United States] and Jexim [Export-Import Bank of Japan]: A Duopoly of ECA Initiative." *Trade Finance* (April 1992): 37–43.

Holden, A. C. "U.S. Official Export-Finance Support: Can American Exporters Expect a Competitive Eximbank To Emerge." *Columbia Journal of World Business* 24 (Fall 1989): 33–46.

U.S. Congress. House. Committee on Banking, Finance and Urban Affairs. *Iraqi and Banca Nazionale del Lavoro Participation in Export-Import Programs: Hearing, April 17, 1992.* 102d Cong., 1st sess. Washington, DC: GPO, 1991. 159 pp.

U.S. Congress. House. Committee on Banking, Finance and Urban Affairs. Subcommittee on International Development, Finance, Trade, and Monetary Policy. *Export-Import Bank: Hearing, April 11, 1991.* 102d Cong., 1st sess. Washington, DC: GPO, 1991. 332 pp.

———. *Export-Import Bank of the United States: Tied Aid Credits and Other Issues: Hearing, May 10, 1990.* 101st Cong., 1st sess. Washington, DC: GPO, 1990. 81 pp.

──────. *Proposal for Export-Import Financing of Defense Articles and Services: Hearing, May 2, 1991.* 102d Cong., 1st sess. Washington, DC: GPO, 1992. 208 pp.

U.S. Congress. House. Committee on Foreign Affairs. Subcommittee on International Economic Policy and Trade. *Export-Import Bank Report to Congress on Tied Aid Credit Practices: Hearing, May 8, 1989.* 101st Cong., 1st sess. Washington, DC: GPO, 1989. 101 pp.

U.S. Congress. House. Committee on Government Operations. Commercial, Consumer and Monetary Affairs Subcommittee. *Export Promotion Programs of the Foreign Commercial Service and the Export-Import Bank: Hearing, September 27, 1983.* 98th Cong., 1st sess. Washington, DC: GPO, 1983. 323 pp.

U.S. Congress. House. Committee on Small Business. Subcommittee on Exports, Tax Policy, and Special Problems. *Increasing Small Business Participation in SBA and Eximbank Export Financing Programs: Hearing, July 9, 1991.* 102d Cong., 1st sess. Washington, DC: GPO, 1991. 274 pp.

U.S. Congress. Senate. Committee on Banking, Housing, and Urban Affairs. Subcommittee on International Finance and Monetary Policy. *The Tied Aid Credit War Chest of the Export-Import Bank of the United States: Hearing, September 13, 1989, To Survey Trends and Developments over the Three Years of the Fund's Existence and To Consider Policy Proposals for the Future.* 101st Cong., 1st sess. Washington, DC: GPO, 1990. 141 pp.

U.S. Congress. Senate. Committee on Small Business. Subcommittee on Export Promotion and Market Development. *Financing of Small Business Exports by the Export-Import Bank: Hearing, May 10, 1984.* 98th Cong., 2d sess. Washington, DC: GPO, 1984. 217 pp.

Foreign Exchange

Alam, M. S. "Transaction Costs of Trade: Some Partial Equilibrium Results." *Southern Economic Journal* 57 (October 1990): 323–329.

Dryden, J., et al. "Comparison of Purchasing Power Parity between the United States and Canada." *Monthly Labor Review* 110 (December 1987): 7–24.

Flood, M. D. "Microstructure Theory and the Foreign Exchange Market." *Federal Reserve Bank of St. Louis Review* 73 (November–December 1991): 52–70.

"Foreign Exchange Review [Special Report]." *Euromoney* (May 1991): 79–102.

Klein, M. W., and E. S. Rosengren. "Foreign Exchange Intervention as a Signal of Monetary Policy [U.S. and West Germany]." *New England Economic Review* (May–June 1991): 39–50.

Trade and Environment

Butler, A. "Environmental Protection and Free Trade: Are They Mutually Exclusive?" *Federal Reserve Bank of St. Louis Review* 74 (May–June 1992): 3–16.

"Free Trade Negotiations with Mexico: Environmental Matters." *International Environmental Affairs* 3 (Summer 1991): 219–231.

Housman, Robert, and Durwood Zaelke. "Trade, Environment, and Sustainable Development: A Primer." *Hastings International and Comparative Law Review* 15 (Summer 1992): 535–612.

Kim, John J., and James P. Cargas. "The Environmental Side Agreement to the North American Free Trade Agreement: Background and Analysis." *Environmental Law Reporter* 23 (December 1993): 10720–10733.

McKeith, Malissa Hathaway. "The Environment and Free Trade: Meeting Halfway at the Mexican Border." *UCLA* (University of California–Los Angeles) *Pacific Basin Law Journal* 10 (Fall 1991): 183–211.

Organization for Economic Cooperation and Development. *The Environmental Effects of Trade.* Paris, France, 1994. 206 pp.

Pastor, Robert A. "NAFTA's Green Opportunity: The Proposed North American Free Trade Agreement Can Make Possible Environmental Progress in All Three Countries." *Science and Technology* 9 (Summer 1993): 47–54.

Schoenbaum, Thomas J., and Edith Brown Weiss. "Agora: Trade and Environment." *American Journal of International Law* 86 (October 1992): 700–735.

Shrybman, Steven. "Trading Away the Environment." *World Policy Journal* 9 (Winter 1991–1992): 93–110.

Stevens, Candice. "Harmonization, Trade, and the Environment." *International Environmental Affairs* 5 (Winter 1993): 42–49.

U.S. Congress. House. Committee on Energy and Commerce: Subcommittee on Health and the Environment. *GATT: Implications on Environmental Laws: Hearing, September 27, 1991.* 102d Cong., 1st sess. Washington, DC: GPO, 1991. 101 pp.

U.S. Congress. House. Committee on Foreign Affairs. *The North American Free Trade Agreement: Environment and Labor Agreements: Joint Hearings, February 24, 1993, Before the Subcommittee on Economic Policy, Trade and Environment and Western Hemisphere Affairs.* 103d Cong., 1st sess. Washington, DC: GPO, 1993. 132 pp.

———. Subcommittee on Economic Policy, Trade and Environment. *U.S. Environmental Exports: Hearing, August 4, 1993, on H.R. 2112.* 103d Cong., 1st sess. Washington, DC: GPO, 1993. 87 pp.

U.S. Congress. House. Committee on Merchant Marine and Fisheries. Subcommittee on Environment and Natural Resources. *Impact of Trade Agreements on U.S. Environmental Protection and National Resource Conservation Efforts: Hearing, March 10, 1993, on Environmental Impacts of a Free Trade Agreement.* 103d Cong., 1st sess. Washington, DC: GPO, 1993. 328 pp.

U.S. Congress. House. Committee on Small Business. Subcommittee on Regulation, Business Opportunities and Energy. *Protecting the Environment in North American Free Trade Agreement Negotiations: Hearing, September 30, 1991.* 102d Cong., 1st sess. Washington, DC: GPO, 1992. 282 pp.

U.S. Congress. Senate. Committee on Commerce, Science and Transportation. Subcommittee on Foreign Commerce and Tourism. *U.S. Environmental Technology in the Global Marketplace: Hearing, June 4, 1993.* 103d Cong., 1st sess. Washington, DC: GPO, 1994. 74 pp.

U.S. Congress. Senate. Committee on Environment and Public Works. *Environmental Aspects of the North American Free Trade Agreement: Hearing, March 16, 1993.* 103d Cong., 1st sess. Washington, DC: GPO, 1993. 126 pp.

U.S. Office of Technology Assessment. *Trade and Environment: Conflicts and Opportunities: Background Paper.* Washington, DC: GPO, 1992. 109 pp.

Certificates of Origin

Foote, Francis W. "The Caribbean Basin Initiative: Development, Implementation and Application of the Rules of Origin and Related Aspects of Duty-Free Treatment." *George Washington Journal of International Law and Economics* 19, 2 (1985): 245–394.

Krueger, Anne. *Free Trade Agreements as Protectionist Devices: Rules of Origin.* NBER Working Paper no. 4352. Cambridge, MA: National Bureau of Economic Research, 1993. 25 pp.

Simon, Lori E. "Appellations of Origin: The Continuing Controversy [Compares the Position of the United States, France, and the Developing Nations, and Highlights the Potential Benefits of Increased United States Protection, Especially for the United States Wine Industry]." *Northwestern Journal of International Law and Business* 5 (Spring 1983): 132–156.

Vermulst, Edwin, and Paul Waer. "European Community Rules of Origin as Commercial Policy Instruments?" *Journal of World Trade* 24 (June 1990): 55–99.

Laws and Regulations

Baldwin, Robert E., and Jeffrey W. Steagall. *An Analysis of Factors Influencing ITC Decisions in Antidumping, Countervailing Duty and Safeguard Cases.* NBER Working Paper no. 4282. Cambridge, MA: National Bureau of Economic Research, 1993. 48 pp.

Boadu, Fred O., and Wesley F. Peterson. "Enforcing United States Foreign Trade Legislation: Is There a Need for Expanded Presidential Discretion?" *Journal of World Trade* 24 (August 1990): 79–93.

Born, Gary B. "A Reappraisal of the Extraterritorial Reach of U.S. Law." *Law and Policy in International Business* 24 (Fall 1992): 1–100.

Butler, A. "The Trade-Related Aspects of Intellectual Property Rights: What Is at Stake?" *Federal Reserve Bank of St. Louis Review* 72 (November–December 1990): 34–46.

Coughlin, C. C. "U.S. Trade-Remedy Laws: Do They Facilitate or Hinder Free Trade?" *Federal Reserve Bank of St. Louis Review* 73 (July–August 1991): 3–18.

Dinopoulos, E., and M. E. Kreinin. "Effects of the U.S.-Japan Auto VER [Voluntary Export Restraints] on European Prices and on U.S. Welfare." *Review of Economics and Statistics* 70 (August 1988): 484–491.

European Communities Committee. *Report on United States Trade and Investment Barriers, 1993: Problems of Doing Business with the U.S.* Brussels, Belgium: Directorate General for External Relations, 1993. 90 pp.

"Export Administration Regulations [Amendments]." *Global Trade & Transportation* 113 (January 1993): 26–31.

Feenstra, R. C., and T. R. Lewis. "Negotiated Trade Restrictions with Private Political Pressure." *Quarterly Journal of Economics* 106 (November 1991): 1287–1307.

Fieleke, N. S. "One Trading World, or Many: The Issue of Regional Trading Blocs." *New England Economic Review* (May–June 1993): 3–20.

Finger, J. Michael, and Tracy Murray. "Policing Unfair Imports: The United States Example." *Journal of World Trade* 24 (August 1990): 39–50.

Forsythe, Kenneth W., Jr., and Mary E. Bredahl. "Strengthening Import Regulations Segments World Markets." *Food Review* 15, 1 (1992): 2–6.

Hazelton, W. A. "The Ins and Outs of Foreign Trade [Value-Added Requirements]." *Management Accounting* 69 (December 1987): 53–58.

Hickok, Susan. "Recent Trade Liberalization in Developing Countries: The Effects on Global Trade and Output." *Federal Reserve Bank of New York Quarterly Review* 18 (Autumn 1993): 6–19.

Hillman, Arye L. "Protectionist Policies as the Regulation of International Industry." *Public Choice* 67 (November 1990): 101–110.

Inman, J. E., and H. H. Fischer. "The Ins and Outs of U.S. Antiboycott Laws." *Business* 38 (July–August–September 1988): 25–32.

Jacobson, C. K., et al. "The Political Embeddedness of Private Economic Transactions [Multinational Firms' Transactions with Soviets Hindered by Government]." *Journal of Management Studies* 30 (May 1993): 453–478.

Kublin, Michael, and Robert Brody. "Parallel Importing and the Law." *Business and Public Affairs* 19 (Spring 1992): 5–9.

Kuttner, R. "How National Security Hurts National Competitiveness [Export Controls Crowd Out Technology Trade Opportunities for U.S. Firms]." *Harvard Business Review* 69 (January –February 1992): 140–149.

"Legal Aspects of Doing Business Overseas." *Business America* 109 (November 21, 1988): 2–18.

"Legal Aspects of Exporting and Investing [Special Report]." *Business America* 112 (February 11, 1991): 2–18.

McCurry, Patrick. "Confusion at the Border: New Rules Hold Up Freight." *Business Mexico* 2 (December 1992): 30–31.

"Message to the Congress Reporting on the Continuation of Export Control Regulations, September 25, 1992." *Weekly Compilation of Presidential Documents* 27 (September 28, 1992): 1740–1745.

Moran, Theodore H. "The Impact of TRIMs on Trade and Development." *Transnational Corps (UN)* 1 (February 1992): 55–65.

Nollen, S. D. "Business Costs and Business Policy for Export Controls." *Journal of International Business Studies* 18 (Spring 1987): 1–18.

Rowe, M. "The International Sales Contract—Central to Trade Transactions [Legal Aspects of Trade]." *International Trade Forum* 23 (July–September 1987): 14–19+.

Rugman, Alan M., and Michael V. Gestrin. "U.S. Trade Laws as Barriers to Globalisation." *World Economics* 14 (September 1991): 335–352.

Swan, P. "A Road Map to Understanding Export Controls: National Security in a Changing Global Environment." *American Business Law Journal* 30 (February 1993): 607–675.

Torre, Fernando Castillo de la. "The EEC New Instrument of Trade Policy: Some Comments in the Light of the Latest Developments." *Common Market Law Review* 30 (August 1993): 687–719.

U.S. Congress. House. Committee on Foreign Affairs. Subcommittee on Economic Policy, Trade and Environment. *Export Controls on Mass Market Software: Hearing, October 12, 1993.* 103d Cong., 1st sess. Washington, DC: GPO, 1994. 139 pp.

U.S. Congress. House. Committee on Government Operations. Legislation and National Security Subcommittee. *Foreign Government Procurement Discrimination and the Effectiveness of Title VII: Hearing, June 10, 1993.* 103d Cong., 1st sess. Washington, DC: GPO, 1993. 142 pp.

U.S. Congress. House. Committee on Science, Space, and Technology. *Export Control Reform in High Technology: Hearing, August 13, 1993.* 103d Cong., 1st sess. Washington, DC: GPO, 1993. 178 pp.

U.S. Congress. House. Committee on Small Business. Subcommittee on Regulation, Business Opportunities and Energy. *Pacific Northwest Trade with the Eastern Bloc: Opportunities and Obstacles for Timber and Electronics: Hearing, February 12, 1990.* 101st Cong., 2d sess. Washington, DC: GPO, 1990. 138 pp.

U.S. Congress. House. Committee on Ways and Means. Subcommittee on Trade. *USTR Identification of Priority Practices and Countries under Super 301 and Special 301 Provisions of the Omnibus Trade and Competitiveness Act of 1988: Hearing: June 8, 1989.* 101st Cong., 1st sess. Washington, DC: GPO, 1989. 138 pp.

U.S. Congress. Senate. Committee on Finance. *Oversight of the Trade Act of 1988: Hearing, pt. 1, March 1, 1989.* 101st Cong., 1st sess. Washington, DC: GPO, 1989. 95 pp.

————. Subcommittee on International Trade. *United States–Japan Trade Policy: Hearing, July 22, 1993.* 103d Cong., 1st sess. Washington, DC: GPO, 1994. 104 pp.

U.S. Congress. Senate. Committee on Foreign Relations. *Nuclear Proliferation: Learning from the Iraq Experience: Hearings, October 17 and 23, 1993.* 102d Cong., 1st sess. Washington, DC: GPO, 1992. 58 pp.

U.S. Congress. Senate. Committee on the Judiciary. *Unfair Trade Practices: Hearings, January 10–27, 1992, on S. 986, a Bill To Amend Title 28 of the United States Code to Expand the Original Jurisdiction of Federal*

District Courts in Certain Civil Actions. 102d Cong., 2d sess. Washington, DC: GPO, 1992. 443 pp.

U.S. International Trade Commission. *Proposed Reorganization of U.S. International Trade Relief Laws.* USITC Publication 2717. Washington, DC: 1993. 366 pp.

"U.S.– Israel Free Trade Area Agreement: A Unique Agreement Offers Unique Opportunities." *Business America* 10 (August 31, 1987): 2–9.

Weidenbaum, Murray, and Harvey S. James, Jr. *Responding to Foreign Competition: Overcoming Government Barriers.* Policy Study no. 113. St. Louis, MO: Center for the Study of American Business, Washington University, 1992. 28 pp.

Finance

Ben-David, D. "Equalizing Exchange: Trade Liberalization and Income Convergence." *Quarterly Journal of Economics* 108 (August 1993): 653–679.

Citrin, D. "The Recent Behavior of U.S. Trade Prices." *International Monetary Fund Staff Papers* 36 (December 1989): 934–949.

Cole, Harold L., and Maurice Obstfeld. *Commodity Trade and International Risk Sharing: How Much Do Financial Markets Matter?* Working Paper no. 3027. Cambridge, MA: National Bureau of Economic Research, 1989. 47 pp.

Hein, John. *Global Economic Trends: What Lies Ahead for the 90's.* Conference Board Report, no. 932. New York: The Conference Board, 1989. 24 pp.

Lipsey, Robert E., et al. *Measures of Prices and Price Competitiveness in International Trade in Manufactured Goods.* Working Paper no. 3442. Cambridge, MA: National Bureau of Economic Research, 1990. 72 pp.

Pozo, S. "Conditional Exchange Rate Volatility and the Volume of International Trade: Evidence from the Early 1900s." *Review of Economics and Statistics* 74 (May 1992): 325–329.

Deficit

Bergsten, C. F. "The Second Debt Crisis Is Coming." *Challenge* 30 (1987): 50–57.

Butler, A. "Trade Imbalances and Economic Theory: The Case for a U.S.-Japan Trade Deficit." *Federal Reserve Bank of St. Louis Review* 73 (March–April 1991): 16–31.

Connock, M., and H. Hillier. "Current Account Deficits and Long-Term Interest Rates: Is There a Risk Premium?" *Applied Economics* 22 (October 1990): 1323–1334.

Chrystal, K. A., and G. E. Wood. "Are Trade Deficits a Problem?" *Federal Reserve Bank of St. Louis Review* 70 (January–February 1988): 3–11.

Clarida, Richard H. "That Trade Deficit, Protectionism and Policy Coordination." *World Economy* (London) 12 (December 1989): 415–437.

Dornbusch, R. "External Balance Correction: Depreciation or Protection?" *Brookings Papers on Economic Activity* 1 (1987): 249–269.

Enders, W., and B-S. Lee. "Current Account and Budget Deficits: Twins or Distant Cousins?" *Review of Economics and Statistics* 72 (August 1990): 373–381.

Fieleke, N. S. "The United States in Debt." *New England Economic Review* (September–October 1990): 34–54.

Hermanson, R. H., and W. C. Stillwagon. "The Foreign Trade Deficit—Causes and Solutions." *Business* 38 (January–February–March 1988): 3–9.

Hickok, S., and J. Hung. "Explaining the Persistence of the U.S. Trade Deficit in the Late 1980s." *Federal Reserve Bank of New York Quarterly Review* 16 (Winter 1991–1992): 29–46.

Hill, John K. "When Will the United States Grow Out of Its Foreign Debt?" *Federal Reserve Bank of Dallas Economic Review* (3d Quarter 1992): 23–31.

Husted, S. "The Emerging U.S. Current Account Deficit in the 1980s: A Cointegration Analysis." *Review of Economics and Statistics* 74 (February 1992): 159–166.

Karier, T. "Unions: Cause or Victim of U.S. Trade Deficit?" *Challenge* 34 (November–December 1991): 34–41.

Klitgaard, Thomas. "The Dollar and U.S. Imports after 1985." *Federal Reserve Bank of New York Quarterly Review* 18 (Autumn 1993): 20–36.

Krugman, P. R., and R. E. Baldwin. "The Persistence of the U.S. Trade Deficit." *Brookings Papers on Economic Activity* 1 (1987): 1–55.

Lipsey, Robert. *Foreign Direct Investment in the U.S. and U.S. Trade.* NBER Working Paper no. 3623. Cambridge, MA: National Bureau of Economic Research, 1991. 38 pp.

Morris, F. E. "The Changing American Attitude toward Debt, and Its Consequences [for Future Economic Policy]." *New England Economic Review* (May–June 1990): 34–39.

Nothdurft, William E. "The Export Game." *Governing* 5 (August 1992): 57–61.

Park, J. H. "Policy Response to Countertrade and the U.S. Trade Deficit: An Appraisal." *Business Economics* 25 (April 1990): 38–43.

Sachs, J. D. "Global Adjustments to a Shrinking U.S. Trade Deficit." *Brookings Papers on Economic Activity* 2 (1988): 639–674.

Thornton, D. L. "Do Government Deficits Matter?" *Federal Reserve Bank of St. Louis Review* 72 (September–October 1990): 25–39.

Whitehill, A. M. "America's Trade Deficit: The Human Problems." *Business Horizons* 31 (January–February 1988): 18–23.

Zietz, J., and D. K. Pemberton. "The U.S. Budget and Trade Deficits: A Simultaneous Equation Model." *Southern Economic Journal* 57 (July 1990): 23–34.

Smuggling

Thursby, M., et al. "Smuggling, Camouflaging, and Market Structure [Cigarette Smuggling in U.S.]." *Quarterly Journal of Economics* 106 (August 1991): 789–814.

Dumping and Antidumping

Anderson, J. E. "Domino Dumping: Competitive Exporters [Voluntary Export Restraints May Increase Dumping." *American Economic Review* 82 (March 1992): 65–83.

Baldwin, Robert E., and Jeffrey W. Steagall. *An Analysis of Factors Influencing ITC Decisions in Antidumping, Countervailing Duty and Safeguard Cases.* NBER Working Paper no. 4282. Cambridge, MA: National Bureau of Economic Research, 1993. 48 pp.

Carbaugh, Robert, and Darwin Wassink. "International Dumping: Final and Intermediate Products." *Journal of Asian Economics* 3 (Fall 1992): 239–251.

Finger, J. Michael. "Dumping and Antidumping: The Rhetoric and the Reality of Protection in Industrial Countries." *World Bank Research Observer* 7 (July 1992): 121–143.

Goehle, D. G. "The Buy American Act: Is It Irrelevant in a World of Multinational Corporations? [Impact of Modifications to 1933 Law]." *Columbia Journal of World Business* 24 (Winter 1989): 10–15.

Guisinger, S. "Total Protection: A New Measure of the Impact of Government Interventions of Investment Profitability." *Journal of International Business Studies* 20 (Summer 1989): 280–295.

Hoekman, Bernard M., and Michael P. Leidy. "Dumping, Antidumping and Emergency Protection." *Journal of World Trade* 23 (October 1989): 27–44.

Louth, C., and E. Rogers. "Impact Administration: Stopping Unfair Trade Practices." *Business America* 111 (November 5, 1990): 2–8.

Matsumoto, Ken, and Grant Finlayson. "Dumping and Antidumping: Growing Problem in World Trade." *Journal of World Trade* 24 (August 1990): 5–19.

Petersmann, Ernst-Ulrich. "Need for Reforming Antidumping Rules and Practices: The Messy World of Fourth-Best Policies." *Aussenwirtschaft* 45 (July 1990): 179–198.

Repp, David M. "Antidumping and Countervailing Duties: Protection at a Cost." *Journal of Corporation Law* 15 (Fall 1989): 65–82.

Schmidt, Ingo, and Sabine Richard. "Conflicts between Antidumping and Antitrust Law in the EC." *Intereconomics* 27 (September–October 1992): 223–229.

Stahl, Tycho H. E. "Problems with the United States Anti-Dumping Law: The Case for Reform of the Constructed Value Methodology." *International Tax and Business Lawyer* 11, 1 (1993): 1–25.

Stegemann, Klaus. "The International Regulation of Dumping: Protection Made Too Easy." *World Economics* 14 (December 1991): 375–405.

Sullivan, Patrick. "Antidumping Law and the Dumping of Services." *New York University Journal of International Law and Politics* 24 (Summer 1992): 1677–1709.

"Symposium: The United States Court of International Trade in a World of Transition." *Law and Policy in International Business* 22, 4 (1991): 643–719.

U.S. Congress. Senate. Committee on Governmental Affairs. Subcommittee on Oversight of Government Management. *Lax Federal Enforcement of the Antidumping and Countervailing Duty Program: Report, October 1991.* 102d Cong., 1st sess. Washington, DC: GPO, 1991. 29 pp.

U.S. General Accounting Office. *Uranium Enrichment: Unresolved Trade Issues Leave Uncertain Future for U.S. Uranium Industry: Report to the Ranking Minority Member, Subcommittee on Nuclear Regulation, Committee on Environment and Public Works, U.S. Senate.* Report B-237747. Gaithersburg, MD: 1992. 39 pp.

Vermulst, Edwin A. "The Anti-Dumping Systems of Australia, Canada, the EEC, and the United States of America: Have Anti-Dumping Laws Become a Problem in International Trade?" *Michigan Journal of International Law* 10 (Summer 1989): 765–806.

Temporary Tariff

Browning, Graeme. "Firepower: `Temporary' Tariff Suspensions Cost the U.S. Treasury Hundreds of Millions of Dollars Every Year: Here's the Story of How One of Them—A Relative Drop in the Bucket as Such Suspensions Go—Managed to Survive for Nearly a Decade and a Half." *National Journal* 25 (July 10, 1993): 1755–1757.

Countertrade

Adkins, R. L. "Competitive Decline: Views of Two Disciples." *Journal of Economic Issues* 21 (June 1987): 869–876.

Lecraw, D. J. "The Management of Countertrade: Factors Influencing Success." *Journal of International Business Studies* 20 (Spring 1989): 41–59.

Ordover, Janusz, and Linda Goldberg. *Obstacles to Trade and Competition.* Washington, DC: Organization for Economic Cooperation and Development, Committee on Competition Law and Policy, 1993. 111 pp.

Park, Jong H. "Policy Response to Countertrade and the U.S. Trade Deficit: An Appraisal." *Business Economics* 25 (April 1990): 38–44.

Schaffer, Matt. "Countertrade as an Export Strategy: For Countries with Limited Funds or Nonconvertible Currencies, Countertrade Provides an Established Trading Vehicle: The Author Describes How This Strategy Can Encourage Trade between the US and Developing Markets." *Journal of Business Strategy* 11 (May–June 1990): 33–38.

Countervailing

Gillen, Mark. "Countervailing Duties: Efficiency and Public Choice." *Ottawa Law Review* 23, 1 (1991): 1–34.

Harvey, M. "A New Way To Combat Product Counterfeiting." *Business Horizons* 31 (July–August 1988): 19–28.

Marketing Barriers

Onkvisit, S., and J. J. Shaw. "Marketing Barriers in International Trade." *Business Horizons* 31 (May–June 1988): 64–72.

Cartels

Ahrari, Mohammed E. "OPEC and the Hyperpluralism of the Oil Market in the 1980s." *International Affairs* (London) 61 (Spring 1985): 263–277.

Casavant, Kenneth L., and Wesley W. Wilson. "Shipper Perspectives of the Shipping Act of 1984." *Transportation Quarterly* 45 (January 1991): 109–120.

Elzinga, Kenneth G. "New Developments on the Cartel Front [Price Fixing Conspiracies]." *Antitrust Bulletin* 29 (Spring 1984): 3–26.

"European Communities–United States: Agreement on the Application of Their Competition Laws (Done at Washington, September 23, 1991)." *International Legal Materials* 30 (November 1991): 1487–1502.

Libecap, Gary D. "The Political Economy of Crude Oil Cartelization in the United States, 1933–1972." *Journal of Economic History* 49 (December 1989): 833–855.

Osterfeld, David. "Voluntary and Coercive Cartels: The Case of Oil." *Freeman* 37 (November 1987): 415–425.

Uesugi, Akinori. "Japan's Cartel System and Its Impact on International Trade." *Harvard International Law Journal* 27 (Special Issue 1986): 389–424.

U.S. Congress. House. Committee on the Judiciary. Subcommittee on Economic and Commercial Law. *Possible Violations of U.S. Antitrust Laws by Foreign Corporations.* 101st Cong., 2d sess. Washington, DC: GPO, 1991. 350 pp.

Export Subsidies

Chambers, R. G., and P. L. Paarlberg. "Are More Exports Always Better? Comparing Cash and In-Kind Export Subsidies." *American Journal of Agricultural Economics* 72 (February 1991): 142–154.

Tariffs

Beladi, H., and S. Samanta. "Uncertainty, Domestic Distortions, and the Optimal Tariff." *Southern Economic Journal* 58 (July 1991): 87–92.

Friman, H. Richard. "Farm Policy Beliefs to Policy Choices: Resurgence of Tariff Retaliation in the U.S. Pursuit of Fair Trade." *Journal of Public Policy* 13 (April–June 1993): 163–182.

Gardner, G. W., and K. P. Kimbrough. "The Behavior of U.S. Tariff Rates." *American Economic Review* 79 (March 1989): 211–218.

Hufbauer, Gary Clyde, and Kimberly Ann Elliott. *Measuring the Costs of Protection in the United States.* Washington, DC: Institute for International Economics, 1994. 125 pp.

Lapan, H. E. "The Optimal Tariff Production Lags, and Time Consistency." *American Economic Review* 78 (June 1988): 395–401.

Lawrence, R. Z., and R. E. Litan. "The Protectionist Prescription: Errors in Diagnosis and Cure." *Brookings Papers on Economic Activity* 1 (1987): 289–310.

Pompelli, G. K., and D. H. Pick. "Pass-Through of Exchange Rates and Tariffs in Brazil-U.S. Tobacco Trade." *American Journal of Agricultural Economics* 72 (August 1990): 676–681.

Ray, E. J. "The Impact of Special Interests on Preferential Tariff Concessions by the United States." *Review of Economics and Statistics* 69 (May 1987): 187–193.

Silverstein, D. "Country-of-Origin Marking Requirements under Section 304 of the Tariff Act: An Importer's Map through the Maze." *American Business Law Journal* 25 (Summer 1987): 285–300.

Sungthong, Chiraporn. "The Steel Bar Industry." Bangkok Bank *Monthly Review* 34 (November 1993): 20–23.

U.S. Congress. House. Committee on Ways and Means. Subcommittee on Trade. *Written Comments on Certain Tariff and Trade Bills: v. 5–6, April 30–June 22, 1992.* 2 vols. 102d Cong., 2d sess. Washington, DC: GPO, 1992.

Nontariff Trade Barriers

Chow, G., and J. J. McRae. "Non-tariff Barriers and the Structure of the U.S.-Canadian (Transborder) Trucking Industry." *Transportation Journal* 30 (Winter 1990): 4–21.

Clark, Don P., and Simonetti Zarrilli. "Non-tariff Measures and Industrial National Imports of GSP-Covered Products." *Southern Economic Journal* 59 (October 1992): 284–293.

European Communities Commission. *Report on United States Trade and Investment Barriers, 1993: Problems of Doing Business with the U.S.* Brussels, Belgium: Directorate General for External Relations, 1993. 90 pp.

———. *Report on United States Trade Barriers and Unfair Practices, 1991: Problems of Doing Business with the U.S.* Brussels, Belgium: Directorate General for External Relations, 1992. 87 pp.

Hughes, Kirsty S. "Trade Performance of the Main EC Economics Relative to the U.S.A. and Japan in 1992—Sensitive Sectors." *Journal of Common Market Studies* 30 (December 1992): 437–458.

Khanna, Ram. "Market Sharing under Multifiber Arrangement: Consequences of Non-tariff Barriers in the Textile Trade." *Journal of World Trade* 24 (February 1990): 71–104.

Knight, C. Foster. "Effects of National Environmental Regulation on International Trade and Investment: Selected Issues." UCLA (University of California–Los Angeles) *Pacific Basin Law Journal* 10 (Fall 1991): 212–223.

Kotabe, Masaaki. "A Comparative Study of U.S. and Japanese Patent Systems." *Journal of International Business Studies* 23, 1 (1992): 147–168.

Naumann, E., and D. J. Lincoln. "Non-tariff Barriers and Entry Strategy Alternatives: Strategic Marketing Implications." *Journal of Small Business Management* 29 (April 1991): 60–70.

Quigley, Kevin F. F., and William J. Long. "Export Controls: Moving beyond Economic Containment." *World Policy Journal* 7 (Winter 1989–1990): 165–188.

Rugman, Alan M., and Michael V. Gestrin. "U.S. Trade Laws as Barriers to Globalisation." *World Economics* 14 (September 1991): 335–352.

Sharkey, T. W., et al. "Export Development and Perceived Export Barriers: An Empirical Analysis of Small Firms." *Management International Review* 29, 2 (1989): 33–40.

Sinha, Radha. "Are EC-Japan-U.S. Trade Relations at the Crossroads?" *Intereconomics* 25 (September–October 1990): 229–237.

Sullivan, D., and A. Bauerschmidt. "Common Factors Underlying Barriers to Export: A Comparative Study in the European and U.S. Paper Industry." *Management International Review* 29, 2 (1989): 17–32.

Tucker, Jonathan L. "The International Car Industry: The Shift from Protection." *Multinational Business* (Winter 1988): 27–36.

U.S. Congress. House. Committee on Banking, Finance, and Urban Affairs. Subcommittee on International Development, Finance, Trade, and Monetary Policy. *Fair Trade in Financial Services Legislation: Hearings, Pt. 2, January 22, 1992.* 102d Cong., 2d sess. Washington, DC: GPO, 1992. 285 pp.

U.S. Congress. House. Committee on Energy and Commerce. Subcommittee on Oversight and Investigations. *Unfair Foreign Trade Practices: Hearings, March 1–2, 1989.* 101st Cong., 1st sess. Washington, DC: GPO, 1989. 403 pp.

U.S. Congress. House. Committee on Ways and Means. Subcommittee on Trade. *USTR Identification of Priority Practices and Countries under Super 301 and Special 301 Provisions of the Omnibus Trade and Competitiveness Act of 1988: Hearing, June 8, 1989.* 101st Cong., 1st sess. Washington, DC: GPO, 1989. 138 pp.

U.S. Congress. Senate. Committee on Commerce, Science, and Transportation. Subcommittee on Foreign Commerce and Tourism. *Effect of the Japanese Patent System on American Business: Hearing, June 24, 1988.* 100th Cong., 2d sess. Washington, DC: GPO, 1988. 102 pp.

U.S. Congress. Senate. Committee on Finance. *Japan Trade Concessions: Hearing, January 23, 1992.* 102d Cong., 2d sess. Washington, DC: GPO, 1992. 207 pp.

U.S. Office of the U.S. Trade Representative. *National Trade Estimate Report on Foreign Trade Barriers, 1993.* Washington, DC: GPO, 1993. 275 pp.

————. *National Trade Estimate Report on Foreign Trade Barriers, 1992.* Washington, DC: GPO, 1992. 267 pp.

————. *National Trade Estimate Report on Foreign Trade Barriers, 1990.* Washington, DC: GPO, 1990. 216 pp.

————. *National Trade Estimate Report on Foreign Trade Barriers, 1989.* Washington, DC: GPO, 1989. 214 pp.

Weidenbaum, Murray, and Harvey S. James, Jr. *Responding to Foreign Competition: Overcoming Government Barriers.* St. Louis, MO: Center for the Study of American Business, Washington University, 1992. 28 pp.

Embargoes

"Continuing Efforts to Restore Democracy to Haiti." *Foreign Policy Bulletin* 2 (January–February 1992): 135–139.

Fraunces, Michel G. "The International Law of Blockade: New Guiding Principles in Contemporary State Practice." *Yale Law Journal* 101 (January 1992): 893–918.

Freeman, Nick J. "United States's Economic Sanctions against Vietnam: International Business and Development Repercussions." *Columbia Journal of World Business* 28 (Summer 1993): 12–22.

Kruis, Elizabeth E. "The United States Trade Embargo on Mexican Tuna: A Necessary Conservationist Measure or an Unfair Trade Barrier." *Loyola of Los Angeles International and Comparative Law Journal* 14 (October 1992): 903–935.

Riefe, Robert H. "Cuban Political Action in the United States." *Journal of Social, Political, and Economic Studies* 14 (Summer 1989): 235–249.

Robinson, William I. "Making the Economy Scream: U.S. Economic Warfare against Nicaragua." *Multinational Monitor* 11 (December 1989): 22–26.

"Vietnam: Capitalist Dawn." *Far Eastern Economic Review* (April 22, 1993): 68–72.

Voitovich, Sergei A. "Legitimacy of the Use of Economic Force in International Relations: Conditions and Limits." *World Competition* 15 (June 1992): 27–36.

Import Quotas

Arnold, Bruce D. *Trade and Restraints and the Competitive Status of the Textile, Apparel, and Nonrubber Footwear Industries.* Washington, DC: U.S. Congress, Budget Office, 1991. 78 pp.

Baughman, Laura M. "Auctioning of Quotas: Lots of Pain for Little Gain." *World Economy* (London) 11 (September 1988): 397–415.

de Melo, J., and D. Tarr. "Welfare Costs of U.S. Quotas in Textiles, Steel, and Autos." *Review of Economics and Statistics* 72 (August 1990): 489–497.

Feenstra, R. C. "Quality Change under Trade Restraints in Japanese Autos." *Quarterly Journal of Economics* 103 (February 1988): 131–146.

Hamilton, Carl B., et al. "Who Wins and Who Loses from Voluntary Export Restraints? The Case of Footwear." *World Bank Research Observer* 7 (January 1992): 17–33.

Krishna, K. "The Case of the Vanishing Revenues: Auction Quotas with Monopoly." *American Economic Review* 80 (September 1990): 828–836.

Maskus, Keith E. "Large Costs and Small Benefits of the American Sugar Programme." *World Economy* (London) 12 (March 1989): 85–104.

Suranovic, S. M. "The Ineffectiveness of Quantitative Restrictions with Production Diversion [Imports and Exports]." *Southern Economic Journal* 58 (October 1991): 379–391.

U.S. Congress. House. Committee on Ways and Means. *Background Materials Relating to the Steel Voluntary Restraint Agreement (VRA) Program, June 2, 1989.* 101st Cong., 1st sess. Washington, DC: GPO, 1989. 167 pp.

U.S. Department of Commerce. International Trade Administration. Office of Textiles and Apparel. *Foreign Regulations Affecting U.S. Textile and Apparel Exports: Foreign Regulations and Trade Barriers Facing U.S. Companies in Sixty Countries.* Washington, DC: GPO, 1992. 179 pp.

Wehr, Elizabeth. "Producers Press for Renewal of Steel Import Quotas: Steelmakers Praise Effects of Trade Restraints, But Users Say the Price Is Too High." *Congressional Quarterly Weekly Report* 47 (March 1989): 629–632.

Trade Promotion

Abrahamsson, Bernhard J. "International Shipping Developments, Prospects, and Policy Issues." *Ocean Yearbook* 8 (1989): 158–175.

Ackerman, K. Z. "Export Promotion Programs Help U.S. Products Compete in World Markets [Agricultural Products]." *Food Review* 16 (May–August 1993): 31–35.

Barrett, G. R. "Finding the Right International Partner for Small Businesses [Seeking Joint Ventures for the Export Market: Department of Commerce and State Programs]." *Journal of Accountancy* 173 (January 1992): 58–64.

Bendow, B. "Evaluating Trade Promotions: Participation in Trade Fairs." *International Trade Forum* 28 (July – September 1992): 12–17+.

Borensztein, E., and A. R. Ghosh. "Foreign Borrowing and Export Promotion Policies." *International Monetary Fund Staff Papers* 36 (December 1989): 904–933.

Dichtl, E., et al. "International Orientation as a Precondition for Export Success." *Journal of International Business Studies* 21, 1 (1990): 23–40.

Feenstra, Robert C., et al. *Designing Policies To Open Trade.* NBER Working Paper no. 3258. Cambridge, MA: National Bureau of Economic Research, 1990. 26 pp.

Fine, Frank L. "EEC Consumer Warranties: A New Antitrust Hurdle Facing Exporters." *Harvard International Law Journal* 29 (Spring 1988): 367–391.

"Foreign Direct Investment in the United States: Detail for Position and Balance of Payments Flows, 1986." *Survey of Current Business* 67 (August 1987): 85–99.

Gerson, R. J. "The ASEAN Market: Its Importance to U.S. Industry and the Need for Closer Industry/Government Cooperation." *Journal of Southeast Asia Business* 8 (Winter 1992): 98–103.

Grossman, G. M., and E. Helpman. "Trade, Innovation, and Growth." *American Economic Review* 80 (May 1990): 86–91.

Jaramillo, C. "Trade Promotion Organizations: A Variety of Approaches." *International Trade Forum* 28 (April–June 1992): 4–9+.

Jensworld, Joel, and William Parle. "The Role of the American States in Promoting Trade Relations with Eastern Europe and the Soviet Union." *Economic Development Quarterly* 6 (August 1992): 320–326.

Kotabe, Masaaki. "The Promotional Roles of the State Government and Japanese Manufacturing Direct Investment in the United States." *Journal of Business Research* 27 (June 1993): 131–146.

Kotabe, Masaaki, and Michael R. Czinkota. "State Government Promotion of Manufacturing Exports: A Gap Analysis." *Journal of International Business Studies* 23, 4 (1992): 637–658.

Naidu, G. M., and T. R. Rao. "Public Sector Promotion of Exports: A Needs-Based Approach." *Journal of Business Research* 27 (May 1993): 85–101.

Nasar, S. "America's Competitive Revival." *Fortune* 117 (January 4, 1988): 44–50+.

Orr, J. "The Trade Balance Effects of Foreign Direct Investment in U.S. Manufacturing." *Federal Reserve Bank of New York Quarterly Review* 16 (Summer 1991): 63–76.

Ray, Edward John. "U.S. Protection and Intra-industry Trade: The Message to Developing Countries." *Economic Development and Cultural Change* 40 (October 1991): 169–187.

Samiee, S., and P. G. P. Walters. "Influence of Firm Size on Export Planning and Performance." *Journal of Business Research* 20 (May 1990): 235–248.

Seifert, B., and J. Ford. "Export Distribution Channels [Small Producers of Industrial Goods; Survey]." *Columbia Journal of World Business* 24 (Summer 1989): 15–21.

Sharkey, T. W., et al. "Export Development and Perceived Export Barriers: An Empirical Analysis of Small Firms." *Management International Review* 29, 2 (1989): 33–40.

Teske, G. R. "Exports: Lead Trade and Growth." *Business America* 110 (September 11, 1989): 2–8.

Therrien, Lois. "Brands on the Run: How Marketers Deal with Eroding Loyalty." *Business Week* (April 19, 1993) 26–29.

Tolchin, M., and S. Tolchin. "The States' Global Hustlers [Officials of Many States Compete for Foreign Dollars]." *Across the Board* 25 (April 1988): 14–22.

U.S. Congress. House. Committee on Energy and Commerce. Subcommittee on Commerce, Consumer Protection, and Competitiveness. *Trade Enhancement: Hearings, March 5 – April 8, 1992, on H.R. 4100, a Bill To Assure Mutually Advantageous International Trade in Motor Vehicles and Motor Vehicle Parts, an Enhanced Market for the Interstate Sale and Export of Domestically Produced Motor Vehicles and Motor Parts, and the Retention and Enhancement of U.S. Jobs.* 102d Cong., 2d sess. Washington, DC: GPO, 1992. 435 pp.

U.S. Congress. House. Committee on Government Operations. Commerce, Consumer, and Monetary Affairs Subcommittee. *Export*

Promotion Activities of U.S. Government Agencies: Hearings, September 28 and October 18, 1989. 101st Cong., 1st sess. Washington, D.C.: GPO, 1990. 241 pp.

U.S. Congress. House. Committee on Merchant Marine and Fisheries. Subcommittee on the Environment and Natural Resources. *Promoting the Export of U.S. Environmental Technologies, Goods, and Services: Hearing, February 25, 1993, on How To Maintain Both a Clean, Healthy Environment and Create Jobs through Development of a U.S. Envirotech Industry and Export These Technologies to Developing Countries.* 103d Cong., 1st sess. Washington, D.C.: GPO, 1993. 197 pp.

"U.S. Direct Investment Abroad: Detail for Position and Balance of Payments Flows, 1986." *Survey of Current Business* 67 (August 1987): 58–84.

Verity, C. W. "Why EXPORT NOW? [Special Issue]." *Business America* 109 (March 28, 1988): 2–40.

Walters, P. G. P., and B. Toyne. "Product Modification and Standardization in International Markets: Strategic Options and Facilitating Policies." *Columbia Journal of World Business* 24 (Winter 1989): 37–44.

Weigand, R. E. "Parallel Import Channels—Options for Preserving Territorial Integrity." *Columbia Journal of World Business* 26 (Spring 1991): 53–60.

Williamson, P. "Successful Strategies for Export [to U.S.: Comparison of British, Japanese, and West German Exporters]." *Long Range Planning* 24 (February 1991): 57–63.

Winders, Rebecca M. "Identifying Opportunities for Georgia's Exports Expansion." *Georgia Business and Economic Conditions* 53 (January–February 1993): 1–9.

Yange, Y. S., et al. "A Market Expansion Ability Approach To Identify Potential Exporters." *Journal of Marketing* 56 (January 1992): 84–96.

Yu, E. S. H., and A. K. Parai. "Factor Immobility and Gains from Trade." *Southern Economic Journal* 55 (January 1989): 601–609.

Government Aid

Kotabe, Masaaki, and Michael R. Czinkota. "State Government Promotion of Manufacturing Exports: A Gap Analysis." *Journal of International Business Studies* 23, 4 (1992): 637–658.

Morrissey, Oliver. "The Mixing of Aid and Trade Policies." *World Economics* 16 (January 1993): 69–84.

Rock, Michael T. "Public Sector Marketing and Production Assistance to South Korea's Manufacturing Exporters: Did It Make a Difference?" *Development Policy Review* 10 (December 1992): 339–357.

U.S. Congress. House. Committee on Foreign Affairs. Subcommittee on Economic Policy and Trade. *Tied Aid and Mixed Credits: Hearing, December 18, 1991.* 102d Cong., 1st sess. Washington, DC: GPO, 1992. 130 pp.

Export Marketing

Borden, Paul, and Jean Kelly. *Marketing in Thailand.* Overseas Business Reports OBR 92–09. Washington, DC: U.S. Department of Commerce, International Trade Administration, 1992. 47 pp.

Seringhaus, F. H. Rolf. "Export Promotion in Developing Countries: Status and Prospects." *Journal of Global Marketing* 6, 4 (1993): 7–31.

U.S. Congress. House. Committee on Banking, Finance, and Urban Affairs. Subcommittee on International Development, Finance, Trade and Monetary Policy. *Practices and Policies of International Institutions: Hearing, January 29, 1992.* 102d Cong., 2d sess. Washington, DC: GPO, 1992. 134 pp.

U.S. Congress. House. Committee on Energy and Commerce. Subcommittee on Commerce, Consumer Protection and Competitiveness. *Trade Enhancement: Hearings, March 5–April 8, 1992, on H.R. 4100, a Bill To Assure Mutually Advantageous International Trade in Motor Vehicle and Motor Vehicle Parts, an Enhanced Market for the Interstate Sale and Export of Domestically Produced Motor Vehicles and Motor Vehicle Parts, and the Retention and Enhancement of U.S. Jobs.* 102d Cong., 2d sess. Washington, D.C.: GPO, 1992. 435 pp.

U.S. Congress. House. Committee on Merchant Marine and Fisheries. Subcommittee on Environment and Natural Resources. *Promoting the*

Export of U.S. Environmental Technologies, Goods and Services: Hearing, February 25, 1993, on How To Maintain Both a Clean, Healthy Environment and Create Jobs through Development of a U.S. Envirotech Industry and Export These Technologies to Developing Countries, 1993. 103d Cong., 1st sess. Washington, D.C.: 1993. 197 pp.

Winders, Rebecca M. "Identifying Opportunities for Georgia's Export Expansion." *Georgia Business and Economic Conditions* 53 (January–February 1993): 1–9.

Commerce

Brand, Diana. "Regional Bloc Formation and World Trade." *Intereconomics* 27 (November–December 1992): 274–281.

Nolle, D. E. "An Empirical Analysis of Market Structure and Import and Export Performance for U.S. Manufacturing Industries." *Quarterly Review of Economics and Business* 31 (Winter 1991): 59–78.

Nunnenkamp, Peter. *The World Trading System at the Crossroads: Multilateral Trade Negotiations in the Era of Regionalism.* Kiel Discussion Papers 204. Kiel, Germany: Institut für Weltwirtschaft, Universitat Kiel, 1993. 20 pp.

Finance

Benvignati, A. M. "Industry Determinants and Differences in U.S. Intrafirm and Arms-Length Exports." *Review of Economics and Statistics* 72 (August 1990): 481–488.

Brauer, D. A. "The Effects of Imports on U.S. Manufacturing Wages." *Federal Reserve Bank of New York Quarterly Review* 16 (Spring 1991): 14–26.

Carnevale, Francesca, and Jack Lowenstein. "Exim and Jexim: A Duopoly of ECA Initiative." *Trade Finance* (April 1992): 37–43.

Citrin, D. "The Recent Behavior of U.S. Trade Prices." *International Monetary Fund Staff Papers* 36 (December 1989): 934–949.

Coughlin, C. C. "The Competitive Nature of State Spending on the Promotion of Manufacturing Exports." *Federal Reserve Bank of St. Louis Review* 70 (May–June 1988): 34–42.

Crookell, H., and A. Morrison. "Subsidiary Strategy in a Free Trade Environment." *Business Quarterly* 55 (Autumn 1990): 33–39.

Devadoss, S. "Market Interventions, International Price Stabilization, and Welfare Implications." *American Journal of Agricultural Economics* 74 (May 1992): 281–290.

Easton, D. "How Regional Banks' Customers Can Become Exporters." *Journal of Commercial Bank Lending* 69 (July 1987): 26–33.

"Financing [Obtaining Government Money for International Business]." *Business America* 12 (March 25, 1991): 18–23.

Froot, K. A., and P. D. Klemperer. "Exchange Rate Pass-Through When Market Share Matters." *American Economic Review* 79 (September 1989): 637–654.

Grossman, G. M., and J. A. Levinsohn. "Import Competition and the Stock Market Return to Capital." *American Economic Review* 79 (December 1989): 1065–1087.

Hooper, P., and C. L. Mann. "Exchange Rate Pass-Through in the 1980s: The Case of U.S. Imports of Manufactures." *Brookings Papers on Economic Activity* 1 (1989): 297–337.

Knetter, M. M. "Price Discrimination by U.S. and German Exporters." *American Economic Review* 79 (March 1989): 198–210.

Letovsky, Robert, "The Export Finance Wars." *Columbia Journal of World Business* 25 (Spring–Summer 1990): 25–35.

Lipsey, Robert E., et al. *Measures of Prices and Price Competitiveness in International Trade in Manufactured Goods.* NBER Working Paper no. 3442. Cambridge, MA: National Bureau of Economic Research, 1990. 72 pp.

Lopez, R. A., and D. Dorsainvil. "An Analysis of Pricing in the Haitian Coffee Market." *Journal of Developing Areas* 25 (October 1990): 93–105.

Ohno, K. "Exchange Rate Fluctuations, Pass-Through, and Market Share [Japan and U.S.]." *International Monetary Fund Staff Papers* 37 (June 1990): 294–310.

Paulus, J. D. "After the Dollar Crash: The World Turned Upside Down [U.S. Economy, Protectionism Overseas]." *Challenge* 31 (January–February 1988): 4–10.

Reinhart, C. M. "Fiscal Policy, the Real Exchange Rate, and Commodity Prices." *International Monetary Fund Staff Papers* 38 (September 1991): 506–524.

Rousslang, D. J. "The Effects of Recent Corporate Tax Changes on U.S. International Trade." *National Tax Journal* 40 (December 1987): 603–615.

Sarris, A. H., and J. Freebairn. "Endogenous Price Policies and International Wheat Prices." *American Journal of Agricultural Economics* 65 (May 1983): 214–224. Discussion 70 (August 1988): 743–749.

Sercu, P., and C. Vanhulle. "Exchange Rate Volatility, International Trade, and the Value of Exporting Firms." *Journal of Banking and Finance* 16 (February 1992): 155–182.

Swanson, P. E. "An Exploratory Empirical Investigation of Vehicle Currency Theory: The Case of the U.S. Dollar [Used To Denominate Third-Country Trade]." *Review of Business and Economic Research* 24 (Spring 1989): 27–42.

Thurow, L. "America's Economy: A Formula for Recovery." *Financial Executive* 4 (May–June 1988): 38–43.

U.S. Congress. Committee on Banking, Finance, and Urban Affairs. Subcommittee on International Development, Finance, Trade, and Monetary Policy. *Practices and Policies of International Financial Institutions: Hearing, January 29, 1992.* 102d Cong., 2d sess. Washington, DC: GPO, 1992. 134 pp.

———. *Proposal for Export-Import Financing of Defense Articles and Services: Hearing, May 2, 1991.* 102d Cong., 1st sess. Washington, D.C.: GPO, 1992. 208 pp.

U.S. Congress. House. Committee on Foreign Affairs. Subcommittee on International Economic Policy and *Trade. Tied Aid and Mixed Credits: Hearing, December 18, 1991.* 102d Cong., 1st sess. Washington, D.C.: GPO, 1992. 229 pp.

U.S. Congress. House. Committee on Small Business. Subcommittee on Exports, Tax Policy, and Special Problems. *Increasing Small Business Participation in SBA and Eximbank Export Financing Programs: Hearing, July 9, 1991.* 102d Cong., 1st sess. Washington, DC: GPO, 1991. 274 pp.

———. *Obstacles That Small Businesses Face in Obtaining Export Financing: Hearing, October 11, 1989.* 101st Cong., 1st sess. Washington, DC: GPO, 1990. 124 pp.

U.S. Congress. Senate. Committee on Banking, Housing, and Urban Affairs. *The Impact of Third World Debt on U.S. Trade: Hearing, October 18, 1989, on Examining the Specific Impact of the Third World Debt Problem on U.S. Trade with Developing Countries.* 101st Cong., 1st sess. Washington, DC: GPO, 1990. 140 pp.

Vachris, Michelle Albert. "Net International Price Series Published by Nation and Region." *Monthly Labor Review* 115 (June 1992): 16–22.

Williamson, P. J. "Domestic Pricing under Import Threat." *Applied Economics* 22 (February 1990): 221–235.

Young, K. H., and A. M. Lawson. "Exchange Rates and the Competitive Price Positions of U.S. Exports and Imports." *Business Economics* 23 (April 1988): 13–19.

Assistance

Chevalier, D. "Freight Forwarders: How To Use Them in Foreign Trade." *International Trade Forum* 25 (July–September 1989): 4–9+.

Cupitt, Richard Thomas, and Margaret Reid. "State Government International Business Promotion Programs and State Export of Manufactures." *State and Local Government Review* 23 (Fall 1991): 127–133.

"Export Promotion Partnership: Working Together To Help Exporters." *Business America* 113 (November 16, 1992): 2–33.

Falvey, R. E., and N. Gemmell. "Explaining Service-Price Differences in International Comparisons." *American Economic Review* 81 (December 1991): 1295–1309.

Fields, G. S., and E. L. Grinols. "Import Competition in the High-Wage Sector and Trade Policy Effects on Labor." *Quarterly Review of Economics and Business* 31 (Summer 1991): 33–56.

Howard, D. G., and I. M. Herremans. "Sources of Assistance for Small Business Exporters: Advice from Successful Firms." *Journal of Small Business Management* 26 (July 1988): 48–54.

"The International Trade Administration Has Many Services To Help U.S. Exporters." *Business America* 114, 9 (1993): 22–28.

Lowry, Houston Putnam. "The United States Joins the Inter-American Arbitration Convention." *Journal of International Arbitration* 7 (September 1990): 83–90.

Uri, N. D., et al. "The Impact of the Export Enhancement Programme on the Soybean Market in the United States." *Applied Economics* 25 (March 1993): 389–402.

U.S. Congress. House. Committee on Banking, Finance, and Urban Affairs. Subcommittee on International Development, Finance, Trade, and Monetary Policy. *Tied Aid Credit Practices: Hearing, May 16, 1989.* 101st Cong., 1st sess. Washington, DC: GPO, 1989. 110 pp.

Quality Control

Raina, H. K. "Measures for Ensuring Quality Conformance in Imports." *International Trade Forum* 28 (April–June 1992): 22–28.

Stokey, N. L. "Human Capital, Product Quality, and Growth." *Quarterly Journal of Economics* 106 (May 1991): 587–616.

Export Marketing

Fitzpatrick, Boyce. *Marketing in the Netherlands.* Washington, DC: U.S. Department of Commerce, International Trade Administration, 1992. 32 pp.

McQueen, Cheryl. *Marketing in Pakistan.* Washington, DC: U.S. Department of Commerce, International Trade Administration, 1992. 56 pp.

Nothdurft, William E. "The Export Game." *Governing* 5 (August 1992): 57–61.

Schares, Gail E., and John Templeman. "Think Small: The Export Lessons To Be Learned from Germany's Midsize Companies." *Business Week* (November 4, 1991): 58–60+.

Sriram, V., and H. J. Sapienza. "An Empirical Investigation of the Role of Marketing for Small Exporters." *Journal of Small Business Management* 29 (October 1991): 33–43.

U.S. Congress. Senate. Committee on Commerce, Science, and Transportation. *Role of Barter and Countertrade in the World Market: Hearing, November 5, 1991.* 102d Cong., 1st sess. Washington, DC: GPO, 1992. 46 pp.

Trading Companies

Carlos, A. M., and S. Nicholas. "Giants of an Earlier Capitalism: The Chartered Trading Companies as Modern Multinationals." *Business History Review* 62 (Autumn 1988): 398–419.

Hipple, F. S. "Multinational Companies and International Trade: The Impact of Intrafirm Shipments on U.S. Foreign Trade 1977–1982." *Journal of International Business Studies* 21, 3 (1990): 495–504.

Holden, A. C. "How To Locate and Communicate with Overseas Customers." *Industrial Marketing Management* 20 (August 1991): 161–168.

Comparative Advantage

Dalal, A. J., and M. Williams. "An Empirical Investigation of Interregional Production Relations and Comparative Advantage in U.S. Manufacturing, 1960–70." *Applied Economics* 22 (June 1990): 823–838.

Erzan, R., and A. J. Yeats. "Implications of Current Factor Proportions Indices for the Competitive Position of the U.S. Manufacturing and Service Industries in the Year 2000." *Journal of Business* 64 (April 1991): 229–254.

Grossman, G. M., and E. Helpman. "Comparative Advantage and Long-Run Growth." *American Economic Review* 80 (September 1990): 796–815.

Management

Brown, D. K., and D. M. Garman. "Human Resource Management and International Trade." *Industrial Relations* 29 (Spring 1990): 189–213.

Cavusgil, S. T., and J. Naor. "Firm and Management Characteristics as Discriminators of Export Marketing Activity." *Journal of Business Research* 15 (June 1987): 221–235.

Jones, J. J. "Earnings Management During Import Relief Investigations [by U.S. International Trade Commission]." *Journal of Accounting Research* 29 (Autumn 1991): 193–228.

Klein, M., et al. "Managing the Dollar: Has the Plaza Agreement Mattered?" *Journal of Money, Credit, and Banking* 23 (November 1991): 742–751.

Korth, C. M. "Managerial Barriers to U.S. Exports." *Business Horizons* 34 (March–April 1991): 18–26.

Export Processing Zones

Krugman, P. "The Move toward Free Trade Zones." *Economic Review* 76 (November–December 1991): 5–35.

Li, K. T. "The Export Processing Zone: A Tool for Promoting Exports." *Industry of Free China* (Taipei) 64 (July 1990): 1–7.

Lindeke, William A. "Export Processing Zones in the Dominican Republic: Implications for the United States." *New Solutions* 4 (Spring 1994): 61–69.

Pissula, Petra, and Dieter Lösch. "Special Economic Zones in the People's Republic of China." *Intereconomics* 25 (September–October 1990): 257–262.

Shayne, William C. *North American Free Trade Agreement: Rules of Origin: 55–955.* Jersey City, NJ: Unz & Co., 1993. 126 pp.

Small Business Trade

Ali, A., and P. M. Swiercz. "Firm Size and Export Behavior: Lessons from the Midwest." *Journal of Small Business Management* 29 (April 1991): 71–78.

DeNoble, Alex F., et al. "Export Intermediaries: Small Business Perceptions of Services and Performance." *Journal of Small Business Management* 27 (April 1989): 33–41.

Kean, Thomas H. "Boosting Small-Business Exports: State Governments Are Pursuing Innovative Programs, But Washington Also Has a Critical Role To Play." *Issues in Science and Technology* 5 (Spring 1989): 37–41.

Lim, J. S., et al. "An Empirical Test of an Adoption Model." *Management International Review* 31, 1 (1991): 51–62.

Mayo, Michael A. "Ethical Problems Encountered by U.S. Small Businesses in International Marketing." *Journal of Small Business Management* 25 (April 1991): 51–59.

Moini, A. H. "Europe 1992: A Challenge to Small Exporters [Problems Faced by U.S. Manufacturers]." *Journal of Small Business Management* 30 (January 1992): 11–20.

Sriram, V., and H. J. Sapienza. "An Empirical Investigation of the Role of Marketing for Small Exporters." *Journal of Small Business Management* 29 (October 1991): 33–43.

U.S. Congress. House. Committee on Small Business. Subcommittee on Exports, Tax Policy, and Special Problems. *EC 1992: How Will American Small Business Develop a Presence: Hearing, September 12, 1989.* 101st Cong., 1st sess. Washington, DC: GPO, 1989. 414 pp.

———. *Increasing Small Business Participation in SBA and Eximbank Export Financing Programs: Hearing, July 9, 1991.* 102d Cong., 1st sess. Washington, DC: GPO, 1991. 274 pp.

———. *Obstacles That Small Businesses Face in Obtaining Export Financing: Hearing, October 11, 1989.* 101st Cong., 1st sess. Washington, DC: GPO, 1990. 124 pp.

———. *Obstacles to Exporting: Hearing, October 4, 1988.* 100th Cong., 2d sess. Washington, DC: GPO, 1989. 105 pp.

U.S. Congress. Senate. Committee on Small Business. *To Examine Small Business Opportunities with the Soviet Union and Eastern Europe: Hearing, March 23, 1990.* 101st Cong., 2d sess. Washington, DC: GPO, 1990. 364 pp.

Vlachoutsikos, Charalambos. "How Small-to-Mid-Sized U.S. Firms Can Profit from Perestroika." *California Management Journal* 31 (Spring 1989): 91–112.

Commodities

Cavusgil, S. T., and V. H. Kirpalani. "Introducing Products into Export Markets: Success Factors." *Journal of Business Research* 27 (May 1993): 1–15.

Flam, H. "Product Markets and 1992: Full Integration, Large Gains?" *Journal of Economic Perspectives* 6 (Fall 1992): 7–30.

"Made in the U.S.A. [Manufactured Exports Cover Story]." *Business Week* (February 29, 1988): 60–71.

Smith, Tim R. "Regional Exports of Manufactured Products." *Federal Reserve Bank of Kansas City Economic Review* 74 (January 1989): 21–31.

U.S. Congress. House. Committee on Science, Space, and Technology. *Product Liability: Hearing, August 4, 1992.* 102d Cong., 2d sess. Washington, DC: GPO, 1992. 459 pp.

————. Subcommittee on Technology and Competitiveness. *Product Liability: Report December 1992).* 102d Cong., 2d sess. Washington, DC: GPO, 1992. 19 pp.

U.S. General Accounting Office. *Technology Transfer: Federal Efforts To Enhance the Competitiveness of Small Manufacturers: Report to the Ranking Minority Member, Committee on Small Business, U.S. Senate.* Gaithersburg, MD, 1991. 46 pp.

Coffee

Bevan, D. L., et al. "Fiscal Response to a Temporary Trade Shock: The Aftermath of the Kenyan Coffee Boom." *World Bank Economic Review* 3 (September 1989): 359–378.

High Technology

Bastos, Maria Ines. "How International Sanctions Worked: Domestic and Foreign Political Restraints on the Brazilian Informatics Policy." *Journal of Development Studies* 30 (January 1994): 380–404.

Browning, Graeme. "Techies in Cahoots: As Japanese Preeminence in Making Semiconductors Threatens a Vital Piece of the American Economy, Debate over the Federal Role in High Technology Has Intensified." *National Journal* 23 (July 6, 1991): 1687–1690.

Evans, Peter B. "Declining Hegemony and Assertive Industrialization: U.S.-Brazil Conflicts in the Computer Industry." *International Organization* 43 (Spring 1989): 207–238.

Janssens, G. K., and L. Cuyvers: "EDI [Electronic Data Interchange]—A Strategic Weapon in International Trade." *Long Range Planning* 24 (April 1991): 46–53.

Kingery, John C. "The U.S.-Japan Semiconductor Arrangement and the GATT: Operating in a Legal Vacuum." *Stanford Journal of International Law* 25 (Spring 1989): 467–497.

Mörth, Ulrika, and Bengt Sundelius. "Dealing with a High Technology Vulnerability Trap: The USA, Sweden, and Industry." *Cooperation and Conflict* 28 (September 1993): 303–328.

National Research Council. Committee on Japan. Office of Japan Affairs. *U.S.-Japan Strategic Alliances in the Semiconductor Industry: Technology Transfer, Competition, and Public Policy.* Washington, DC: National Academy Press, 1992. 118 pp.

Parkhe, A. "U.S. National Security Export Controls: Implications for Global Competitiveness of U.S. High Tech Firms." *Strategic Management Journal* 13 (January 1992): 47–66.

Sununu, John E., and Kevin Keegan. "The Solid States: European Manufacturing Strategies in the Electronics Industry." *Journal of European Business* 2 (September–October 1990): 9–16+.

U.S. Congress. House. Committee on Energy and Commerce. Subcommittee on Oversight and Investigations. *Unfair Foreign Trade Practices: Hearings, March 1–2, 1989.* 101st Cong., 1st sess. Washington, DC: GPO, 1989. 403 pp.

U.S. Congress. House. Committee on Foreign Affairs. Subcommittee on International Economic Policy and Trade. *Policy Implications and Proposed Legislation Concerning the Toshiba/Kongsberg Case: Hearing, June 30, 1987.* 100th Cong., 1st sess. Washington, DC: GPO, 1989. 93p.

————. *United States Exports of Sensitive Technology to Iraq: Hearings, April 8 and May 22, 1991.* 102d Cong., 1st sess. Washington, DC: GPO, 1991. 28 pp.

U.S. Congress. House. Committee on Government Operations. Legislation and National Security Subcommittee. *Is the Administration Giving Away the U.S. Supercomputer Industry? Hearings, July 1 and 8, 1992.* 102d Cong., 2d sess. Washington, DC: GPO, 1992. 452 pp.

U.S. Congress. House. Committee on Science, Space, and Technology. *Export Control Reform in High Technology: Hearing, August 13, 1993.* 103d Cong., 1st sess. Washington, DC: GPO, 1993. 178 pp.

————. Subcommittee on Science, Research, and Technology. *The Federal Research Policy for Semiconductors: Hearing, March 29, 1990.* 101st Cong., 2d sess. Washington, DC: GPO, 1990. 113 pp.

U.S. Congress. House. Committee on Small Business. Subcommittee on Regulation, Business Opportunities, and Energy. *Pacific Northwest Trade with the Eastern Bloc: Opportunities and Obstacles for Timber and Electronics: Hearing, February 12, 1990.* 101st Cong., 2d sess. Washington, DC: GPO, 1990. 138 pp.

U.S. Congress. Senate. Committee on Banking, Housing, and Urban Affairs. *The Defense Production Act Amendments of 1989: Hearing, November 17, 1989, on the Industry's Ability To Meet Defense Needs for Innovation and Production.* 101st Cong., 1st sess. Washington, DC: GPO, 1990. 261 pp.

U.S. National Advisory Committee on Semiconductors. *A National Strategy for Semiconductors: An Agenda for the President, the Congress, and the Industry.* Washington, DC: GPO, 1992. 21 pp.

Wallerstein, Mitchel B. "Controlling Dual-Use Technologies in the New World Order." *Issues in Science and Technology* 7 (Summer 1991): 70–77.

Textiles

Ahmad, Jaleel. "Import Competition, Government Subsidies, and Trade Developing Countries." *Journal of Economic Studies* 19, 2 (1992): 48–57.

Courtless, Joan C. "Recent Trends in Clothing and Textiles." *Family Economic Review* 3, 2 (1990): 8–12.

de Melo, J., and D. Tarr. "Welfare Costs of U.S. Quotas in Textiles, Steel and Autos." *Review of Economics and Statistics* 72 (August 1990): 489–497.

Friman, H. Richard. "Rocks, Hard Places, and the New Protectionism: Textile Trade Policy Choices in the United States and Japan." *International Organization* 42 (Autumn 1988): 689–723.

Kraiprayune, Nicananong. "The Thai-U.S. Textile Agreement 1991." *Bangkok Bank Monthly Review* 32 (September 1991); 343–345.

Ramesh, M. "Explaining Cross-Industry Variations in Trade Protection: Textiles, Clothing and Footwear in Canada." Review of International Studies 20 (January 1994): 75–96.

Reinert, Kenneth A. "Textile and Apparel Protection in the United States: A General Equilibrium Analysis." *World Economics* 16 (May 1993): 359–376.

Richman, Louis S. "How NAFTA Will Help America" *Fortune* 127 (April 19, 1993): 95–96+.

"The Textile and Apparel Trade Act: Pro & Con." *Congressional Digest* 68 (January 1989): 1–32.

U.S. Congress. House. Committee on Government Operations. Commerce, Consumer, and Monetary Affairs Subcommittee. *The North American Free Trade Agreement (NAFTA) and Its Impact on the Textile/Apparel/Fiber and Auto and Auto Parts Industries: Hearing, May 4, 1993.* 103d Cong., 1st sess. Washington, DC: GPO, 1993. 233 pp.

U.S. Department of Commerce. International Trade Administration. Office of Textiles and Apparel. *Foreign Regulations Affecting U.S. Textile Apparel Exports.* Washington, DC: GPO, 1990. 240 pp.

———. *Foreign Regulations Affecting U.S. Textile and Apparel Exports: Foreign Regulations and Trade Barriers Facing U.S. Companies in Sixty Countries.* Washington, DC, 1992. 179 pp.

Energy

Becker, Joanna M. "The Regulation of Nuclear Trade in the United States." *Nuclear Law Bulletin* (June 1993): 26–56.

Bernard, Jean-Thomas, and Robert J. Weiner. *Multinational Corporations, Transfer Prices, and Taxes: Evidence from the U.S. Petroleum Industry.* NBER Working Paper no. 3013. Cambridge, MA: National Bureau of Economic Research, 1989. 40 pp.

Cooper, Mary H. "Oil Imports: U.S. Energy Dependence Remains High after the Gulf War." *CQ Researcher* 1 (August 23, 1991): 585–607.

D'Amato, Anthony, and Kirsten Engel. "State Responsibility for the Exportation of Nuclear Power Technology." *Virginia Law Review* 74 (September 1988): 1011–1066.

Ebel, Robert E. "Out of Gas: Jimmy Carter Meets Mikhail Gorbachev in the Great Coming Soviet Energy Crisis." *International Economics* 5 (July–August 1991): 63–67.

"Gulf Conflict Special." *Petroleum Economist* 57 (September 1990): 5–11+.

Hausker, Karl. "Oil Import Fees: Measuring the Costs and Benefits." *Journal of Energy and Development* 13 (Spring 1988): 171–185.

Kase, R. D. "Petroleum Perestroika [Soviet Oil and Gas Free Market and Investment Prognosis]." *Columbia Journal of World Business* 26 (Winter 1992): 16–28.

Linde, Colby van der. "Empty Barrels Make the Most Sound: Energy Markets in Eastern Europe and the Soviet Union." *World Competition* 15 (December 1991): 127–162.

Looney, Robert E. "World Oil Market Outlook: Implications for Stability in the Gulf States." *Middle East Review* 22 (Winter 1989–1990): 30–37.

McDougall, John N. "The Canada-U.S. Free Trade Agreement and Canada's Energy Trade." *Canadian Public Policy* 19 (June 1991): 473–479.

Minogue, Diane C. *A Review of International Power Sales Agreements.* Industry and Energy Department Working Paper, Energy Series Paper no. 42. Washington, DC: International Bank for Reconstruction and Development, Industry and Energy Department, 1991. 94 pp.

"North American Energy Markets after Free Trade." *Energy Journal* 14, 3 (1993): 1–248.

Plourde, André. "The NEP Meets the FTA." *Canadian Public Policy* 17 (March 1991): 14–24.

Powell, Stephen J., and Valerie A. Slater. "Ramifications of U.S. Trade and National Security Laws for Petroleum Imports." *Journal of Energy and Development* 14 (Spring 1989): 293–317.

Schlesinger, J. R. "Inherent Difficulties in Producer-Consumer Cooperation [Oil-Market Stability]." *Energy Journal* 12, 2 (1991): 9–15.

Subroto. "Will the Trade Blocs Affect Sustainable Development Positively?" *OPEC* (Organization of Petroleum Exporting Countries) *Bulletin* 24 (July–August 1993): 7–11.

True, W. R. "Canadian Gas Imports to New York, New England Surging in 1992." *Oil Gas Journal* 90 (March 2, 1992): 33–39.

U.S. Congress. House. Committee on Banking, Finance, and Urban Affairs. Subcommittee on Economic Stabilization. *National Energy Policy: Implications for Economic Growth: Hearings, October 7 and November 6, 1991.* 102d Cong., 1st sess. Washington, DC: GPO, 1992. 262 pp.

U.S. Congress. House. Committee on Energy and Commerce. *Energy Impact of the Persian Gulf Crisis: Hearing, January 9, 1991.* 102d Cong., 1st sess. Washington, DC: GPO, 1991. 189 pp.

———. Subcommittee on Energy and Power. *Energy: Free Trade with Canada: Hearings, March 1, 1988, Oil and Natural Gas; March 9, 1988, Electricity and Uranium.* 100th Cong., 2d sess. Washington, DC: GPO, 1988. 286 pp.

U.S. Congress. House. Committee on Foreign Affairs. *North American Free Trade Agreement: Mexico's Petroleum Sector: Joint Hearings, March 26 and May 5, 1992, Before the Subcommittees on International Economic Policy and Trade and Western Hemisphere Affairs.* 102d Cong., 2d sess. Washington, DC: GPO, 1993. 104 pp.

U.S. Congress. House. Committee on Ways and Means. Subcommittee on Trade. *Fuel Ethanol Imports from Caribbean Basin Initiative Countries: Hearing, April 25, 1989.* 101st Cong., 1st sess. Washington, DC: GPO, 1989. 238 pp.

U.S. Congress. Senate. Committee on Energy and Natural Resources. *Key Elements of a National Energy Policy: Hearing, October 2, 1990.* 101st Cong., 2d sess. Washington, DC: GPO, 1991. 189 pp.

———. Subcommittee on Renewable Energy, Energy Efficiency, and Competitiveness. *Industrial Competitiveness through Energy Efficiency and Waste Minimization: Hearing, April 29, 1993.* 103d Cong., 1st sess. Washington, DC: GPO, 1993. 101 pp.

U.S. Congress. Senate. Committee on the Judiciary. Subcommittee on Antitrust, Monopolies, and Business Rights. *Anticompetitive Practices in the Retail Gasoline Market: Hearing, May 6, 1992, on S. 790, S. 2401, and S. 2043.* 102d Cong., 2d sess. Washington, DC: GPO, 1992. 608 pp.

U.S. Energy Information Administration. Office of Energy Markets and End Use. *International Energy Outlook, 1990.* Washington, DC, 1990. 56 pp.

U.S. General Accounting Office. *Mexican Oil: Issues Affecting Potential U.S. Trade and Investment: Report to the Chairman, Subcommittee on International Economic Policy and Trade, Committee on Foreign Affairs, House of Representatives.* Report B-247884. Gaithersburg, MD, 1992. 36 pp.

U.S. Office of Technology Assessment. *U.S. Oil Import Vulnerability: The Technical Replacement Capability.* Washington, DC: GPO, 1991. 136 pp.

Wolak, F. A., and C. D. Kolstad. "A Model of Homogeneous Input under Price Uncertainty [Risk-Diversification Framework as Applied to the Japanese Steam-Coal Import Market]." *American Economic Review* 81 (June 1991): 514–538.

Yucel, Mine K., and Carol Dahl. "Reducing U.S. Oil-Import Dependence: A Tariff, Subsidy or Gasoline Tax?" *Federal Reserve Bank of Dallas Economic Review* (May 1990): 17–25.

Motor Vehicles
Barry, Steven, et al. *The Automobile Industry and the Mexico-U.S. Free Trade Agreement.* NBER Working Paper no. 4152. Cambridge, MA: National Bureau of Economic Research, 1992. 75 pp.

Bussmann, W. V. "The Trade Deficit in Autos with Japan: How Much Improvement?" *Business Economics* 23 (April 1988): 20–25.

"Competitiveness of the North American Auto Industry." *UMTRI* (University of Michigan Transportation Research Institute) *Research Review* 23 (November–December 1992): 1–16.

Monica, John C., Jr. "United States Exports with a Japanese Label: Potential Effects of EC '92 on Automobiles Manufactured by Japanese on U.S. Soil." *George Washington Journal of International Law and Economics* 24, 3 (1991): 623–645.

O'Kane, Gerry. "Long Way To Go for Car Makers: Asia Offers Huge Potential for the World's Major Car Makers: But It Also Has Big Headaches for Them." *Asian Business* 28 (December 1992): 60–62+.

Stokes, Bruce. "Protection—For a Price: Congress Is Warning the U.S. Auto Industry That If It Wants To Be Protected against Japanese Car Imports It Will Have To Show What It Is Willing To Do for Itself." *National Journal* 24 (April 4, 1992): 794–799.

Taylor, Alex, III. "U.S. Cars Come Back." *Fortune* 126 (November 16, 1992): 52–59+.

U.S. Congress. House. Committee on Energy and Commerce. Subcommittee on Commerce, Consumer Protection, and Competitiveness. *Trade Enhancement: Hearings, March 5 – April 8, 1992, on H.R. 4100, a Bill To Assure Mutually Advantageous International Trade in Motor Vehicles and Motor Vehicle Parts, an Enhanced Market for Domestically Produced Motor Vehicles and Motor Vehicle Parts, and the Retention and Enhancement of U.S. Jobs.* 102d Cong., 2d sess. Washington, DC: GPO 1992. 435 pp.

U.S. Congress. House. Committee on Energy and Commerce. Subcommittee on Energy and Power. *What's Ailing the U.S. Auto Industry?* 102d Cong., 2d sess. Washington, DC: GPO, 1992. 161 pp.

U.S. Congress. House. Committee on Ways and Means. *Customs' Enforcement of the Rules-of-Origin Provisions of the United States–Canada Free Trade Agreement: Hearing, October 16, 1991, Before the Subcommittee on Trade, and the Subcommittee on Oversight.* 102d Cong., 1st sess. Washington, DC: GPO, 1992. 141 pp.

———. Subcommittee on Trade. *U.S. International Trade Performance and Outlook: Competitive Position in the Automotive, Aerospace, and Chemical and Pharmaceutical Sectors: Hearings, March 11–April 7, 1992.* 102d Cong., 2d sess. Washington, DC: GPO, 1992. 669 pp.

Warf, Barney. "International Automobile Trade of the United States during the 1980s." *Geographical Review* 80 (July 1990): 252–265.

Womack, James P. "Awaiting NAFTA: Investment Dilemmas in the Auto Sector." *Business Mexico* 3 (April 1993): 4+.

Glass

U.S. Congress. Senate. Committee on Commerce, Science, and Transportation. Subcommittee on Foreign Commerce and Tourism. *Competitiveness in the Glassware Industry: Hearing, October 30, 1989, on Competitiveness in the Glassware and Commercial Chinaware Industry.* 101st Cong., 1st sess. Washington, DC: GPO, 1990. 70 pp.

Iron and Steel

Denzau, Arthur. *The Unlevel Playing Field: How High Steel Prices and Trade Protection Help Deindustrialize America.* Working Paper 128. St. Louis, MO: Center for the Study of American Business, Washington University, 1989. 24 pp.

de Silva Neto, Alfredo Lopes. "The International Effects of Mining Projects: The Case of Carajás Iron Ore." *Resource Policy* 19 (June 1993): 124–130.

European Communities. Statistics Office. *Iron and Steel Yearly Statistics, 1992.* Luxembourg: European Communities Official Publications Office, 1993. 137 pp.

Lenway, S., et al. "The Impact of Protectionism on Firm Wealth: The Experience of the Steel Industry." *Southern Economic Journal* 56 (April 1990): 1079–1093.

Murphy, Brendan, and John Erkkila. "Steel Trade between the U.S. and Canada: There Is More to It Than Market Share." *World Competition* 12 (December 1988): 69–80.

Stokes, Bruce. "Saving Steel: The Bush Administration May Soon Seek New Deals with World Steel Producers To Limit Exports to the United States, But the Industry Needs More Than Another Quick Fix." *National Journal* 21 (March 25, 1989): 735–739.

U.S. Congress. House. Committee on Ways and Means. *Background Materials Relating to the Steel Voluntary Restraint Agreement (VRA) Program, June 2, 1989.* 101st Cong., 1st sess. Washington, DC: GPO, 1989. 167 pp.

Wehr, Elizabeth. "Producers Press for Renewal of Steel Import Quotas: Steelmakers Praise Effects of Trade Restraints, But Users Say the Price Is Too High." *Congressional Quarterly Weekly Report* 47 (March 1989): 629–632.

Agriculture

Ackerman, K., and S. MacDonald. "International Trade." *National Food Review* 12 (April–June 1989): 40–48.

"Agricultural Trade and Mexico's Foreign Debt: Mexican and United States Perspectives." *American Journal of Agricultural Economics* 71 (December 1989): 1117–1137.

Alston, Julian M., et al. "Discriminatory Trade: The Case of Japanese Beef and Wheat Imports." *Canadian Journal of Agricultural Economics* 38 (July 1990): 197–214.

Anania, Giovanni, et al. "United States Export Subsidies in Wheat: Strategic Trade Policy or Expensive Beggar-Thy-Neighbor Tactic?" *American Journal of Agricultural Economics* 74 (August 1992): 534–545.

Anderson, M., and P. Garcia. "Exchange Rate Uncertainty and the Demand for U.S. Soybeans." *American Journal of Agricultural Economics* 71 (August 1989): 721–729.

Ashley, Gregory A., and James E. Epperson. *An Analysis of Potential International Market Penetration of U.S. Vegetables: Foreign Importers' Perspective.* Research Bulletin 380. Athens, GA: Agriculture Experiment Stations, 1989. 34 pp.

Barkema, Alan. "How Will Reform of the Soviet Farm Economy Affect U.S. Agriculture?" *Federal Reserve Bank of Kansas City Economic Review* 76 (September–October 1991): 5–19.

———. "The North American Free Trade Agreement: What Is at Stake for U.S. Agriculture?" *Federal Reserve Bank of Kansas City Economic Review* 77, 3 (1992): 5–20.

Barkema, Alan, et al. "Agriculture and the GATT: A Time for Change; The Link to U.S. Farm Policy." *Federal Reserve Bank of Kansas City Economic Review* 7 (February 1989): 21–42; 7 (May 1989): 3–24.

Baroudi, Sami. "Egyptian Agriculture Exports since 1973." *Middle East Journal* 47 (Winter 1993): 63–76.

Barry, R. D. "The U.S. Sugar Program in the 1980's." *National Food Review* 88 (October 8, 1990): 55–61.

Blackburn, Joseph. "The Time Factor." *National Productivity Review* 9 (Autumn 1990): 395–408.

Braga, F. S., and L. J. Martin. "Hedging Strategies for Exports of Cereals and Cereal Products to the European Community." *Journal of Futures Markets* 11 (June 1991): 347–369.

"Canada-U.S. Agricultural Trade: The Current Agenda." *Canada-U.S. Outlook* 2 (May 1991): 3–48.

Casavant, Kenneth L., and Wesley W. Wilson. "Shipper Perspectives of the Shipping Act of 1984." *Transportation Quarterly* 45 (January 1991): 109–120.

Chambers, R. G., and P. L. Paarlberg. "Are More Exports Always Better? Comparing Cash and In-Kind Export Subsidies." *American Journal of Agricultural Economics* 73 (February 1991): 142–154.

Cohn, Theodore H. *Emerging Issue in Canada-U.S. Agricultural Trade under the GATT and FTA.* Canadian American Public Policy no. 10. Orono, ME: Canadian-American Center, University of Maine, 1992. 57 pp.

———. *The Intersection of Domestic and Foreign Policy in the NAFTA Agricultural Negotiations,* Canadian-American Public Policy no. 14. Orono, ME: Canadian-American Center, University of Maine, 1993. 58 pp.

Creason, Jared R., and C. Ford Runge. *Agricultural Competitiveness and Environmental Quality: What Mix of Policies Will Accomplish Both Goals.* St. Paul, MN: Center for International Food and Agricultural Policy, University of Minnesota, 1990. 47 pp.

Duffy, P. A., et al. "The Elasticity Demand for U.S. Cotton." *American Journal of Agricultural Economics* 72 (May 1990): 468–474.

Filipek, Jon G. "Agriculture in a World of Comparative Advantage: The Prospects for Farm Trade Liberalization in the Uruguay Round of GATT Negotiations." *Harvard International Law Journal* 30 (Winter 1989): 123–170.

Forsythe, Ken, and Liana Neff. "Enterprise for the American Initiative." *Agricultural Outlook* (August 1992): 35–39.

Grennes, Thomas, and Barry Krissoff. "Agricultural Trade in a North American Free Trade Agreement." *World Economics* 16 (July 1993): 483–502.

Haniotis, T. "European Community Enlargement Impact on U.S. Corn and Soybean Exports." *American Journal of Agricultural Economics* 72 (May 1990): 289–297.

Harper, Richard K., and John Aldrich. "The Political Economy of Sugar Legislation." *Public Choice* 70 (June 1991): 299–314.

Hine, R. C., et al. "Agriculture in the Uruguay Round: From the Punta del Este Declaration to the Geneva Accord." *Journal of Agricultural Economics* 40 (September 1989): 385–396.

Huffman, W. E., and R. E. Evenson. "Supply and Demand Functions for Multiproduct U.S. Cash Grain Farms: Biases Caused by Research and Other Policies." *American Journal of Agricultural Economics* 71 (August 1989): 761–773.

"International Trade [Agricultural Trade]."*National Food Review* 37 (1987): 40–47.

Jaffee, Steven. *Exporting High-Value Food Commodities: Success Stories from Developing Countries.* Washington, DC: International Bank for Reconstruction and Development, 1993. 105 pp.

Janvry, Alain de, and Elisabeth Sadoulet. "The Conditions for Compatibility between Aid and Trade in Agriculture." *Economic Development and Cultural Change* 37 (October 1988): 1–30.

Lo, Ming-Che, and Tsorng-Chyi Hwang. "Agricultural Trade Policy in Taiwan." *Industry of Free China* (Taipei) 80 (November 1993): 37–53.

McFaul, Francis G. *U.S. Foreign Trade Highlights, 1992.* Washington, DC: U.S. Department of Commerce, International Trade Administration, Office of Trade and Analysis, 1993. 207 pp.

McGregor, Andrew, et al. *Commercial Management Companies in the Agricultural Development of the Pacific Islands.* Research Report Series no. 15. Honolulu, HI: University of Hawaii Press, 1992. 43 pp.

Maskus, Keith E. "Large Costs and Small Benefits of the American Sugar Programme." *World Economy* (London) 12 (March 1989): 85–104.

Mendelson, Richard, et al. "Wine Trade with Canada: A Case Study in Trade Deregulation." *International Tax and Business Lawyer* 7 (Winter 1989): 91–119.

Monahan, Katherine E. "U.S. Sugar Policy: Domestic and International Repercussions of Sour Law." *Hastings International and Comparative Law Review* 15 (Winter 1992): 325–362.

"The New Round of Japan—U.S. Friction." *Tokyo Business Today* (November 1988): 16–23.

"The 1990 Farm Bill and the GATT Outcome." *American Journal of Agricultural Economics* 73 (August 1991): 905–925.

Orden, D. "International Capital Markets and Structural Adjustment in U.S. Agriculture." *American Journal of Agricultural Economics* 72 (August 1990): 749–757.

Oskam, Arie, and Harald von Witzke. *Agricultural Policy Preferences: Wheat in the United States, 1981–1990.* Staff Papers Series P90-68. St. Paul, MN: Department of Agricultural and Applied Economics, Institute of Agriculture, Forestry, and Home Economics, University of Minnesota, 1990. 17 pp.

Paarlberg, Robert L. "The Upside-Down World of U.S.-Japanese Agricultural Trade." *Washington Quarterly* 13 (Autumn 1990): 131–147.

Palmeter, N. David. "Agriculture and Trade Regulation: Selected Issues in the Application of U.S. Antidumping and Countervailing Duty Laws." *Journal of World Trade* 23 (February 1989): 47–68.

Pick, D. H. "Exchange Rate Risk and U.S. Agricultural Trade Flows." *American Journal of Agricultural Economics* 72 (August 1990): 694–700.

Pick, D. H., and T. A. Park. "The Competitive Structure of U.S. Agricultural Exports." *American Journal of Agricultural Economics* 73 (February 1991): 133–141.

Pitcher, Andrew. "Nebraska's Exports of Agricultural Commodities." *Business in Nebraska* 44 (May 1989): 1–6.

Rauch, Jonathan. "Subsidized Ads: Under the Agriculture Department's Controversial Market Promotion Program, Taxpayers Help Pay for Business Advertising Overseas; Is That Strategic Trade Policy—or Corporate Welfare?" *National Journal* 24 (June 27, 1992): 1509–1512.

Raup, Philip M. *Some Expected Changes in World Trade in Wheat and Coarse Grains.* Staff Paper P92-7. St. Paul, MN: Department of Agricultural and Applied Economics, College of Agriculture, University of Minnesota, 1992. 12 leaves.

Rayner, A. J., et al. "Agriculture in the Uruguay Round: An Assessment." *Economic Journal* 103 (January 24, 1994): 56–61.

Ritchie, Mark. "Free Trade versus Sustainable Agriculture; The Implications of NAFTA." *Ecologist* 22 (September–October 1992): 221–227.

Runge, C. Ford. *Agricultural Trade in the Uruguay Round: Into Final Battle.* Staff Papers Series P89-34. St. Paul, MN: Institute of Agriculture, Forestry and Home Economics, Department of Agricultural and Applied Economics, University of Minnesota, 1989. 21 pp.

———. *Illusion and Reality in International Agricultural Trade Negotiations.* St. Paul, MN: Department of Agricultural and Applied Economics. Institute of Agriculture, Forestry, and Home Economics, University of Minnesota, 1990. 17 pp.

———. *Trading with Canada: The Impact of the U.S./Canada Free Trade Agreement on North American Agriculture.* Staff Paper P91-5. St. Paul, MN: Department of Agricultural and Applied Economics, Institute of Agriculture, University of Minnesota, 1991. 21 pp.

Runge, C. Ford, and D. Halbach. "Export Demand, U.S. Farm Income and Land Prices: 1949–1985." *Land Economics* 66 (May 1990): 150–162.

Runge, C. Ford, and Steven J. Taff. "Changing the Rules for Agricultural Trade." *Minnesota Agricultural Economist* (February 1989): 1–5.

Sigalia, Fiona D. "Regional Effects of Liberalized Agricultural Trade." *Federal Reserve Bank of Dallas Economic Review* (2d Quarter 1992): 43–54.

Smith, Mark E. "New Era in Trade with Former USSR." *Agricultural Outlook* (June 1992): 20–23.

"Trade Issues for the 1990s." *Journal of Agricultural Economics* 71 (December 1989): 1219–1243.

United Nations. Conference on Trade and Development. *Studies in the Processing, Marketing and Distribution of Commodities: The Marketing of Bovine Meat and Products: Areas for International Co-operation.* New York: U.N. Agency, 1989. 76 pp.

U.S. Congress. Budget Office. *Agricultural Progress in the Third World and Its Effect on U.S. Farm Exports.* Washington, DC, 1989. 78 pp.

U.S. Congress. House. Committee on Agriculture. *Third World Debt and Its Impact on the U.S. Agricultural Sector: Hearing, May 11, 1989.* 101st Cong., 1st sess. Washington, DC: GPO, 1989. 179 pp.

––––––. Subcommittee on Wheat, Soybeans, and Feed Grains. *Effect of Grain Imports on U.S. Commodity Programs and Markets: Hearing, November 18, 1991.* 102d Cong., 1st sess. Washington, DC: GPO, 1992. 83 pp.

U.S. Congress. House. Committee on Foreign Affairs. *Thirty-First Meeting of the Canada–United States Interparliamentary Group, February 22–26, 1990: Report by the Chairman of the House of Representatives Delegation.* 101st Cong., 2d sess. Washington, DC: GPO, 1990. 31 pp.

––––––. Subcommittee on International Economic Policy and Trade. *National Policy Related to the U.S. Fishery Export Promotion: Hearings, November 6, 1987, and March 9, 1988.* 100th Cong., 2d sess. Washington, DC: GPO, 1988. 189 pp.

––––––. *U.S. Agriculture Exports and Economic Embargoes: Hearing, June 8, 1988.* 100th Cong., 2d sess. Washington, DC: GPO, 1988. 119 pp.

U.S. Congress. House. Committee on Ways and Means. Subcommittee on Trade. *Conditions of Competition between the United States and Canadian Durum Wheat Industries: Hearing, December 7, 1989.* 101st Cong., 1st sess. Washington, DC: GPO, 1990. 111 pp.

––––––. *Country-of-Origin Labeling Requirements for Imported Meat and Other Food Products: Hearing, September 27, 1988.* 100th Cong., 2d sess. Washington, DC: GPO, 1989. 185 pp.

———. *U.S. Sugar Policy, Implications for International Trade, and Options for Reform: Hearing, February 20, 1990*. 101st Cong., 1st sess. Washington, DC: GPO, 1990. 226 pp.

U.S. Congress. Joint Economic Committee. *The Effects of the Third World Debt Crisis on U.S. Agriculture: Hearing, May 18, 1989*. 101st Cong., 1st sess. Washington, DC: GPO, 1989. 58 pp.

U.S. Congress. Senate. Committee on Agriculture, Nutrition, and Forestry. *China: Agricultural Trade Prospects*. 100th Cong., 2d sess. Washington, DC: GPO, 1988. 33 pp.

———. *Fast Track Procedures for Agricultural Trade Negotiations: Hearing, May 8, 1991, on Reviewing the Extension of Fast Track Procedures for International Trade Negotiations as Related to the Uruguay Round of the General Agreement on Tariffs and Trade, the North American Free Trade Area, and the Enterprise for the American Initiative*. 102d Cong., 1st sess. Washington, DC: GPO, 1992. 139 pp.

U.S. Congress. Senate. Committee on Agriculture, Nutrition, and Forestry. Subcommittee on Domestic and Foreign Market and Product Promotion. *Importation of Subsidized Grains from Sweden: Hearing, July 8, 1991, on the Importation of Swedish Feed Barley into the United States, Focusing on Market Conditions at the Time of These Imports and Unfair Trade Practices*. 102d Cong., 1st sess. Washington, DC: GPO, 1992. 62 pp.

U.S. Congress. Senate. Committee on Finance. Subcommittee on International Trade. *Extending International Trading Rules to Agriculture: Hearing, November 3, 1989*. 101st Cong., 1st sess. Washington, DC: GPO, 1990. 105 pp.

———. *Trade between Montana and the Pacific Rim: Hearing, December 8, 1989*. 101st Cong., 1st sess. Washington, DC: GPO, 1990. 61 pp.

U.S. Congress. Senate. Committee on Governmental Affairs. Subcommittee on Oversight of Government Management. *Oversight of U.S. Trade Policy with Japan: Hearing, May 8, 1991*. 102d Cong., 1st sess. Washington, DC: GPO, 1991. 283 pp.

U.S. Congress. Senate. Committee on the Budget. *United States/Mexico International Agricultural Trade Situation: Hearing, January 10, 1990*. 101st Cong., 2d sess. Washington, DC: GPO, 1990. 162 pp.

U.S. Department of Agriculture. Foreign Agriculture Service. Information Division. *Foreign Agriculture,* 1992. Washington, DC, 1992. 207 pp.

U.S. General Accounting Office. *Drug Policy and Agriculture: U.S. Trade Impacts of Alternative Crops to Andean Cocoa: Report to Congressional Requesters.* Report B-245867. Gaithersburg, MD, 1991. 58 pp.

————. *International Trade: Canada and Australia Rely Heavily on Wheat Boards To Market Grain: Report to the Chairman, Subcommittee on Domestic and Foreign Marketing and Product Promotion, Committee on Agriculture, Nutrition and Forestry, U.S. Senate.* Report B- 114824. Gaithersburg, MD, 1992. 60 pp.

U.S. Office of Technology Assessment. *Enhancing the Quality of U.S. Grain for International Trade.* Washington, DC, 1989. 293 pp.

Wisner, Robert N., and Hamid Tabesh. *World Food Trade and U.S. Agriculture, 1960–1987: U.S. Share of World Exports.* Ames, IA: World Food Institute, Iowa State University, 1988. 90 pp.

Communication Equipment Industry

Dörrenbacher, Christoph, and Oliver Fischer. "Telecommunications in the Uruguay Round." *Intereconomics* 25 (July–August 1990): 185–192.

Johnson, Leland L. *U.S.-Japan Trade Relations in Telecommunications and Equipment Markets.* Santa Monica, CA: Rand Corporation, 1993. 77 pp.

Neu, Werner, and Thomas Schnöring. "The Telecommunications Equipment Industry: Recent Changes in Its International Trade Pattern." *Telecommunications Policy* 13 (March 1989): 25–39.

U.S. Congress. House. Committee on Energy and Commerce. Subcommittee on Oversight and Investigations. *Unfair Foreign Trade Practices: Hearings, March 1–2, 1989.* 101st Cong., 1st sess. Washington, DC: GPO, 1989. 403 pp.

————. Subcommittee on Telecommunications and Finance. *Telecommunication Opportunities in Eastern Europe: Hearing, May 17, 1990.* 101st Cong., 2d sess. Washington, DC: GPO, 1990. 148 pp.

U.S. Department of Commerce. International Trade Administration. *A Guide to Telecommunications Markets in Latin America.* Washington, DC: 1989. 84 pp.

Forest Products

Button, Kenneth R. "The United States–Canada Free Trade Agreement: An Overview and an Assessment for the U.S. Non-ferrous Metals and Forest Products Industries." *Law and Policy in International Business* 20, 4 (1989): 765–793.

Hammett, A. L., and Kevin T. McNamara. *Shifts in the Southern Share of United States Wood Product Exports from 1980 to 1988.* Research Report 594. Athens, GA: Agriculture Experiment Station, 1990. 11 pp.

U.S. Congress. House. Committee on Energy and Commerce. Subcommittee on Commerce, Consumer Protection, and Competitiveness. *Tropical Wood Labeling: Hearing, May 13, 1992, on H.R. 2854, a Bill To Provide for the Labeling or Marking of Tropical Wood and Tropical Wood Products Sold in the United States, and Related Issues.* 102d Cong., 2d sess. Washington, DC: GPO, 1992. 79 pp.

Waggener, Thomas R. *Forests, Timber and Trade: Emerging Canadian and U.S. Relations under the Free Trade Agreement.* Canadian-American Public Policy no. 4. Orono, ME: University of Maine Press, 1990. 45 pp.

Lumber Industry

Chase, Brian F. "Tropical Forests and Trade Policy: The Legality of Unilateral Attempts To Promote Sustainable Development under the GATT." *Third World Quarterly* 14, 4 (1993): 749–774.

U.S. Congress. House. Committee on Agriculture. Subcommittee on Forests, Family Farms, and Energy. *Review of Proposals To Restrict Timber Exports: Hearing, May 8, 1990, on H.R. 1037.* 101st Cong., 1st sess. Washington, DC: GPO, 1991. 140 pp.

U.S. Congress. House. Committee on Foreign Affairs. Subcommittee on International Economic Policy and Trade. *Log Exports: Hearings, v. 1–2, November 7, 1987–April 27, 1988, on H.R. 1587.* 2 vols. 100th Cong., 1st and 2d sess. Washington, DC: GPO, 1988.

U.S. Congress. House. Committee on Small Business. Subcommittee on Regulation, Business Opportunities, and Energy. *1986 United*

States–Canada Memorandum of Understanding on Softwood Lumber: Hearing, February 22, 1991. 102d Cong., 1st sess. Washington, DC: GPO, 1991. 195 pp.

————. *Pacific Northwest Trade with the Eastern Bloc: Opportunities and Obstacles for Timber and Electronics: Hearing, February 12, 1990.* 101st Cong., 2d sess. Washington, DC: GPO, 1990. 138 pp.

U.S. Congress. Senate Committee on Banking, Housing, and Urban Affairs. Subcommittee on International Finance and Monetary Policy. *Log Export Legislation: Hearing, November 7, 1989, on S. 754, To Restrict the Export of Unprocessed Timber from Certain Federal Lands, and for Other Purposes; S. 755, To Authorize the States to Prohibit or Restrict the Export of Unprocessed Logs Harvested from Lands Owned or Administered by States.* 101st Cong., 1st sess. Washington, DC: GPO, 1990. 269 pp.

Waggener, Thomas R. *Forests, Timber, and Trade: Emerging Canadian and U.S. Relations under the Free Trade Agreement.* Canadian-American Public Policy no 4. Orono, ME: University of Maine Press, 1990. 45 pp.

Pesticides

Hill, Raymond. "Problems and Policy for Pesticide Exports to Less Developed Countries." *Natural Resources Journal* 28 (October 1988): 699–720.

Kablack, Mark A. "Pesticide Abuses in Third World Countries and a Model for Reform." *Boston College Third World Law Journal* 11 (Summer 1991): 277–305.

Powledge, Fred. "Toxic Shame: Foreign Policy Is Becoming Environmental and Consumer Policy, But the Circle of Poison Remains Unbroken." *Americus Journal* 13 (Winter 1991): 38–44.

U.S. Congress. House. Committee on Foreign Affairs. Subcommittee on International Economic Policy and Trade. *U.S. Pesticide Exports and the Circle of Poison: Hearing, February 20, 1992.* 102d Cong., 2d sess. Washington, DC: GPO, 1992. 149 pp.

U.S. Congress. House. Committee on Government Operations. Environment, Energy, and Natural Resources Subcommittee. *The Uncontrolled Export of Unregistered Pesticides: Hearing, May 3, 1989.* 101st Cong., 1st sess. Washington, DC: GPO, 1989. 267 pp.

U.S. Congress. Senate. Committee on Agriculture, Nutrition, and Forestry. *Circle of Poison: Impact of U.S. Pesticides on Third World Workers: Hearing, June 5, 1991.* 102d Cong., 1st sess. Washington, DC: GPO, 1991. 210 pp.

———. *Circle of Poison: Impact on American Consumers: Hearing, September 20, 1991, on Improving the Safety of Exported Pesticides Manufactured in the United States on the American Consumer.* 102d Cong., 1st sess. Washington, DC: GPO, 1992. 528 pp.

Aircraft

Contracting Parties to the General Agreement on Tariffs and Trade. *Agreement on Trade in Civil Aircraft: Including the Protocol (1986) Amending the Annex to the Agreement.* Geneva, Switzerland, 1990. 29 pp.

European Communities Commission. *Proposal for a Council Decision Concerning the Conclusion of an Agreement between the European Economic Community and the United States of America on Trade in Large Civil Aircraft.* Luxembourg, 1992. 17 pp.

March, Artemis. "The Future of the U.S. Aircraft Industry: Amidst a Dramatically Changed Environment at Home, U.S. Aviation Manufacturers Face a Serious Challenge from Abroad." *Technology Review* (June 1990): 26–34+.

Yang, Dori Jones, and Michael Oneal. "How Boeing Does It: America's Export Machine Is Ready To Bet Big on Its Embryonic 777." *Business Week* (July 9, 1990): 46–50.

Hazardous Material

Applegate, John S. "The Perils of Unreasonable Risk: Information, Regulatory Policy, and Toxic Substances." *Columbia Law Review* 91 (March 1991): 261–333.

Handl, Günther, and Robert E. Lutz. "An International Policy Perspective on the Trade of Hazardous Materials and Technologies." *Harvard International Law Journal* 30 (Spring 1989): 351–374.

Kablack, Mark A. "Pesticide Abuses in Third World Countries and a Model for Reform." *Boston College Third World Law Journal* 11 (Summer 1991): 277–305.

Mehri, Cyrus. "Prior Informed Consent: An Emerging Compromise for Hazardous Exports." *Cornell International Law Journal* 21 (Summer 1988): 365–389.

Chemicals

Anderson, E. V. "Canadian Chemical Industry Backs North American Free Trade Pact." *Chemical Engineering News* 70 (January 27, 1992): 9–15.

Thomas, James, et al. "Chemical Trade Prospers in the 1980s." *Monthly Labor Review* 114 (June 1991): 3–11.

U.S. Congress. House. Committee on Ways and Means. Subcommittee on Trade. *U.S. International Trade Performance and Outlook: Competitive Position in the Automotive, Aerospace, and Chemical and Pharmaceutical Sectors: Hearings, March 11–April 7, 1992.* 102d Cong., 2d sess. Washington, DC: GPO, 1992. 669 pp.

U.S. Congress. Senate. Committee on Commerce, Science, and Transportation. Subcommittee on Foreign Commerce and Tourism. *U.S. Chemical Exports to Latin America: Hearings, February 6, 1990.* 101st Cong., 2d sess. Washington, DC: GPO, 1990. 87 pp.

———. *U.S. Chemical Exports to Latin America: Hearings, February 6 and August 1, 1990.* 2 pts. 101st Cong., 2d sess. Washington, DC: GPO, 1990.

Weigand, R. E. "Parallel Import Channels—Options for Preserving Territorial Integrity." *Columbia Journal of World Business* 26 (Spring 1991): 53–60.

Apparel

Ahmad, Jaleel. "Import Competition, Government Subsidies, and Trade in Developing Countries." *Journal of Economic Studies* 19, 2 (1992): 48–57.

Goto, Junichi. "The Multifibre Arrangement and Its Effects on Developing Countries." *World Bank Research Observer* 4 (July 1989): 203–227.

Haggblade, Steven. "The Flip Side of Fashion: Used Clothing Exports to the Third World." *Journal of Development Studies* 26 (April 1990): 505–521.

Majmudar, Madhavi. "Indian Garment Exports to the U.S.A., 1980–8: Market Access or Supply-Side Response?" *Development Policy Review* 8 (June 1990): 131–153.

U.S. Congress. House. Committee on Government Operations. Commerce, Consumer and Monetary Affairs Subcommittee. *The North American Free Trade Agreement (NAFTA) and Its Impact on the Textile/Apparel/Fiber and Auto and Auto Parts Industries: Hearing, May 4, 1993*. 103d Cong., 1st sess. Washington, DC: GPO, 1993. 233 pp.

U.S. Congress. Senate. Committee on Finance. *Textile, Apparel and Footwear Trade Act of 1990: Hearing, June 7, 1990 on S. 2411*. 101st Cong., 1st sess. Washington, DC: GPO, 1991. 97 pp.

U.S. Department of Commerce. International Trade Administration. Office of Textiles and Apparel. *Foreign Regulations Affecting U.S. Textile/Apparel Exports*. Washington, DC, 1990. 240 pp.

———. *Foreign Relations Affecting U.S. Textile and Apparel Exports: Foreign Relations and Trade Barriers Facing U.S. Companies in Sixty Countries*. Washington, DC, 1992. 179 pp.

Tobacco

Heise, Lori. "Unhealthy Alliance: With U.S. Government Help, Tobacco Firms Push Their Goods Overseas." *World Watch* 1 (September–October, 1988): 19–28.

Joyce, D., and P. Joyce. "U.S. Cigarette Manufacturers in Asia: The Emerging Battlefield." *Southeast Asia Business* 7 (Spring 1991): 15–35.

Mackay, Judith. "China's Tobacco Wars." *Multinational Monitor* 13 (January–February 1992): 9–12.

Marshall, Patrick G. "Tobacco Industry: On the Defensive, But Still Strong." *Editorial Research Reports* (September 21, 1990): 538–551.

Schwartz, Robbie Danielle. "Exporting Cigarettes: Do Profits Trump Ethics and International Law?" *Vanderbilt Journal of Transnational Law* 24, 5 (1991): 1009–1045.

Thursby, M., et al. "Smuggling, Camouflaging, and Market Structure [Cigarette Smuggling in U.S.]," *Quarterly Journal of Economics* 106 (August 1991): 789–814.

"The Tobacco Trade." *Economist* (London) 323 (May 16, 1992): 21–22+.

U.S. Congress. House. Committee on Agriculture. Subcommittee on Tobacco and Peanuts. *Review of Exported Tobacco Issues: Hearing, June 15, 1988.* 100th Cong., 2d sess. Washington, DC: GPO, 1988. 96 pp.

————. *Review of Imported Tobacco Issues: Hearing, May 25, 1988.* 100th Cong., 2d sess. Washington, DC: GPO, 1988. 35 pp.

U.S. Congress. House. Committee on Energy and Commerce. Subcommittee on Health and the Environment. *Tobacco Control and Marketing: Hearings, May 17 and July 12, 1990.* 101st Cong., 2d sess. Washington, DC: GPO, 1990. 833 pp.

U.S. Congress. Senate. Committee on Labor and Human Resources. *Smoking and World Health: Hearing, May 4, 1990, Examining Certain Issues Surrounding the Export of Tobacco to Foreign Countries, Focusing on U.S. Advertising Techniques Used To Promote Smoking in Foreign Countries and the Health Effects of Smoking on World Health.* 101st Cong., 2d sess. Washington, DC: GPO, 1990. 260 pp.

U.S. General Accounting Office. *Trade and Health Issues: Dichotomy between U.S. Tobacco Export Policy and Antismoking Initiatives: Report to Congressional Requesters.* Gaithersburg, MD, 1990. 49 pp.

Drugs

Andreas, Peter, and Coletta Youngers. "U.S. Drug Policy and the Andean Cocaine Industry." *World Policy Journal* 6 (Summer 1989): 529–562.

Lee, Rensselaer W., III. "Why the U.S. Cannot Stop South American Cocaine." *Orbis* 32 (Fall 1988): 499–519.

U.S. Congress. House. Committee on Agriculture. *Review of Bolivian Soybeans, U.S. Drug Policy and the Food for Peace Program: Joint Hearing, June 27, 1990, Before the Subcommittee on Wheat, Soybeans, and Feed Grains, and the Subcommittee on Department Operations, Research, and Foreign Agriculture.* 101st Cong., 2d sess. Washington, DC: GPO, 1990. 97 pp.

U.S. Congress. House. Committee on Foreign Affairs. *The Future of Colombian Narcotics Control Efforts and the Andean Initiative: Hearing, July 10, 1991.* 102d Cong., 1st sess. Washington, DC: GPO, 1991. 116 pp.

———. *U.S. Licit Opium Imports: Foreign Policy Issues; Report of a Staff Study Mission to Turkey, India, and Australia, May 1988.* 101st Cong., 1st sess. Washington, DC: GPO, 1989. 12 pp.

U.S. Congress. House. Committee on the Judiciary. Subcommittee on Crime. *The Licit Importation of Opium: Hearing, February 27, 1990.* 101st Cong., 2d sess. Washington, DC: GPO, 1990. 309 pp.

Arms

Albright, David, and Mark Hibbs. "Iraq's Shop-Till-You-Drop Nuclear Program: IAEA (International Atomic Energy Agency) Inspectors Found German Fingerprints on Much of Iraq's Nuclear Weapon Technology." *Bulletin of the Atomic Scientists* 48 (April 1992): 26–37.

Anthony, Ian. "The Global Arms Trade." *Arms Control Today* 21 (June 1991): 3–8.

———. "The International Arms Trade." *Disarmament* (UN) 13, 2 (1990): 231–256.

Cobb, Jean, and John M. Zindar. "Dealing Arms: American Taxpayers Are Subsidizing the Global Arms Buildings." *Common Cause Magazine* 15 (March–April 1989): 23–27.

Daffron, Stephen C. "U.S. Arms Transfers: New Rules, New Reasons." *Parameters* 21 (Spring 1991): 77–91.

Fieleke, Norman S. "A Primer on the Arms Trade." *New England Economic Review* (November–December 1991): 47–63.

Goldstein, Lyle, et al. *Fueling Balkan Wars: The West's Arming of Greece and Turkey.* Washington, DC: British American Security Information Council, 1993. 15 pp.

Hartung, William D. "Why Sell Arms? Lessons from the Carter Years." *World Policy Journal* 10 (Spring 1993): 57–64.

Hicks, D. Bruce. "Internal Competition over Foreign Policy-Making: The Case of U.S. Arms Sales to Iran." *Policy Studies Review* 9 (Spring 1990): 471–484.

Hwang, Byong-Moo. "The Evolution of U.S. China Security Relations and Its Implications for the Korean Peninsula." *Asian Perspective* 14 (Spring–Summer 1990): 69–90.

Kamal, Nazir. "China's Arms Export Policy and Responses to Multilateral Restraints." *Contemporary Southeast Asia* 14 (September 1972): 112–141.

Karp, Aaron. "Arming Ethnic Conflict." *Arms Control Today* 23 (September 1993): 8–13.

Klare, M. T. "Who's Arming Who? The Arms Trade in the 1900's." *Technology Review* 93 (May–June 1990): 42–50.

Krauland, Edward J., et al. "Recent Developments in U.S. Export Licensing and Civil Enforcement Procedures: What They Mean to Exporters." *International Tax and Business Lawyer* 7 (Summer 1989): 202–238.

Laurence, Edward J. "Political Implications of Illegal Arms Exports from the United States." *Political Science Quarterly* 107 (Fall 1992): 501–533.

———. "The U.N. Register of Conventional Arms: Rationales and Prospects for Compliance and Effectiveness." *Washington Quarterly* 16 (Spring 1993): 163–172.

Lefebvre, Jeffrey A. "Globalism and Regionalism: U.S. Arms Transfers to Sudan." *Armed Forces and Society* 17 (Winter 1991): 211–227.

Miskel, James F. "National Defense Requirements: The Foreign Connection." *Global Affairs* 7 (Winter 1992): 150–169.

Montgomery, Peter. "Re-arm the World: The Bush Administration May Be Talking a New World Order, But It's Hawking U.S. Weapons Like Never Before." *Common Cause Magazine* 17 (May–June 1991): 25–29+.

Morrison, David C. "Still Open for Business: Now That the Cold War and the Persian Gulf Conflict Are Over, the Nations of the World—with the White House in the Lead—Are Taking Steps To Close Down the Middle East Arms Bazaar, Right? Guess Again." *National Journal* 23 (April 13, 1994): 850–854.

Neuman, Stephanie G. "The Arms Market: Who's on Top?" *Orbis* 33 (Fall 1989): 509–529.

O'Hanlon, Michael, et al. "Controlling Arms Transfers to the Middle East: The Case for Supplier Limits." *Arms Control Today* 22 (November 1992): 18–24.

Segal, Gerald. "Managing New Arms Races in the Asian Pacific." *Washington Quarterly* 15 (Summer 1992): 83–101.

Smyth, Frank. *Arming Rwanda: The Arms Trade and Human Rights Abuses in the Rwanda War.* New York: Human Rights Watch, 1994. 64 pp.

Steinberg, Gerald M. "Toward Real Arms Control in the Middle East." *Issues in Science and Technology* 7 (Summer 1991): 63–69.

Tansey, Kevin, and Ross Johnson. "The Pentagon's Dependence on Foreign Sources: When So Much of the "Smarts" in Our Smart Weapons Come from Abroad, Is There Cause for Concern?" *GAO* (General Accounting Office) *Journal* (Winter 1991–1992): 28–33.

Timmons, Jeffrey. "U.S. Policy and the Arming of Iraq: Anatomy of a Policy Failure." *World Outlook* 16 (Spring 1993): 1–26.

Twinam, Joseph W. "Controversial Arms Sales to Saudi Arabia: An American Tragedy in Possibly Four Acts." *American-Arab Affairs* (Summer 1989): 47–55.

U.S. Arms Control and Disarmament Agency. *World Military Expenditures and Arms Transfers, 1990.* Washington, DC, 1992. 148 pp.

U.S. Congress. House. *Examines the Link between an Illegal Military Procurement Network That Fueled the Iraqi War Machine and the U.S. Department of Agriculture's Export Credit Guarantee Programs: Joint Hearing, August 1, 1991, Before the Subcommittee on Department Operations, Research, and Foreign Agriculture of the Committee on International Economic Policy and Trade of the Committee on Foreign Affairs.* 102d Cong., 1st sess. Washington, DC: GPO, 1992. 117 pp.

U.S. Congress. House. Committee on Agriculture. Subcommittee on Department Operations, Research and Foreign Agriculture. *Review of the Department of Agriculture's Export Credit Guarantees Extended to Iraq: Hearing, March 14, 1991.* 102d Cong., 1st sess. Washington, DC: GPO, 1991. 418 pp.

U.S. Congress. House. Committee on Armed Services. Investigations Subcommittee. *Examination of the M-16 Coproduction Agreement between the United States and Korea: Hearing, May 5, 1988.* 100th Cong., 2d sess. Washington, DC: GPO, 1989. 337 pp.

————. *Review of Arms Coproduction Agreements: Hearing, March 22, 1989.* 101st Cong., 1st sess. Washington, DC: GPO, 1989. 58 pp.

U.S. Congress. House. Committee on Banking, Finance, and Urban Affairs. Subcommittee on International Development, Finance, Trade, and Monetary Policy. *Proposal for Export-Import Financing of Defense Articles and Services: Hearing, May 2, 1991.* 102d Cong., 1st sess. Washington, DC: GPO, 1992. 208 pp.

U.S. Congress. House. Committee on Foreign Affairs. *Arms Restraint Policy: Joint Hearing, March 24, 1992, Before the Subcommittees on Arms Control, International Security and Science and Europe and the Middle East.* 102d Cong., 1st sess. Washington, DC: GPO, 1992. 114 pp.

————. *Connection between Arms and Narcotics Trafficking: Hearing, October 31, 1989.* 101st Cong., 1st sess. Washington, DC: GPO, 1990. 142 pp.

————. *Proposed Arms Sales to Kuwait: Hearing, July 17, 1988, Before the Subcommittee on Arms Control, International Security and Science, and on Europe and the Middle East.* 100th Cong., 2d sess. Washington, DC: GPO, 1988. 90 pp.

————. *Proposed Sales and Upgrades of Major Defense Equipment to Saudi Arabia: Hearing, June 19, 1990, Before the Subcommittee on Arms Control, International Security and Science, and on Europe and the Middle East.* 101st Cong., 2d sess. Washington, DC: GPO, 1990. 65 pp.

————. *Sale of AEGIS Weapon Systems to Japan: Hearing, June 16, 1988, Before the Subcommittees on Arms Control, International Security and Science and on Asian and Pacific Affairs.* 100th Cong., 2d sess. Washington, DC: GPO, 1988. 81 pp.

Munitions

U.S. Congress. House. Committee on Government Operations, Legislation and National Security Subcommittee. *The Operations of the Department of Defense Memorandums of Understanding and Related Issues: Hearing, November 21, 1989.* 101st Cong., 2d sess. Washington, DC, 1990. 123 pp.

U.S. Congress. House. Committee on Ways and Means. Subcommittee on Trade. *Banning the Importation of Assault Weapons and Certain*

Accessories into the United States: Hearing, April 10, 1989, on HR 1154. 101st Cong., 1st sess. Washington, DC: GPO, 1989. 116 pp.

———. *United States–China Trade Relations: Hearing, June 8, 1993.* 103d Cong., 1st sess. Washington, DC: GPO, 1993. 195 pp.

U.S. Congress. House. Select Committee on Narcotics Abuse and Control. *The Flow of Precursor Chemicals and Assault Weapons from the United States into the Andean Nations: Hearing, November 1, 1989.* 101st Cong., 1st sess. Washington, DC: GPO, 1990. 285 pp.

U.S. Congress. Senate. Committee on Armed Services. Subcommittee on Defense Industry and Technology. *Ballistic and Cruise Missile Proliferation in the Third World: Hearing, May 2, 1989.* 101st Cong., 1st sess. Washington, DC: GPO, 1989. 85 pp.

U.S. Congress. Senate. Committee on Banking, Housing, and Urban Affairs. *United States Export Policy toward Iraq Prior to Iraq's Invasion to Kuwait: Hearing, October 27, 1992, on Did U.S. Exports Aid Iraq's Military Capabilities and Did the Administration Accurately Disclose Its Licensing of Dual-Use Exports to Iraq?* 102d Cong., 2d sess. Washington, DC: GPO, 1992. 497 pp.

U.S. Congress. Senate. Committee on Foreign Relations. Subcommittee on East Asian and Pacific Affairs. *Sino-American Relations: Current Policy Issues: Hearings, June 13–27, 1991.* 102d Cong., 1st sess. Washington, DC: GPO, 1991. 141 pp.

———. Subcommittee on European Affairs. *America and Europe: Creating an Arms Suppliers' Cartel: Hearing, April 23, 1991.* 102d Cong., 1st sess. Washington, DC: GPO, 1991. 47 pp.

U.S. Congress. Senate. Committee on Governmental Affairs. Permanent Subcommittee on Investigations. *Arms Trafficking, Mercenaries and Drug Cartels: Hearings, February 27–28, 1991.* 102d Cong., 1st sess. Washington, DC: GPO, 1991. 148 pp.

———. Subcommittee on Federal Services, Post Office and Civil Service. *Federal Licensing Procedures for Importing and Selling Firearms: Hearing, March 26, 1993.* 103d Cong., 1st sess. Washington, DC: GPO, 1993. 74 pp.

U.S. General Accounting Office. *European Initiatives: Implications for U.S. Defense Trade and Cooperation; Report to the Chairman, Subcommittee on Investigations, Committee on Armed Services, House of Representatives.* Gaithersburg, MD, 1991. 68 pp.

————. *Export Controls: Issues in Removing Militarily Sensitive Items from the Munitions List: Report to the Chairman, Committee on Governmental Affairs, U.S. Senate.* Gaithersburg, MD, 1993. 70 pp.

U.S. General Accounting Office. Committee on Government Operations. Commerce, Consumer and Monetary Affairs Subcommittee. *U.S. Government Controls on Sales to Iraq: Hearing, September 27, 1990.* 101st Cong., 2d sess. Washington, DC: GPO, 1991. 343 pp.

U.S. Office of Technology Assessment. *Global Arms Trade.* Washington, DC, 1991. 179 pp.

Countries and Regions

Asia

Bradford, Colin L., Jr. *From Trade-Driven Growth to Growth-Driven Trade: Reappraising the East Asian Development Experience.* Development Centre Documents. Paris, France: Organization for Economic Co-operation and Development, 1994. 46 pp.

Brownstein, Ronald. "Facing West Nervously: California, Oregon and Washington on the Front Line of the Pacific Rim, Share America's Ambivalence about the Nation's Growing Economic Links to Asia." *National Journal* 21 (October 28, 1989): 2624–2629.

Choi, Yearn Hong. "U.S. Congress and the Press: Odd Couple? The Case of the Omnibus Trade Law." *Korea Observer* 21 (Summer 1990): 225–249.

Funabashi, Yoichi. "Japan and America: Global Partners." *Foreign Policy* (Spring 1992): 24–39.

Goddin, Scott, et al. *Marketing in Korea.* Washington, DC: U.S. Department of Commerce, International Trade Administration, 1990. 92 pp.

Goldstein, Carl. "Join the Club: China Could Win GATT Membership by Year-End: It Has Made Important Concessions on U.S. and

European Demands for Special Safeguards against Surge in Chinese Imports." *Far Eastern Economic Review* 157 (March 17, 1994): 42–44.

Hickock, Susan, and James Orr. "Shifting Patterns of U.S. Trade with Selected Developing Asian Economies." *Federal Reserve Bank of New York Quarterly Review* 14 (Winter 1989–1990): 36–47.

Ho, Y. P., and Y. Y. Kueh. "Whither Hong Kong in an Open-Door: Reforming Chinese Economy?" *Pacific Review* 6, 4 (1993): 333–351.

Kim, Youn-suk. "Korea-U.S. Trade Friction and the Japan Factor." *Asian Profile* 18 (February 1990): 79–87.

Lee, Yong S., et al. "Agricultural Policy Making under International Pressures: The Case of South Korea, a Newly Industrialized Country." *Food Policy* 15 (October 1990): 418–433.

Majumdar, Madhavi. "Indian Garment Exports to the USA, 1980–8: Market Access or Supply-Side Response?" *Development Policy Review* 8 (June 1990): 131–153.

Thaveechaiyagarn, Suthiphon. "Current Developments: The Section 301 Cigarette Case against Thailand: A Thai Perspective." *Law and Policy in International Business* 21, 3 (1990): 367–387.

U.S. Congress. House. Committee on Foreign Affairs. *Proposed Tank Sale to Saudi Arabia: Hearing, November 7, 1989, Before the Subcommittees on Arms Control, International Security and Science, and on Europe and the Middle East.* 101st Cong., 1st sess. Washington, DC: GPO, 1990. 97 pp.

U.S. International Trade Commission. *Saccharin from China and Korea.* Publication 2716. Washington, DC, 1994. Various paging.

"U.S.-Korea and U.S.-Taiwan Trade Symposium." *Michigan Journal of International Law* 11 (Winter 1990): 273–524.

Young, Alwyn. *Lessons from the East Asian NICs: A Contrarian View.* NBER Working Paper no. 4482. Cambridge, MA: National Bureau of Economic Research, 1993. 16 pp.

China

Cai, Wenguo. "Canadian and U.S. Antidumping Laws and Chinese Exports." *World Competition* 14 (September 1990): 123–134.

Mosher, Steven W. "Made in the Chinese Laogai: China's Use of Prisoners to Produce for Export." *Asian Outlook* (Taipei) 25 (August 1990): 10–39.

"President Announces Renewal of MFN [Most-Favored-Nation] Status for China with Conditions for Renewal Next Year." *Foreign Policy Bulletin* 4 (September–October 1993): 44–49.

U.S. Congress. House. Committee on Foreign Affairs. Subcommittee on International Economic Policy and Trade. *Technology Transfer to China: Hearing, July 8, 1987.* 100th Cong., 1st sess. Washington, DC: GPO, 1989. 95 pp.

U.S. Congress. House. Committee on Merchant Marine and Fisheries. Subcommittee on Oversight and Investigations. *Fair Trade Practices with the People's Republic of China: Hearing, July 17, 1991, on the Republic of China's Trade Practices and the Report of Forced Labor Goods Being Exported to the United States.* 102d Cong., 1st sess. Washington, DC: GPO, 1991. 83 pp.

U.S. Congress. House. Committee on Ways and Means. Subcommittee on Trade. *United States–China Trade Relations: Hearing, June 8, 1993.* 103d Cong., 1st sess. Washington, DC: GPO, 1993. 195 pp.

Japan

Adams, L. Jerold. "The Law of United States–Japan Trade Relations." *Journal of World Trade* 24 (April 1990): 37–65.

Alston, Julian M., et al. "Discriminatory Trade: The Case of Japanese Beef and Wheat Imports." *Canadian Journal of Agricultural Economics* 38 (July 1990): 197–214.

Cargill, T. F. "A Perspective on Trade Imbalances and U.S. Policies toward Japan." *Columbia Journal of World Business* 22 (Winter 1987): 55–60.

Choate, Pat. "Political Advantage: Japan's Campaign for America." *Harvard Business Review* 68 (September–October 1990): 87–103.

Ichioka, Yoichiro. "Laying the Groundwork for a Single Global Market." *Economic Eye* 11 (Autumn 1990): 9–12.

Kim, Youn-suk. "Korea-U.S. Trade Friction and the Japan Factor." *Asian Profile* 18 (February 1990): 79–87.

McCreary, Don R., and Chris J. Noll, Jr. "Cultural, Psychological, and Structural Impediments to Free Trade with Japan." *Asian Perspective* 15 (Fall/Winter 1991): 75–97.

Paarlberg, Robert L. "The Upside-Down World of U.S.-Japanese Agricultural Trade." *Washington Quarterly* 13 (Autumn 1990): 131–142.

Reich, R. B. "We Need a Strategic Trade Policy [U.S.-Japan Trade]." *Challenge* 33 (July–August 1990): 38–42.

Salvatore, D. "How To Solve the U.S.-Japan Trade Problem." *Challenge* 34 (January–February 1991): 40–46.

Sinha, Radha. "Are EC-Japan-U.S. Trade Relations at the Crossroads?" *Intereconomics* 25 (September–October 1990): 229–237.

Staiger, R. W., et al. "The Effects of Protection on the Factor Content of Japanese and American Foreign Trade." *Review of Economics and Statistics* 70 (August 1988): 475–483.

Tobin, J. "The Adam Smith Address on Living and Trading with Japan: United States Commercial and Macroeconomic Policies." *Business Economics* 26 (January 1991): 5–16.

U.S. Congress. Joint Economic Committee. *The Japanese Market: How Open Is It? Hearing, October 11, 1989.* 101st Cong., 1st sess. Washington, DC: GPO, 1990. 83 pp.

U.S. Congress. Senate. Committee on Governmental Affairs. Subcommittee on Oversight of Government Management. *Oversight of U.S. Trade Policy with Japan: Hearing, May 8, 1991.* 102d Cong., 1st sess. Washington, DC: GPO, 1991. 283 pp.

Yamagata, Yuichiro, and David Williams. "Remaking Japan: Remaking America." *Tokyo Business Today* 57 (November 1989): 14–19.

Yamawaki, H. "Exports and Foreign Distributional Activities: Evidence on Japanese Firms in the United States." *Review of Economics and Statistics* 73 (May 1991): 294–300.

Europe

Alexakis, Panayotis, and Manolis Xanthakis. "Export Performance of Greek Manufacturing Companies: Export Subsidies and Other Factors." *Economia Internazionale* 45 (May 1992): 143–157.

Blomstrom, Magnus, and Robert E. Lipsey. "The Export Performance of U.S. and Swedish Multinationals." *Review of Income and Wealth* 35 (September 1989): 245–264.

Blomstrom, Magnus, et al. *What Do Rich Countries Trade with Each Other? R&D and the Composition of U.S. and Swedish Trade.* NBER Working Paper no. 3140. Cambridge, MA: National Bureau of Economic Research, 1989. 33 pp.

U.S. Congress. House. Committee on Ways and Means. Subcommittee on Trade. *Written Comments on Certain Tariff and Trade Bills and Agreement on Trade Relations between the Government of the United States of America and the Government of the Czechoslovak Federative Republic, September 28, 1990.* 101st Cong., 2d sess. Washington, DC: GPO, 1990. 49 pp.

Latin America

Gitli, Eduardo, and Gunilla Ryd. "Latin American Integration and the Enterprise for the American Initiative." *Journal of World Trade* 26 (August 1992): 25–45.

"Latin America and the Free Trade Agreement." *Business Economics* 27 (April 1992): 7–16+.

"Latin America: The Big Move to Free Markets." *Business Week* (June 15, 1992): 50–57+.

Mahon, James E., Jr. "Was Latin America Too Rich To Prosper? Structural and Political Obstacles to Export-Led Industrial Growth." *Journal of Development Studies* 28 (January 1992): 241–263.

Saghafi, Massoud M., et al. "Why U.S. Firms Don't Buy from Latin American Companies." *Industrial Marketing Management* 20 (August 1991): 207–213.

"Symposium: Free Trade and the Environment in Latin America." *Loyola of Los Angeles International and Comparative Law Journal* 15 (December 1992): 1–147.

U.S. Department of Commerce. International Trade Administration. *Latin America Trade Review, 1988: A U.S. Perspective.* Washington, DC, 1989. 53 pp.

Willmore, Larry, and Jorge Máttar. "Industrial Restructuring, Trade Liberalization and the Role of State in Central America." *CEPAL Review* (August 1991): 7–19.

Mexico

"Agricultural Trade and Mexico's Foreign Debt: Mexican and United States Perspectives." *American Journal of Agricultural Economics* 71 (December 1989): 1117–1137.

Alarcón, Diana, and Terry McKinley. "Beyond Import Substitution: The Restructuring Projects of Brazil and Mexico." *Latin American Perspectives* 19 (Spring 1992): 72–87.

Gibbons, Thomas. "Tough Trade-Offs: A Free Trade Proposal with Mexico Raises Doubts about Our Country's Commitment to Human Rights." *Human Rights* (American Bar Association) 19 (Spring 1992): 26–30.

Laurell, Asa Cristina, and Maria Elena Ortega. "The Free Trade Agreement and the Mexican Health Sector." *International Journal of Health Services* 22, 2 (1992): 331–337.

Morici, Peter. *Trade Talks with Mexico: A Time of Realism.* CIR Report no. 22. NPAR Report no. 253. Washington, DC: National Planning Association, Committee on Changing International Realities, 1991. 124 pp.

Ramirez, Miguel D. "Stabilization and Trade Reform in Mexico: 1983–1989." *Journal of Developing Areas* 27 (January 1993): 173–190.

Smith, Guy C. "The United States–Mexico Framework Agreement: Implications for Bilateral Trade." *Law and Policy in International Business* 20, 4 (1989): 655–681.

Taylor, Lynda. "The Fast Track Agreement: Help or Hurt for the U.S.-Mexico Border Environment?" *Workbook* (Southwest Research and Information Center) 17 (Summer 1992): 50–64.

U.S. Congress. House. Committee on Banking, Finance, and Urban

Affairs. Subcommittee on International Development, Finance, Trade, and Monetary Policy. *The U.S.-Mexican Free Trade Agreement: Hearing, April 16, 1991.* 102d Cong., 1st sess. Washington, DC: GPO, 1991. 158 pp.

U.S. Congress. House. Committee on Education and Labor. *Hearing on Implications for Workers of the Fast Track Process and the Mexican Free Trade Agreement: Joint Hearing, April 30, 1991, Before the Subcommittee on Labor-Management Relations and the Subcommittee on Employment Opportunities.* 102d Cong., 1st sess. Washington, DC: GPO, 1991. 126 pp.

U.S. Congress. Senate. Committee on Finance. *United States–Mexico Free Trade Agreements: Hearings, February 6 and 20, 1991.* 102d Cong., 1st sess. Washington, DC: GPO, 1991. 505 pp.

U.S. Congress. Senate. Committee on Foreign Relations. Subcommittee on Western Hemisphere and Peace Corps Affairs. *Issues Relating to a Bilateral Free Trade Agreement with Mexico: Hearings, March 14–April 11, 1991.* 102d Cong., 1st sess. Washington, DC: GPO, 1991. 190 pp.

Weintraub, Sidney. "U.S.-Mexico Free Trade: Implications for the United States." *Journal of Interamerican Studies and World Affairs* 34 (Summer 1992): 29–52.

Weiss, John. "Trade Policy Reform and Performance in Manufacturing: Mexico 1975–1988." *Journal of Development Studies* 29 (October 1992): 1–23.

Whalen, C. "Will Mexico Make It? [U.S.-Mexico Free Trade Agreement]." *Across the Board* 27 (June 1990): 36–43.

Soviet Union

U.S. Congress. House. Committee on Foreign Affairs. *United States–Soviet Trade Relations: Hearing, June 14, 1989, Before the Subcommittees on Europe and the Middle East, and on International Economic Policy and Trade.* 101st Cong., 1st sess. Washington, DC: GPO, 1989. 187 pp.

Africa

Solomon, Emily. *Marketing in Zimbabwe.* Washington, DC: U.S. Department of Commerce, International Trade Administration, 1990. 29 pp.

United States

Murray, Matthew N. "Influence of the International Sector on the Tennessee Economy." *Survey of Business* (University of Tennessee) 25 (Fall 1989): 69–79.

Winders, Rebecca M. "Identifying Opportunities for Georgia's Export Expansion." *Georgia Business and Economic Conditions* 53 (January–February 1993): 1–9.

Selected Journal Titles

The journals listed below publish articles on many aspects of international trade. Because of the growing importance of trade, new journals are continuously appearing. For new journals and additional information, please consult *Ulrich's International Periodical Directory 1993–1994*, 32d ed. (New York: R. R. Bowker Company, 1993), 3 vols. Information on the journals listed is arranged as in the following sample entry:

Journal Title

1. Editor
2. Year first published
3. Frequency of publication
4. Code
5. Special features
6. Address of publisher

American Business Law Journal

1. Michael J. Phillips
2. 1963
3. 4 issues per year
4. ISSN 0002-7766
5. Adv., bk. rev., charts, illus., index
6. Academy of Legal Studies in Business
   c/o Daniel J. Herron, School of Business
   Western Carolina University
   Cullowhee, NC 28723

American Economic Review

1. —
2. 1911
3. Quarterly
4. ISSN 0002-8282
5. Adv., charts, illus., stat., index
6. American Economic Association
   2014 Broadway
   Suite 305
   Nashville, TN 37203

Business America

1. Douglas Carroll
2. 1880
3. Fortnightly
4. ISSN 0190-6275
5. Bk. rev., bibl.
6. U.S. Department of Commerce
   14th Street between Constitution Avenue and
      Pennsylvania Avenue, NW
   Washington, DC 20230

Business Week

1. Stephen Shepard
2. 1929
3. Weekly
4. ISSN 0007-7135
5. Adv., bk. rev., illus., stat., index
6. McGraw-Hill
   1225 Avenue of the Americas
   New York, NY 10020

Columbia Journal of World Business

1. Mary Anne Devanna
2. 1965
3. Quarterly
4. ISSN 0022-5428
5. Adv., bk. rev., charts, illus., index
6. Columbia University
   Trustees of Columbia University
   310 Uris Hall
   New York, NY 10027

Economic Journal

1. John D. Hey
2. 1891
3. 6 issues per year
4. ISSN 0013-0133
5. Adv., bk. rev., index
6. Basil Blackwell
   108 Cowley Road
   Oxford OX4 1JF
   England

Economic Review

1. Rubin Ratliff and Tess Ferg
2. 1919
3. Quarterly
4. ISSN 0013-0281
5. Charts, stat.
6. Federal Reserve Bank of Cleveland
   Box 6387
   Cleveland, OH 44101

Federal Reserve Bank of Dallas Economic Review

1. —
2. 1916
3. Every two months
4. ISSN 0149-5364
5. Charts, illus., stat.
6. Federal Reserve Bank of Dallas
   Station K
   Dallas, TX 75222

Federal Reserve Bank of Kansas City Economic Review

1. Lowell C. Jones
2. 1914
3. Quarterly
4. ISSN 0161-2387
5. —
6. Federal Reserve Bank of Kansas City
   925 Grand Avenue
   Kansas City, MO 64198

Federal Reserve Bank of New York Quarterly Review

1. —
2. 1976
3. Quarterly
4. ISSN 0147-6580
5. Charts, stat.
6. Federal Reserve Bank of New York
   Public Information
   33 Liberty Street
   New York, NY 10045-0001

Federal Reserve Bank of Richmond Economic Review

1. Thomas M. Humphrey
2. 1914
3. Every two months
4. ISSN 0094-6893
5. Bibl., charts, stat.
6. Federal Reserve Bank of Richmond
   Research Department
   701 E. Byrd Street
   Richmond, VA 23219

Federal Reserve Bank of St. Louis Review

1. Daniel P. Brennan
2. 1917
3. Every two months
4. ISSN 0014-9187
5. Charts, stat., index
6. Federal Reserve Bank of St. Louis
   Box 442
   St. Louis, MO 63166

Harvard Business Review

1. Rosabeth Moss Kanter
2. 1922
3. Every two months
4. ISSN 0017-8012
5. Adv., bk. rev., charts, cum. index
6. Harvard University
   Graduate School of Business Administration
   Soldiers Field Road
   Boston, MA 02163-1099

Harvard International Law Journal

1. —
2. 1959
3. 2 issues per year
4. ISSN 0017-8063
5. Bk. rev., cum. index
6. Harvard University
   Law School
   Publications Center
   Hastings Hall
   Cambridge, MA 02138

Hastings International and Comparative Law Review

1. Brian Keating
2. 1977
3. Quarterly
4. ISSN 0149-9246
5. Adv., bk. rev., cum. index every 5 years
6. University of California, San Francisco
   Hastings College of the Law
   200 McAllister Street
   San Francisco, CA 92102-4978

Intereconomics

1. Otto G. Mayer
2. 1966
3. Every two months
4. GW ISSN 0020-5346
5. Adv., index
6. Transaction Publishers
   Department 3091
   Rutgers University
   New Brunswick, NJ 08903

International Environmental Affairs

1. K. von Moltke
2. 1989
3. Quarterly
4. ISSN 1041-4665
5. Adv., bk. rev.

6. University Press of New England
   22 South Main Street
   Hanover, NH 03755-1540

International Trade Forum

1. J. Goertz
2. 1964
3. Quarterly
4. UN ISSN 0020-8957
5. Bk. rev., bibl., charts, illus., index
6. International Trade Center
   Palais des Nations
   1211 Geneva 10
   Switzerland

Journal of Agricultural Economic Research

1. J. Latham and G. Schulter
2. 1949
3. Quarterly
4. ISSN 1043-3309
5. Bk. rev., bibl., charts, index
6. U.S. Department of Agriculture
   Economic Research Service
   International Economics Division
   1301 New York Avenue, NW
   Washington, DC 20005-4788

Journal of Business Strategy

1. Robert Lamb
2. 1980
3. 6 issues per year
4. ISSN 0275-6668
5. Adv., illus.
6. Warren, Gorham, and Lamont
   One Penn Plaza
   New York, NY 10119

Journal of Corporation Law

1. —
2. 1975

3. 4 issues per year
4. ISSN 0360-7951
5. Bk. rev.
6. University of Iowa
   College of Law
   Iowa City, IA 52242

Journal of International Business Studies

1. David A. Ricks
2. 1970
3. 4 issues per year
4. ISSN 0047-2506
5. Adv., bk. rev., charts
6. University of South Carolina
   College of Business Administration
   Columbia, SC 29208

Journal of Public Policy

1. Richard Rose
2. 1981
3. 4 issues per year
4. UK ISSN 0143-814X
5. —
6. Cambridge University Press
   40 W. 20th Street
   New York, NY 10011

Journal of World Trade

1. Jacques Werner
2. 1967
3. Every two months
4. SZ ISSN 0022-5444
5. Adv., bk. rev., index
6. Werner Publishing
   P.O. Box 93
   12 11 Geneva 11
   Switzerland

Monthly Labor Review

1. Henry Lowenstern
2. 1915

3. Monthly
4. ISSN 0098-1818
5. Bk. rev., index
6. U.S. Bureau of Labor Statistics
   441 G Street, NW
   Washington, DC 20212

National Journal

1. Richard S. Frank
2. 1969
3. Weekly
4. ISSN 0360-4217
5. Adv., bk. rev., charts, illus., index
6. National Journal, Inc.
   1730 M Street, NW
   Suite 1100
   Washington, DC 20036

Quarterly Journal of Economics

1. Editorial Board
2. 1886
3. Quarterly
4. ISSN 0033-5533
5. Adv., charts, index
6. MIT Press
   55 Hayward Street
   Cambridge, MA 02142

Southern Economic Journal

1. Vincent J. Tarascio
2. 1933
3. Twice monthly
4. ISSN 0038-4038
5. Adv., bk. rev., bibl., index
6. University of North Carolina at Chapel Hill
   Southern Economic Association
   300 Hanes Hall
   CB 3540
   Chapel Hill, NC 27514

Traffic World

1. —
2. 1907
3. Weekly
4. ISSN 0041-073X
5. Adv., illus., stat.
6. Journal of Commerce
   741 National Press Bldg.
   Washington, DC 20045

World Policy Journal

1. Richard Caplan
2. 1983
3. Quarterly
4. ISSN 0740-2775
5. Adv., bk. rev., charts
6. World Policy Institute
   777 United Nations Plaza
   New York, NY 10017

Audio-Visual Aids 6

The audio-visual aids listed in this chapter provide some background for understanding international trade relationships. A graphic presentation can often convey information more vividly than the written word. Although the films vary greatly in date of production, all provide a present-day picture of international trade.

The following sources list audio-visual aids in English:

Educational Film/Video Locator of the Consortium of College and University Media Centers and R. R. Bowker. 2 vols. 4th ed. New York: R. R. Bowker, 1990–1991.

Film & Video Finder. 3 vols. 3d ed. Medford, NJ: Plexus, 1991.

Films & Video for Business and Economics. 3d ed. University Park, PA: Penn State Audio-Visual Services, Pennsylvania State University, 1993.

New Media Dealing with Business and Economics. University Park, PA: Penn State Audio-Visual Services, Pennsylvania State University, 1994.

The Video Source Book. 2 vols. and supplement. 15th ed. Detroit, MI: Research Inc., 1994.

293

The following data are provided for each film:

Title of film
Distributor
Data on film
Description

Commerce
Film Australia
636 Fifth Avenue
New York, NY 10020
Color, 11 minutes, sound, 16mm, 1982.

The film shows Australia's contribution to world trade, its products, and its competitive international markets.

Doing Business in Japan: Negotiating a Contract
Vision Associates
665 Fifth Avenue
New York, NY 10022
Color, 34 minutes, sound, 16mm, 1976.

Provides an analysis of the negotiating process, exploring such complex elements as language and communication, industry, cultural and pragmatic disparities, use of interpreters, and other aspects relating to a successful trading agreement.

Embargo
Coronet/MTI Film and Video
108 Wilmot Road
Deerfield, IL 60015
Color, 29 minutes, sound, ½" VHS, 1986.

Discusses the political reality of economic sanctions imposed by one nation or another. Reveals the advantages and disadvantages of economic restrictions. Analyzes the U.S. embargo on banana imports from Nicaragua in 1980. From the Enterprise 4 Series.

Exchange Rates: What in the World Is a Dollar Worth?
(Revised Edition)
Annenberg/CPB Project
P.O. Box 2345
South Burlington, VT 05407-2345
Color, 29 minutes, sound, ½" VHS, 1992.

Shows the effect of exchange rates on trade, inflation, and domestic economic growth and the effect of domestic economic events on foreign exchange rates.

International Economy
Journal Films
930 Pitner Avenue
Evanston, IL 60202
Color, 26 minutes, sound, 16mm, 1980.

Reveals the alteration of the world's economy due to the imbalance of wealth between the poor and rich nations. This change has led to problems of inflation and economic recession. Emphasizes the need for a new economic order to increase the flow of goods throughout the world.

International Marketing/The Philadelphia Phillies
CPS Inc.
c/o Mr. Ron Roby
53 Wellington Blvd.
Wyomissing, PA 19610
Color, 27 minutes, sound, VHS, 1992.

Shows the relation of such companies as Mitsubishi, Chrysler, Caterpillar, and McDonald's to the economies of Kuwait, China, and the former Soviet Union in an effort to understand the new world order. The second section studies the marketing of services.

International Trade
Dallas County Community College District
Dallas, TX
Color, 29 minutes, sound, $\frac{3}{4}$" U-matic, 1979.

The film describes the U.S. involvement in international trade and its importance in the world.

International Trade
Dallas Community College District
4343 N. Highway 67
Mesquite, TX 75150
Color, 30 minutes, sound, $\frac{3}{4}$" video, n.d.

Discusses international trade. Part of the "Everybody's Business Series."

International Trade—For Whose Benefit

Annenberg/CPB Collection
1213 Wilmette Avenue
Wilmette, IL 60091
Color, 30 minutes, sound, $\frac{3}{4}$" or $\frac{1}{2}$" video, 1985.

Discusses international trade. Economics USA Series.

New York Faces the Sea

Cornell University
Audio-Visual Research Center
8 Research Park
Ithaca, NY 14850
Color, 13 minutes, sound, 16mm, $\frac{3}{4}$" U-matic, $\frac{1}{2}$" VHS, $\frac{1}{2}$" Beta, 1973.

Problems of the use of coastal waters, power plant development, and shipping. Describes New York's Sea Grant Program.

Shipping

AIMS Media
9710 DeSoto Avenue
Chatsworth, CA 91311-4409
Color, 16 minutes, sound, Beta, VHS, $\frac{3}{4}$" U-matic, 1974.

Traces the changes in cargo shipping from the 1890s to the present and its importance in world trade.

Trade and Economics

Film Video Library
University of Michigan
919 S. University Avenue
Room 207
Ann Arbor, MI 48109-1185
Color, 30 minutes, sound, $\frac{3}{4}$" U-matic, 1980.

Discusses methods by which China is trying to modernize its commerce and the problems associated with international business dealings with China. Part of the "China after Mao" Series.

U.S.–Chinese Relations

Film Video Library
University of Michigan
919 S. University Avenue
Room 207
Ann Arbor, MI 48109-1185

Color, 30 minutes, sound, $\frac{3}{4}$" U-matic, 1980.

A reflection upon the economic transitions and the motives upon which they are based. Part of the "China after Mao" Series.

United States–Japan Trade War
Downtown Community TV Center
87 Lafayette Street
New York, NY 10013
Color, 25 minutes, sound, Beta, VHS, $\frac{3}{4}$" U-matic, 1988.

Discusses reasons behind the trade war and the complex issues of bigotry, psychological pressure, and cultural isolation.

Appendix

U.S. International Banks

The following list of banks is organized according to amount of assets. Each entry supplies the bank's address, assets, and number of employees.

Citicorp
399 Park Avenue
New York, NY 10043
$213,701,000,000
86,000

Bankamerica Corp.
Bank of America Center
PO Box 37000
San Francisco, CA 94137
$180,646,000,000
96,428

Chemical Banking Corporation
270 Park Avenue
New York, NY 10017-2036
$139,655,000,000
41,567

NationsBank Corporation
NationsBank Corporate Centre
Charlotte, NC 28255
$118,059,300,000
57,463

J. P. Morgan & Company
60 Wall Street
New York, NY 10005-2807
$102,941,000,000

Chase Manhattan Corporation
Chase Manhattan Plaza
New York, NY 10081
$95,862,000,000
34,390

Bankers Trust New York Corporation
280 Park Avenue
New York, NY 10017
$72,448,000,000
13,571

Bank One Corporation
100 East Broad Street
Columbus, OH 43271
$61,417,400,000

Wells Fargo & Company
420 Montgomery Street
San Francisco, CA 94163
$52,537,000,000
19,700

PNC Bank Corporation
One PNC Plaza
Fifth Avenue and Wood Street
Pittsburgh, PA 15265
$51,379,900,000
21,100

First Union Corporation
Two First Union Center
Charlotte, NC 28288-0570
$51,326,700,000
32,861

First Interstate Bankcorp
633 West Fifth Street
Los Angeles, CA 90071
$50,863,000,000
26,589

First Chicago Corporation
One First National Plaza
Chicago, IL 60670
$49,281,000,000
17,355

Fleet Financial Group, Inc.
50 Kennedy Plaza
Providence, RI 02903
$46,938,500,000
27,500

Norwest Corporation
Norwest Center
Sixth and Marquette
Minneapolis, MN 55479
$44,557,100,000
35,000

NBC Bancorporation
611 Woodward Avenue
Detroit, MI 48226
$40,937,200,000
18,700

Bank of New York Company, Inc.
48 Wall Street
New York, NY 10286
$40,909,000,000
15,621

Barnett Banks
P.O. Box 40789
Jacksonville, FL 32203-0789
$39,464,800,000
18,000

Republic New York Corporation
452 Fifth Avenue
New York, NY 10018
$37,146,400,000
5,262

Suntrust Banks, Inc.
25 Park Place, NE
Atlanta, GA 30303
$36,648,600,000
19,532

Wachovia Corporation
301 North Main Street
P.O. Box 3099
Winston-Salem, NC 27150
$33,366,500,000
15,531

Bank of Boston Corporation
100 Federal Street
P.O. Box 1987
Boston, MA 02110
$32,346,100,000
23,633

Mellon Bank Corporation
1 Mellon Bank Center
500 Grant Street
Pittsburgh, PA 15258-0001
$31,574,000,000
22,000

First Fidelity Bancorporation
2673 Main Street
15th Floor
Newark, NJ 08648
$31,480,300,000
10,600

Keycorp
127 Public Square
Cleveland, OH 44114-1306
$30,114,100,000
30,054

International Bank for Reconstruction and Development (IBRD) (World Bank)
1818 H Street, NW
Washington, DC 20433

International Monetary Fund (IMF)
700 19th Street, NW
Washington, DC 20431

Glossary

aid In trade relations, economic assistance by means of grants of credit for purchases generally from an industrialized nation to Third World countries. Aid may come from voluntary organizations or governmental agencies.

antidumping regulation Rules to prevent the export of goods and services to another nation at prices below the cost level.

asset In the context of economics, any property that can be used to discharge a debt, including capital.

automation The use in industry of machines that perform sequences of operations according to instructions supplied by other machines, with the minimum of human intervention.

bankability Ease of access of a company or other organization to bank credit.

bilateral treaty A treaty enacted between two countries.

binding A commitment, usually negotiated, by a government not to impose a tariff rate higher than the rate agreed upon in a trade agreement.

border tax adjustments The remission of taxes on exported goods, including sales and value-added taxes, designed to ensure that national taxes do not impede exports of goods and services.

bound rates Most-favored-nation tariff rates resulting from GATT negotiations and incorporated in a country's schedule of concessions. A bound rate higher than the existing rate is called a "ceiling rate."

buffer stock A number of commodities held under an international commodity agreement and increased or decreased with the goal of keeping the price of the commodity stable.

cartel A market arrangement between producers to manipulate prices, generally by controlling output.

cash crop A crop grown for sale, often for export, and not for direct consumption.

clearinghouse Institution for settling accounts between banks or trading nations.

code of conduct A trade agreement that specifies acceptable standards for implementing national trade legislation and cooperating with governments on trade matters.

collateral A pledge of assets accepted by a lender as guarantee for repayment of a loan.

counterpart funds Money made available by a government to complement aid received from outside, such as the Marshall Fund.

countertrade Any exchange of goods or services in which there is a nonmonetary element, such as barter.

credit Funds provided, generally at a rate of interest, for goods or services or supplies before delivery of a commodity.

currency Any form of money accepted as a means of exchange within a nation that can be converted to another currency used between nations.

customs union A group of nations that have eliminated trade barriers among themselves and have imposed a common tariff on all goods imported from other countries.

database Organized collection of information on specific topics, generally available in machine readable form.

debt Money owed by an individual, organization, or government to another.

deficit Sum by which outgoing funds exceed receipts.

deflation Reduction of a price level, either by government in a national economy or by an industry, to a base year or to other set prices.

demand In economics, the ability to buy a certain quantity of goods or services at an established price.

depreciation The amount by which the value of goods has fallen over a period of time.

division of labor Distribution of economic activities among persons or countries according to the theory of comparative economic advantage.

dummy company Name applied to a company that does no business but invoices payments for goods or services moving between subsidiaries of a transnational company so as to conceal the profits being made.

dumping Exporting goods at prices below local costs of producing in order to gain international markets.

economic boom A rapid increase in economic activity in one or more industries or nations.

enterprise zone An area designated to increase the trade of a nation by providing special conditions.

equal exchange The concept that trade should involve exchanges of equal value more fairly than the marketplace provides.

equilibrium A situation in which supply and demand are in balance, achieved, for example, by varying the levy on imports and the refunds on exports.

escalating tariffs The increase in the rate of taxation on imports based on the extra degree of processing applied to a primary product in the exporting country.

escape clause Any one of a number of provisions of U.S. trade law designed to provide relief to domestic producers adversely affected by import competition.

exchange rate The rate at which one country's currency is exchanged for another's, determined by the relative prices of goods and services traded between them.

exclusivity The removal of rival suppliers of competing products.

export promotion zone An area designated to display export commodities to potential buyers.

export restitution A term applied to a refund or subsidy granted to European farmers in order bring their prices down to world levels for agricultural exports.

export subsidies A form of governmental assistance that benefits companies that export goods or services.

fair trade mark An emblem made by accrediting organizations for goods or a service to indicate that it has complied with certain advertised criteria of fair treatment of the producers.

fair value The established value compared to the U.S. purchase price of imported goods.

farmgate price The price at which agricultural produce is sold by a farmer.

First World Name given to the developed industrialized countries of the world.

free trade International trade that is unrestricted by tariffs, subsidies, or other trade barriers.

free trade zone A zone, usually in a port or airport, where imports may be stored free of tariffs.

General Agreement on Tariffs and Trade (GATT) Initiated in 1944 as part of the Bretton Woods agreement in Washington, D.C., GATT establishes procedures to develop free international trade by removing barriers, tariffs, and other restrictive measures.

gross national product (GNP) The total value of goods and services produced in a year before allowing for depreciation (capital consumption) of assets.

gross trade Total trade applied to products, income expenditures, and other items before allowing for depreciation, taxes, and other deductions.

growth rate Measure of economic activity, generally calculated by gross domestic product (GDP) per capita. A doubling of the GDP takes place in ten years at an interest rate of 7 percent a year.

hard currency A convertible and widely accepted currency, such as U.S. dollars.

hedging The buying or selling of futures with the aim of compensating for possible trading losses owing to price changes.

imperialism Protection by advanced industrialized countries of their foreign trade by establishing colonial rule or economic dependency in other countries.

incentive Extra wage, subsidy, tax concession, or other payment to encourage investment in international markets.

index Number indicating relative price of volume changes at a particular date compared with a base rate.

infant industry An industry established in a developing country and normally protected from outside competition in its early development.

insider (trading) The use of knowledge gained as a privilege from a particular company or organization for personal gain in a market.

International Cooperative Alliance (ICA) A worldwide organization of cooperatives.

International Monetary Fund (IMF) An institution established by the United Nations at Bretton Woods in 1944 to provide finances for governments having short-term deficits on their foreign balance of payments.

Interpress A nongovernmental organization for encouraging international networking.

leads and lags The transfer of funds either before or after delivery of goods or services, depending upon the advantage or disadvantage to be gained from the interest-rate levels and exchange rates.

less developed country One of the 43 countries defined by the United Nations as having a low per capita income and little industrialization.

letter of credit A promise of credit that may be used as collateral for borrowing.

levy A tax on persons, capital, or goods entering a country.

licensing Defined by the Tokyo Round of GATT on import licensing. It is the practice of requiring an application to the relevant administrative body for approval as a prior condition to import.

market A specific place where commodities are assembled for sale.

marketing board An organization to promote trade in certain commodities, mainly for export.

Marshall Plan Financial program to aid countries of Western Europe after World War II.

merchanting Buying and selling of goods and services produced by others to make a profit.

middlemen Intermediaries between direct producers of goods and services and the market.

monopoly The dominance of a single seller of any goods or services in a market.

monopsony A single or dominant buyer in the market.

most-favored-nation treatment A country's commitment to another country that it will extend the lowest tariff rates or the most favorable nontariff policies it applies to any Third World country. All GATT countries agree to this policy.

Multi-Fibre Agreement (MFA) An agreement whereby industrialized countries place quotas on import of textiles and clothing from less developed countries, one of the exceptions permissible under GATT.

multilateral agreement An international agreement in which three or more parties establish trade relations.

multilateral aid Aid given through international agencies such as the World Bank.

national income The total annual income of a nation.

net The amount left after deduction of taxes, depreciation, or other charges.

networks Horizontal linkages between organizations for the purpose of exchanging information or coordinating action in trade.

nondiscrimination Procedures in which no preference is given to any trading partner.

nontariff barrier Barriers to trade such as import quotas or variable levies other than tariff barriers, and the restriction or prevention of the international exchange of goods or services.

option In a market, the right to buy or sell by a certain date, not the actual purchase or sale of goods.

Organization of Petroleum Exporting Countries (OPEC) An organization to control oil production and raise oil prices.

parastatal Organization established by a government, but not a government department such as a nationalized industry.

per capita From the Latin, meaning according to the number of heads.

preference Advantages given to a nation in trade relations.

premium Extra charge in trade relations due to special values or quality of a product.

primary commodities Defined by GATT as "any product of farm, forest, or fishing or any mineral in its natural form which has undergone such processing as is customarily required to prepare it for marketing in substantial volume in international trade."

principal supplier The country that is the most important source of a particular product imported by another country. Under GATT, a country offering to reduce import duties or other barriers on a particular item and expecting the other country to respond in like manner.

product differentiation A procedure to attract buyers to a particular product by advertising its advantages and using distinctive labeling.

productivity Usually labor productivity, the measure of output per person, generally in relation to increased productivity due to the application of an advanced technology.

profit margin An addition to the cost of producing or marketing goods or a service in order to increase the total income.

protection In foreign trade, device used by a nation to give advantages to their own national products.

Protocol of Provisional Accession (PPA) An agreement that enables the original GATT countries to accept general obligations and benefits despite the fact that some of their existing domestic legislation discriminated against imports in a manner inconsistent with GATT.

quality mark (QM) A distinguishing mark, such as a trademark, of a high-quality product to designate a trading organization.

quantum A term used in the United States to denote the volume of goods produced or moving in foreign trade.

quarantine, sanitary, and health laws and regulations Government measures to protect human, animal, and plant health from specific diseases.

quota A fixed amount or share measured in monetary value or quantity of goods permitted to be imported or exported as a result of agreements reached between national governments.

real terms Value of goods or services, e.g., imports or exports, expressed at the prices current in an established base year to enable year-by-year comparisons to be made.

reciprocity principle In tariff reductions, one country's reductions are matched by reciprocal concessions in another country.

re-exports Goods brought into custom areas in one country, not for importing into that country, but for re-export after being sold on the commodity market.

regulations Rules applied by a government to control the workings of the market.

rescheduling Delaying payment of part or all of a debt, either interest or principal, due in any one year, by adding to the principal sum to be repaid.

reserves The monies, especially hard currency, held by a company, bank, or government, to finance foreign trade exchanges.

restrictive action or agreement In foreign trade, an action or agreement that limits commodities, markets, or trading partners.

retour A trade transaction financed by the exporter with credit from another transaction.

reverse transfer Flow of funds back from borrowers to lenders or from poor to rich countries as a result of debt repayment for goods or services received.

risk capital Capital provided by the owner of a business, who has the last claim to repayment in the event of failure.

rolling over (of debt) Agreement by creditors to defer repayment of the principal and even the interest on loans made to businesses, organizations, or governments in financial difficulties.

safeguards Temporary import trade restrictions to protect domestic industry.

scale Refers to the production capacity of a business.

slump Decline in economic activity in one or more industry or nation.

special and differential treatment Special and differential treatment of imports from developing countries, permitted after 1964 GATT.

special deposit reserve (SDR) A form of money issued by the World Bank and backed by member states to provide a common unit account that can provide gold or hard currency revenue to finance international trade.

speculation Buying commodities, including money, not for use but for resale in the expectation that prices will rise, or selling in the expectation that prices will fall.

stabilization schemes Designed to correct volatile movements in the prices of commodities.

standards Refers to a wide variety of technical barriers to trade, such as product standards such as food, plant, and animal health regulations, defined by the Tokyo Round Agreements as technical barriers to trade.

staple The basic product of a country, either for domestic use or foreign trade.

state trading The practice of conducting trade exclusively through a government agency. Nonmarket economies follow this practice exclusively.

stocks Goods or money accumulated and held for further use.

subsidies code The subsidies code, elaborated in the Tokyo Round Agreements, prohibits the use of export subsidies on nonprimary products. The use of export subsidies on primary products is not to displace other exports from the market or undercut their prices.

takeover Action by one company to obtain a majority of the shares in another.

tariff Tax imposed by a nation, generally ad valorem, on goods imported from other nations.

tariff escalation A situation in which tariffs are high on manufactured goods, moderate on semimanufactured goods, and very low on raw materials. This situation normally discourages developing of manufacturing industries in Third World countries.

tariff quotas Application of a higher tariff rate to imported goods after a certain quantity of items has entered the country at the usual tariff rate during a specified period.

terms of trade Refers to the establishment of the volume and prices of the exports and imports of a nation.

transfer pricing Prices determined by a company for goods and services moved from one place to another, sometimes between nations.

trend Having a certain general direction over a period of time.

unfair trade practices Unusual government support to firms, such as export subsidies, or certain anticompetitive practices by governments or companies, such as dumping, boycotts, or discriminary shipping arrangements, that benefit a company or nation.

unilateral An action taken by a country independently of other countries.

unit An individual item or quantity chosen as the minimum in production or trade for calculating price or quantity.

valuation The process of appraising the value of imported goods in which duties are assessed according to the tariff schedule of the country. The Tokyo Round Agreements established a custom valuation code based on transaction value.

value added Addition made to the value of a product due to processing, refining, packaging, and so on.

value-added tax Tax placed on the value added to a commodity as a result of refining or manufacturing.

variable levy An import charge subject to change as world market prices change. The alterations are designed to assure that the import price after payment of the charge will equal a predetermined domestic price.

voluntary restraint agreements Informal bilateral or multilateral agreements in which exporting countries voluntarily limit exports of certain products to a particular country in order to avoid the imposition of import restrictions.

wholesale Sale and purchase of goods in large quantities to be retailed by others.

working party A committee made up of GATT countries that deals with special issues, normally other than dispute settlements. The GATT committee reports to the GATT Council and makes recommendations on the course of action.

yield The return, usually expressed as money or as the return on investments in economic activity.

zone An area specifically assigned to a particular purpose, such as trade or industry.

Index